Rakka

Resafa

PALMYRENA

Halebiyah

Deir-ez-Zor

R. Khabur

Kasr-el-Heir

Sukna

Palmyra

R. Euphrates

RIA

D1272307

SYRIA

English miles

0   50   100   150 C.W.B

SYRIA

THORUMQUE, ET PRIMA IN DISCORDIA SEMPER UTRIMQUE CURA, ABEST A SELEUCIA PARTHORUM, M PROPIUS. Plin. Nat. Hist. Lib. V

SYRIA

AN HISTORICAL APPRECIATION

BY

ROBIN FEDDEN

Syria is a land of blessing, a country of cheapness,
abounding in fruits, and peopled by holy men.

A TENTH CENTURY TRAVELLER

ILLUSTRATED FROM PHOTOGRAPHS
MAINLY BY A. COSTA

ROBERT HALE LIMITED
63 Old Brompton Road London S.W.7

First published August 1946
Reprinted June 1947
Revised edition February 1955
Reprinted June 1956

By the same author :

The Land of Egypt, 1939
Crusader Castles, 1950

PRINTED IN GREAT BRITAIN BY
A. WHEATON & CO., LTD., EXETER, DEVON

PREFACE

—————————————— ❦ ——————————————

T HIS book could not have been written without the friendly
co-operation of the authorities in Syria and the Lebanon,
to whom I am deeply grateful. I wish also to thank the
following for their help and advice: Monsieur R. Demonts,
Monsieur J. Gaulmier, Professor T. S. R. Boase, Professor A.
Guillaume, Monsieur Daniel Schlumberger, Monsieur Fady
Bustros, Professor H. S. Deighton, and above all Mr Albert
Hourani to whose wide and various knowledge of Syria I am
deeply indebted.

I also wish to thank those who have allowed me to use their
photographs, and in particular A. Costa who is responsible
for all the illustrations with the exceptions of Nos. 2, 8, 11, 15,
22, 24, 26, 27 (by courtesy of the Antiquities Service at Beyrouth); Nos. 12, 21, 29 (by Lee Miller); No. 4 (by Mr John
Gough); No. 5 (by Lieut.-Colonel T. Clarke); and No. 23 (by
Mrs Wrinch).

LONDON 1955

CONTENTS

ILLUSTRATIONS

◦◦

The ruins of Palmyra *Frontispiece*

SYRIA

———— ·❦· ————

INTRODUCTION

·❦·

THE ancients seem to have regarded Syria as a place where abnormal things happened, a land of prodigies, of rare coincidences in time and of curious objects in space. They had some excuse for doing so. The rapid growth of religious faiths and frenzies, each with an attendant crop of miracles, and queer natural phenomena observed under the snows of Mons Libanus or in the deserts, had given the country a strange and provoking reputation. Not least there was the enigmatic Syrian Goddess, of many forms and names – Ishtar, Ashtoreth, Astarte – whose rites and person fascinated the Mediterranean world.

Syria today – and this must be emphasized – has not lost its strangeness. The pleasure which the sensitive traveller finds in Byblos, Palmyra or the dead Byzantine towns is continually sharpened by a sense of the curious and the unusual. This sense does not operate only, or even mainly, in the past. The Adonis River still runs blood-red to the sea, and the contemporary scene appears, with a little perception and goodwill, as strange as anything the Romans wondered at. There are many of those surprising juxtapositions which the march of time is so well able to produce: ski tracks beside the cedars of Lebanon; paramount sheiks shooting gazelle from Ford motor-cars; Orthodox monks in a mountain monastery listening to the incantations of Bing Crosby; the hammer and sickle nine thousand feet up on the Temple of Baal-Hermon. Other things bear the mark of a strangeness altogether different. In an isolated village they still practise communally those rites of Astarte on which the sensual goddess insisted and against which the early church so eloquently declaimed. Not long ago in the Alawi territory a fat bandit, heralded by signs and wonders, appeared as the last incarnation of the deity; and the peasantry were bled for the jealous god.[1] Every night in Beyrouth an old woman who has been dead several years struggles from

[1] The notorious Suleiman Merched.

her cerements, is seen coming at sunset along the cobbled street in front of the wharves, and later sings French songs behind the bar in a packed *boîte*. A wig hides the bald skull, and lace-work gloves cover the hands. The eyes are glass. The face is nothing but a structure of bone. Yet every gesture is exquisite, and has the perfection of something exactly remembered. She sings salacious songs that the early twenties knew, but death takes the salt from the *esprit Gaulois*. There is no bawdry without blood. The words change their meaning; palpable enough in the throat of a living person, in hers they are etherealized. The people, crowded against the bar and crowded at smoky tables, cheer themselves hoarse for her, having heard they hardly know what.

Again, farther south in the village of Djoun, there is a boy who assumes the shape of a faun, though this fewer travellers have seen, for the metamorphosis is temporary and only occurs in the depth of the summer heats. The ragged boy who sprouts the horns is about fourteen and few of the villagers appear to be aware of his curious dual nature. There is indeed at first sight nothing remarkable about him, though travellers who have witnessed the metamorphosis claim to have been struck from the first by the rather elongated shape of his ears, and by his legs, abnormally hairy for an adolescent. The boy goes by the name of Ahmad and has assumed the role of guide to the few strangers who in the course of the year penetrate to Djoun to visit the house and tomb of Lady Hester Stanhope.

The manor where Chatham's granddaughter made her headquarters, now a tumbledown half-deserted farm, lies across-country some twenty minutes from the village. The path, such as it is, winds among olive-trees and boulders. Since, owing to distances, it is almost impossible to arrive at Djoun except in the doldrums of noon or the early afternoon, there will be hardly a breath of air, not a man in the fields, and only the monotonous grating of the cicadas. The journey out is uneventful enough. It is only when the stranger turns from the empty rooms where Lady Hester with her imperturbable dignity received native homage and the suspicious emissaries of the West, and emerges into the sudden hot sunlight that the possibility of the curious begins. Ahmad suggests an alternative route back. There is no path he says, but the way is shorter. He points eastward. With only a steep ravine between, Djoun sleeps in the sun, a bare half mile away. The traveller, lured down that hillside in the white stillness of the afternoon, has soon gone too far to retrace his steps; the walk has become a mountaineering descent, and return is impossible. It is at this point that his guide begins to change.

The traveller notes at first only the changed enigmatic smile with which the boy watches his progress and the amazing bird-like ease with which he flits from rock to rock, now lost in the shade, now beckoning from a well of sunlight thirty feet below. The ascent up the other side of the ravine to Djoun is even longer and tougher. It is there that the traveller, worming his way through the rocks and scrub, finds the head with rudimentary horns staring down at him. He looks again and knows he is climbing with a faun. From that point accounts vary, and are naturally suspect since no traveller is likely to remain objective in such circumstances. Some accounts have been published in learned journals, and some are unpublishable. On one or two points there is unanimity: the horns which appear to be about four inches in length spring from the hair just above the forehead and in front of the little skull cap which the faun-boy, like many of the peasants, habitually wears; again, the silky legs and haunches and the hooves are apparently referable to the eastern wild goat (*Capra aegagrus*) and not to the domestic variety. The experience always ends in the same way: when the traveller reaches the hilltop and sinks exhausted on the level ground, Ahmad is sitting quietly on a boulder. *Saab iktir*, 'very steep', he says, with an expressionless smile. The village lies a stone's-throw away.

The curious and the strange persist in Syria and the traveller will find them for himself and in the degree that he wishes. This book is not about them. Nor is it about the far people: the reed men on the Euphrates who build their huts like birds; the camel men whose tents are made of hair and who chew the cud, testy as their beasts; the men who live in the mud-built beehive villages around Aleppo and give you goats' milk in leather bowls; the men who live in caves. Nor is it about the nearer people: the merchants with three thousand years of chaffering behind them; the new business men; the coffee-drinkers who talk their politics; the veiled ghosts of Hama and Damascus; the Maronite priests in their eyries; and the dudes of Beyrouth, tight-hipped in European reach-me-downs. Nor is it about the Syrian peasant: the perennial tilling Syrians who, as the Allied columns in 1941 rolled across the Hauran plain towards Damascus, danced their harvest dance upon the last span of a dynamited bridge, oblivious of the West and uninterested, conscious only that once again their meagre crops were in. Nor is it the fascinating book that might be written about the landscape with its flora and fauna: the Orontes soil red as blood, the dusty Hauran, the green hidden valley of Marj Hine; the leopards in the Alawi Mountains, the pin-tailed grouse, the ridiculous jerboa, and the affronted bustard;

the black and scarlet tulips and the grape hyacinths of the desert spring,
Rosa phoenicia, the grey-blue *Crocus damascenus* which the Bedouin use
for food, or the rare sea-lavender known only from the Palmyra lake.

All over Syria there stand in the deserts, in the mountains, along the
shore, astonishing and romantic monuments which dispute with the
people and the natural world the foremost place in the Syrian scene.
This book is mainly about these monuments and the way in which they
have accumulated on Syrian soil in the stratifications of time. The book
attempts quite simply to relate them to their background, and in doing
so to answer the questions which normally arise in the mind of the
inquisitive traveller when faced with the ruins of places such as Ruad,
Baalbeck, the Oasis of Resafa and the castles of the Crusaders. The
approach is chronological and each stratum of history with its embedded
monuments is taken in turn, beginning with the Phoenician towns and
ending with our own time.

Such a book includes much both of past history and present colour,
and these serve to emphasize a point which it is essential to grasp if the
nature of Syria's past and present is to be understood: Syria is a battle-
ground. Owing to its geographical position it is the area where for
centuries the dialectic of the Near East and the West has been fought
out in ideas and arms: Phoenician versus Greek, Greek versus Persian,
Roman versus Parthian, Byzantine versus Arabo-Persian, Crusader
versus Saracen. So it remains today. Syria has always been a frontier,
the frontier and meeting-point of East and West, and thus it has
rarely known security. A stake between greater empires and greater
forces, Syria throughout the millenniums of its history has enjoyed
only the briefest moments of independence, the briefest expressions
as a kingdom. The temporary heyday of Tyre and Sidon in a thousand
B.C.; the Seleucid kingdom; the Umayyad glory of the seventh century;
a bare fifty years of Hamdanid power at Aleppo in the tenth: such
political emergences have been no more than punctuations in a long
provincial history. Alexander the Great appointed as regent Abdolony-
mus, a gardener (or so the *Anatomy of Melancholy* maintains); the
Abbasids brought jealous neglect; the Fatimids incompetence; and
the Mamelukes and Turks slow death; with the twentieth century came
the League Mandates. Even prosperity when it visited the country went
usually hand in hand with intelligent exploitation, and Syrian wealth
was the product of Roman rule. Subject now to this power and now to
that, Syria in history has had no chance to find itself, no chance to
crystallize into an unambiguous and homogeneous form. It is a

kingdom that has rarely managed to exist. The boundaries are there, as definite as any state could wish for – the Taurus northward, the Euphrates to the east, the deserts to the south, and westward the sea – but no sovereign state has ever permanently filled them. It is a puzzle which has never been put together, and thus the unified picture has failed to emerge.

There is consequently no single Syrian type or personality. There have been continually the elements of such a personality and an obscure straining towards it, visible for instance in the nationalist character of the Syrian heresies and the native twist which Syria always gives to the arts of the foreigner,[1] but there has never been the rounded fulfilled whole.[2] Hence the intense variety of Syria – a variety of faith, culture, outlook, aspiration – which makes it so complex a place, and at the same time so fascinating and so richly coloured.

It is because of this variety that Syria is difficult to write about. No formula will cover it all. It is, moreover, not simply that the Syro-Phœnician merchant and the Bedouin sheik, the Maronite priest and the Armenian refugee, the Beyrouth intellectual and the Hauran peasant, the mountain men and the men of the plain, cannot be subsumed under one head. Nature itself complicates the problem. Nine-thousand-foot snows overhang a scorched desert; and the extraordinary variation between summer and winter temperatures creates everywhere a totally different country at each season. Where you have a sea of flowers in April, there is, literally, only desert sand in July. Even the things that grow along the littoral and in the hinterland are utterly different, and the very plants multiply the confusion. Thus the Lebanon (and for some odd reason Hermon and the Jebel Druze) enjoy a Mediterranean vegetation, while the rest of Syria falls within the Irano-Turanian plant zone, typical of the desertic countries of the Middle East. The writer, therefore, unless he is to qualify every statement, must run the danger of generalization both in speaking of the people and of the country itself. The present book runs this danger throughout; it does so in the interest of brevity.[3]

[1] This twist is particularly clear in architecture. Graeco-Roman, Byzantine and Islamic architecture, all become something different on Syrian soil.

[2] Syrian parochialism is a symptom of this non-fulfilment. The local inhabitant, when asked what he is, will often enough fail to give the obvious replies, such as 'Syrian', 'Lebanese', 'Muslim' or 'Christian'. He will say instead that he is a *Homsi*, a *Baalbecki* (a man of Homs, a man of Baalbeck), or a native of whatever city or village he happens to have been born in. Units of loyalty often remain small.

[3] One such generalization should perhaps be pointed out. The term *Syria* is in this book used to mean: (1) Syria; (2) Syria and the Lebanon. The reader will usually realize readily enough in which sense the term is being used in any given context.

The dialectic of East and West, that has so wrung Syria, has oriented the country in turn either mainly towards the Mediterranean or towards the Euphrates. For a thousand years of Graeco-Roman rule Syria looked west; it was an integral part of Mediterranean civilization, and its long coastline was intensely active. Politics and geography were in harmony and the country prospered. The population was at least twice as large as in our own time and the area under cultivation infinitely greater. Then came Islam and for a thousand years Syria turned eastward and faced the deserts. The sea lapped in vain along the western littoral, the ports silted up, and only the enterprise of a few Frankish merchants maintained the trade links with the Mediterranean world. Politics and geography were at variance, and the country little by little decayed.[1] The pathos of this decay will not cease to haunt the traveller as he explores the ruins of the past. Palmyra is a scrubby village, the aqueducts of the Hauran are waterless, the Byzantine towns and Umayyad palaces are abandoned, and only the bird's-eye view of the aeroplane reveals the lines of the great Imperial roads. There is an intense melancholy in the Syrian hinterland, and time and again the traveller will be led to reflect on the impermanence of all achievement. To attribute the decline of Syria and the atrophy of its life, as the traveller might be tempted to do, mainly to the influence of Islam would be altogether wrong. Factors purely geographical and political played a major role. Syria was simply turned the wrong way and the descendants of the men who invented the alphabet, explored the west coast of Africa, turned the Orontes into the Tiber, contributed to the Greek anthology, and built the great basilica of St Simeon Stylites, were disorganized and impoverished by the conscious political policy of a Persianized Baghdad, by Mongol destruction, by neglect and incompetence from Cairo, and finally by the intransigent rule of the Turks.

The middle of the nineteenth century saw the beginning of a new era in Syrian history. The country painfully and at first slowly began to turn back towards the West, to reintegrate itself into the Mediterranean orbit and economy. The process is still a painful one, and though the economic advantages are palpable, the social and cultural dislocation is enormous. Western techniques, thought processes, clothes, have all invaded the life of Syria, and will continue to do so in ever greater measure. In spite of a vigorous political nationalism, Syria again looks

[1] It is symptomatic that today little grows in the deserted and desertic steppe between Homs and Palmyra, where in the third century the Emperor Aurelian maintained an army of forty to fifty thousand troops upon the produce of the country during an operation of several months.

westward. This *volte face* imposes a tremendous strain on the social and cultural structure of the country. How is the Syrian to preserve all that is fruitful in his Islamic culture when assimilating so much that runs directly counter to all that it stands for? How is he to evolve a stable framework of ideas, a dignified and decent way of life, from this amalgam of old and new? These are the problems which in Syria exceed in importance all others and which the thinking people of the country will have to solve in the course of the next generation. A situation exists that is appallingly difficult and complex; it calls for the greatest understanding and sympathy on the part of the West.

CHAPTER II

THREE TOWNS

---- ·‹‹ ›· ----

Though Beyrouth, Damascus and Aleppo are the pivotal points of Syrian and Lebanese life, they have little in common. Each exerts its own influence, each claims for itself a special position, and each shows a strongly marked individuality.

For most travellers Beyrouth is their first contact with Syria, and very beautiful it seems to one coming in from the sea. The mountains climb tier on tier into a blue sky, olive groves encircle the town with a belt of soft grey and, to the south of the promontory on which Beyrouth is so comfortably placed, spread orange sand-hills dotted with clumps of umbrella pine.[1] Seen from the sea, the palms with which the town is sprinkled appear to sprout mysteriously from very stone, and there is an impression of gaiety and colour in the quays and houses that crowd along the foreshore; while down the coast stretch pleasant bays where the waves break lazily on the sand and coves invite the bather. Nor does a first acquaintance with the town disappoint. The gaiety and the colour do not disappear as you land. The streets are full of movement, the *suks* are crowded, and there is a good-tempered clanging of trams. Delightful fruit stalls display an amazing variety from all the rich hillsides around, and amusing antique shops sell the usual medley of genuine and fake.

The natural setting of Beyrouth never fails to enchant. On some coasts the sea ends abruptly, defined and terminated by the shore. Not so here. It is almost as if the Mediterranean, grudging the strip of green between its waves and the mountains, extended its influence inland. From every window you look out to sea, from every orchard and olive grove through wreaths of leaves you glimpse the inevitable blue. The warm clinging sea air washes in lazy tides across the cultivation to the

---

[1] There is an odd legend that the pines were planted by the Emir Fakr-ed-Din in the seventeenth century. This is quite untrue, since the Crusaders built ships with timber from this same forest.

8

mountains' feet and excites the narrow coastal fringe to lush bewildering growth. Hibiscus, acacia, huge overgrown sunflowers, and the towers of grey-green eucalyptus that line the roads outside Beyrouth, bathe in the tidal air. No seed falls but it sprouts; and they are, in a sense, sea crops that the overloaded donkey-carts ferry into the town. Above, the mountains climb, deliberate and stair-like, steadily away from the sea's encroachment into the high clear air. Overhanging Beyrouth they are as inescapable as the sea. Constant yet changeable, they are always there yet never twice the same; each change that the day brings to their still flanks and snow-capped summits lifts the eyes with a new surprise and pleasure from the movement of the streets. Even on dark nights they remain present, for the lights of Aley and the mountain villages shine in clusters too emphatic to be mistaken for the stars. Under a full moon the nine-thousand-foot snows of Sannine positively throb with light and hang so deceptively close that it seems you could almost stretch out your hand to them, feel on your forearm the freezing air.

These things Beyrouth has always had and can never lose, yet the longer you stay in the town the more you feel that they are not enough. There is something missing and a sense of dissatisfaction grows upon you daily, perhaps to crystallize without your knowing why into an almost unbearable antipathy. It takes time to discover that the movement in the streets is superficial and the life fictitious; nothing stands behind it. Only chaffering thrives, only trade quickens; it is *negotiationis ardor* that stirs the town and creates a semblance of living. When not in Alexandria, the Spirit of the Levant here makes its capital, and under its jealous rule the town prospers – and languishes. It is hard to think of a more sudden change of air than you meet dropping from Aley to Beyrouth. Driving with your windscreen down, the moist sea air at a certain point strikes you like a wall of fog. It seems incredible that you should be able to see through so heavy and palpable a vapour. Indeed, for months at a time it *is* impossible to see Beyrouth in detail from the mountains above, a haze envelops the town and promontory, creeps even into the foot-hills. The obscurity is symbolic of the change from the ascetic deserts behind, and the mountain villages, down into the miasmic Levant. Rich and uncertain, heady and oppressive, the air blurs shapes and principles, precludes clarity of action and thought. But it drives trade, it is the heavy fuel on which the Levantine works. Under this haze enterprises spawn and coin turns rapidly. The obscure deal and the close contract burgeon into fortunes.

Any criticism of Beyrouth is also a criticism of the West, for the town

is superficially westernized. Here, however, as elsewhere in the Middle
East, though our machines find no difficulty in acclimatizing themselves,
our ideas are not in the same case. Further, though our machines are
good, the level of our cultural exports is lamentably low. In the West
a lack of taste and shoddy values are sometimes offset by traditional
feeling and culture which temper the futility of the time. On the Levantine seaboard Turkish tradition and culture have been swept away
pell-mell by the sudden onset of twentieth-century technology and its
curious novelties. We have uprooted an old culture but have not
supplied a new. Beyrouth is a town without a tradition. Neither the
politicians who manipulate public opinion, nor the wealthy families
who disregard it, are likely to provide one.

The Beyrouth of history hardly pierces through the commercial
tegument of the twentieth century and the new prosperity of eighty
years. A few dignified Turkish houses behind high walls are almost all
that at first indicates a long and not altogether fortunate past. Further
searching reveals little more than whispers of history. These, however,
as everywhere in Syria and the Lebanon, speak of layer on layer of
civilization. Phoenician, Roman, Byzantine, Arab, Crusader, Turk and
contractor in ferro-concrete: each of these has conspired to wipe out the
record of his predecessors. The erasures have been sadly successful. The
excellent new museum, attempting to reverse the process of history,
resurrects almost all that remains of the Phoenician period and the great
Roman heyday. The grubby mosque at El Khader, an ancient chapel
once dedicated to St George, preserves a relic of Christian antiquity and
claims with disarming lack of evidence to celebrate the spot on which
the saint slew the dragon. The Middle Ages survive in the Great Mosque
where layers of plaster hide the fine capitals, and a large doorway pierces
what was once the apse of the Crusader Cathedral of St John the Baptist.
It is in a sense significant of Beyrouth's lack of contact with its past that
this, the town's most important monument, should remain neglected.

Beyrouth's great days came when Augustus, favouring the Phoenician
town of Berytus with the name both of his daughter and family,
baptized it *Julia Augusta Felix* and created it a Roman colony. As such
it enjoyed the usual colonial constitution, and local government was in
the hands of a senate who appointed the chief magistrates and among
other things arranged for a quinquennial census. Herod the Great and
his successors, probably courting Imperial favour, proceeded to adorn
the town with temples, and in the middle of the third century the Severi
gave it an Academy of Law which was to make it famous for three

hundred years and of which no trace now remains. Earliest of the law
schools of the Empire – previously in Rome law had been taught by
private professors and the School of Constantinople was not founded
until A.D. 425 – Beyrouth soon acquired an unrivalled prestige. Throughout the East, the *cachet* of a Beyrouth education came to be almost
essential to young men ambitious of administrative office or scholarly
repute. Studies were completed in a four years' course, later increased to
five years. Students were privileged by exemption from taxes and
military service, and professors can hardly have been discouraged by
salaries amounting to two thousand pounds a year. Around the Academy
grew up a typical university life with athletic clubs, clashes with a
tolerant police, and inevitably in the fourth and fifth centuries brawls
between Christian and paganizing students. We know the names of the
lost churches – St Jude, the Church of the Virgin, the Church of the
Resurrection – that the Christian students frequented, and have kept a
description of the greatest of the lost lecture halls where, in a setting of
marble and mosaic, they assembled to listen to the foremost jurists of
the Empire. Gaius, Papinian and Ulpian – last of the great lawyers –
were among the Academy's many eminent professors. The list of its
brilliant scholars includes a large proportion of the talent of the East
from the third to the sixth centuries – theologians of the eminence of
Gregory Thaumaturgus, Gregory Nazianus, and that warring schismatic, the Patriarch Severus; writers such as Eusebius, the historian of
the early church, and Ammianus Marcellinus who recorded the life and
wars of Julian the Apostate. It was not only a graduate's partiality that
led the poet Nonnus to describe Beyrouth as 'the source of life, the
mother of cities, the home of equity, and the bulwark of the law'. The
town's contribution to civilization was without doubt considerable. So
important had been the work of Gaius, Papinian and Ulpian, that later
jurists recommended that in doubtful cases their judgments should be
regarded as decisive. Two Beyrouth professors sat on the Commission
appointed by Justinian to draw up the legal code which for fourteen
centuries has inspired the legislation of the West. Not least, it seems
probable that through its actively Christian element the university
played a part in bringing about much of the moderate legislation of the
period, such as the mitigation of the slavery laws.

In the sixth century it looked as though the glory of the town and
university were securer than ever before and that both might look
forward to a long and prosperous future. The appalling earthquakes of
A.D. 551 and succeeding years disposed otherwise. The shocks that

devastated the whole Phoenician coast were particularly catastrophic at Beyrouth, where thirty thousand are said to have lost their lives. The university never rose from its ruins and the last professor whose name is known to us left the town in A.D. 555. With the eclipse of the university the town failed to recapture its former importance. The Muslim invasion found it not yet rebuilt, and only centuries later did the commerce of the Italian trading cities bring to the port something of its old prosperity. Even so its fortunes for a long time fluctuated, flourishing during the independence of efficient Lebanese emirs such as Molhem, Bechir and the remarkable Fakr-ed-Din, and losing ground at other times under the burden of Turkish neglect and obstruction. Paradoxically enough this same Turkish administration finally assured the prosperity of the town and its pre-eminence up and down the coast, since it was as a result of the Christian massacres of 1860 that Beyrouth received a large influx of population from the insecure mountain regions. After that date the commercial importance of the town grew steadily.

It would be unjust to leave Beyrouth on the unkind and in some sense superficial contrast that the traveller discovers between the classical past and the Levantine present. Beyrouth in its prime was a university town; it remains such today. Behind the commerce and the *salons* of the rich, behind the tasteless goods that represent the worst the West can give, a university town leads its autonomous life and preserves its permanent values. Though not at first readily perceptible to the stranger, the humanizing influence of Beyrouth's two universities – the Université St Joseph and the American University – is a very real force and one that grows year by year. It is a sign of great good omen that though these institutions are both the outcome of western capital and initiative they produce first-rate Syrian scholars. Many of these in due course serve with distinction on their respective academic bodies and carry on the work of the universities, as indeed it is so desirable that it should be carried on, by Syrians for Syrians. The Jesuit University of St Joseph received canonical confirmation of its university status in 1881. Both its Faculty of Theology and its more recently established Institute of Oriental Letters have a justly acquired reputation. Further, the university press, more particularly with its publication of historical, archaeological and philological studies, fills a vital role in the intellectual life of the country. The American University moved into Beyrouth from the countryside in 1868. Under a series of remarkable presidents it has played, through its various Faculties, a tremendously important part in the formation of a *cadre* of men with the sense of social and moral responsibility which is so hardly come by in the Levant. With these two institutions lies much of the future of Beyrouth, and not only of Beyrouth, but of all Syria, for it is to these universities that the most promising talent comes from all over the country. Further, probably stimulated by these nuclei and the congenial atmosphere they offer, there has arisen in Beyrouth a group of poets, painters and writers, who, even if they represent, so far, more in the way of useful interest than achievement, are a hopeful sign. It is in its role as a progressive intellectual centre for Syria and the Lebanon that the valuable future of Beyrouth lies. It is a role of infinite possibility and one which most appropriately links the modern town to the creative period of its history. It may perhaps revive for Beyrouth in the Middle East something of the hegemony of thought once exercised by imperial Berytus.

Where the road from Beyrouth to Damascus strays across the desertic eastern slopes of the Anti-Lebanon Mountains, and the landscape is at its barest – a wilderness of stone and shale and sun-baked earth – a slip of water hurrying between the rocks makes its almost miraculous appearance. The road follows it and together they set off downhill. At first the water is little more than a precarious thread urging its way between arid slopes. But as it moves it grows, and fed by subterranean springs it strengthens almost momently. The fringe of green along its banks deepens, and soon the stream is mistress of a narrow gorge-like valley. But the burnt hills still overhang it, it still trespasses in the desert. It is not long, however, before brief orchards and meadows are wedged beside its banks; spare trees multiply into serried ranks of poplar, walnut and alder; branch touching branch makes a close-packed sea of green. Though the desert rocks still sharply define on either side the limit of its kingdom, the stream has become a small river. As the water races eastward down its twisting course, the stranger is aware of a queer sense of anticipation. This precipitate onrush, this strip of green pouring down between the hills, must have some objective; such energy must find release. It does. With dramatic suddenness the imprisoning desert hills are at an end; river and road cease to twist and hurry. The waters, freed, flow out into the *Ghouta*, the Oasis of Damascus.

Near this point of release there stands a café-restaurant above the road, which might well claim to be the most attractive spot in the Oasis. The waters there, diverted from the main stream, race along on different levels, and between these waterways stretches the café terrace shaded with huge mulberry-trees and garlanded with vines. The spray of a

waterfall cools the air and its sound blends with the long conversations
to which wine and the discreet weather-worn tables invite. The kitchen is
itself a delightful whitewashed place, decorated with naïve Utrilloesque
wall-paintings, the work of the proprietor. Ducks waddle in and out
unconscious of intruding, and *habitués* are always to be found smoking
long Turkish pipes. A porcelain charm hangs above the door, whose
influence undoubtedly reigns over the primitive grill whence they carry
out to you, in the shade of the garden, hot *kebab* on skewers, and rounds
of native bread. This is followed by white cheese and large succulent
figs. With the waters running above and below you and spilling into
fountain basins at your feet, it is a fit spot in which to begin your acquaintance with Damascus, a city which has been so patently created
and maintained by the licence and bounty of this single stream, the
Barada.

The ancients not inaptly called the Barada, the 'River of Gold', and
Naiman the Syrian was surely right to claim that for non-medicinal
purposes at any rate the Rivers of Damascus were 'better than all the
waters of Israel'. The Barada very literally *makes* Damascus and its
Oasis, and the fortuitous nature of things comes home to you on
reflecting that a few chance springs in the Anti-Lebanon have accounted
for over three thousand years of history. Under a fine old bridge, which
spring rains and the efforts of the authorities have as yet been unable to
remove, the river flows on through gardens into the city and the road
runs beside it.[1] It is necessary to insist on the Barada, since not only
does it make possible the existence of the town, but contributes perhaps
more than anything else to its particular atmosphere. 'As a man falls
flat,' says Kinglake, 'face forward on the brook, that he may drink and
drink again; so Damascus, thirsting for ever, lies down with her lips to
the stream, and clings to its rushing waters.' The complex manner in
which this osculation is made to irrigate the town dates mainly from the
Aramaic, Roman and Umayyad periods. Parcelled into seven streams,
the river carries into streets and houses the sound of running water, and
the energy of its hemmed course between the hills is spent in the coolness of grave basins. Water, placid in tessellated pools, slopping into
stone troughs, gurgling in worn runnels, spraying up into the sunlight
of courtyards, is of the essence of Damascus. To water, many of the
mosques owe half their charm and the private houses much of their air of
leisure and abundance. In an eastern country, pent in by deserts, there
is something deliciously extravagant about this profuse expense of so

[1] The bridge has now been destroyed.

precious a commodity. Into the bargain this generosity of water is surprisingly and wonderfully cold, whether to drink or trail your fingers in, and thus it cools innumerable streets, and courts, and merchants' houses. Even in the depth of summer the water retains the subterranean chill of the springs, not so very distant, whence it rose. To most parts of Damascus the waters of the Barada arrive by 'free flow', but there are sections of the old suburb of Salhiyeh above the highest of the river's channels. The cunning with which succeeding generations have there raised the water, and led it on from building to building, illustrates perhaps better than anything else the companionship of water and stone which in Damascus is so characteristic. From a channel of the Barada a wheel lifts the water to an aqueduct which feeds the enchanting thirteenth-century Maristan of El Kaimari, thence it passes to the Mosque of Mouy ed Din (sixteenth century), and finally is led away to the crowded *suk* of El Seiman, built in the seventeenth century.

In Damascus, unlike Beyrouth, history does not have to be pieced together from fragments or found in the pages of books. It exists in a profusion of monuments. Nor does that sad gap exist which, so often in Syria, separates the ruins of a Roman or Byzantine past from the modern world. In Damascus, on the contrary, the coming of Islam maintained and increased the commercial and intellectual activity of the old Roman colony, and gave the town a special position and a special history, together with an architecture worthy of these. For most people indeed the interest of the town does not begin with the ancient city, Rimmon's 'delightful seat'; nor with the biblical quarrels of Israel and Damascus; nor even with the Roman town which received the converted St Paul; but precisely with the coming of the Umayyads. Under these caliphs the town as the capital of the Islamic world enjoyed from the middle of the seventh to the middle of the eighth centuries a hundred years of incomparable splendour. Of this vivid century which so touches the imagination, unfortunately little architecture remains. Perhaps the studied neglect of the town during the ensuing period is in part responsible, for the Abbasids removing the Caliphate to the banks of the Tigris – a removal fraught with such tragic consequences for Syria – did their best to ruin the older capital. Under Saladin and the Ayyubids in the twelfth and thirteenth centuries the town again burst into magnificence and there arose countless buildings – mosques, mausoleums, hospitals, fountains and public baths – many of which are still to be visited. That they remain is a miracle, since the Mongol invasions that followed were here particularly cruel, and after Tamerlane's holocaust in 1400 the town is said to have remained a desert for two generations. These destructive visitations were preceded and followed by an inefficient Mameluke rule exercised from Cairo, during which any governor who showed the least capability was at once removed on the grounds that he might grow ambitious. The same policy was conscientiously pursued after the Turkish conquest. Turkish rule in Damascus, however, was not the disaster that it sometimes was elsewhere; intelligent and effective administrators, such as the Azem Pasha who built the delightful palace that bears his name, were by rare good fortune appointed from time to time, and the period has left several interesting monuments. The so-called Tekkiyeh built by Suleiman the Magnificent shows what the Turks could do in Damascus when they had a mind. The mosque with its pencil-shaped minarets, its cloisters built in alternating courses of black basalt and white stone, its basin of grey-green water and perpetually bubbling fountain, creates a delightful effect of elegance and sobriety. To this, the quiet sun and shade between the arches, the trees in the courtyard, and the singing birds, as decorative and ostentatious as in a Persian miniature, add something further and emphasize the note of graceful leisure which (however inappropriate it may be in a religious institution) the western imagination will always seek to associate with the buildings of the Turks.

There is a lot to see and Wulzinger's *Damaskus*, Sauvaire's *Description de Damas*, and the publications of the Institute of Archaeology – appropriately housed in the Azem Palace – have conveniently sorted it out for the traveller. He will find none the less that there is more to the Great Mosque than archaeology or guide-books can ever reveal. Though it has been so often described, the emotional impact of the immense and echoing court is unexpected and overwhelming. This is the more remarkable, since fire and mason in the centuries have destroyed as much as now remains. The mosque stands on the site of the temple of *Jupiter Damascenus*, once the centre of the Roman town. Avenues led up to it from east and west, and the temple buildings comprised two tremendous and concentric peristyle courts, having their colonnades facing inwards. The interior court, which occupied more or less the area covered by the present great courtyard and mosque, held the sanctuary and the offices of the cult; under the colonnades of the outer *enceinte* were situated the bazaars of the Roman town. The triumphal arch through which one passes on emerging from the Hamidieh *suk* marks the entrance to this outer *enceinte*. The rites of the god were on the same scale as his accommodation, and when revived in the days of Julian the Apostate

astounded the public by their magnificence. Christianity not long after
swept away the pagan sanctuary and a large basilica dedicated to St
John appeared on the south side of the great court, where the prayer
hall of the mosque is at present situated. A Greek inscription over one
of the cathedral doors, now walled up and situated in the south wall
near the present *mihrab*, still testifies to the period of Christian owner-
ship. It reads, ironically enough in the circumstances, 'Thy Kingdom,
O Christ, is an everlasting Kingdom; and Thy Dominion is from
Generation to Generation.' Under the Umayyads the basilica changed
its function, but not apparently its form, and became a mosque. Only
later was it actually destroyed. Such a sequence – Pagan temple,
Christian basilica, Muslim mosque – could be paralleled in numbers of
monuments in Syria. It is not in fact its history but its atmosphere –
and its mosaics – that 'make' the Great Mosque. It is difficult to convey
a sense of the spaciousness and dignity of the courtyard with its silence
and its echoes. The stones are worn and pale, and many of the piers and
arches, pale too, are picked out with decoration in just the right faded
red and blue. The whole place gives a certain agreeable impression of
being semi-organic, of having grown and changed and aged in the
irregular and unexpected way that people do, rather than of having
originated on drawing-boards and in the heads of architects. Varied
batterings and misfortunes, though they have obscured the symmetry of
its original plan, have contributed to the growth of its very particular
personality. Its every feature speaks of a long adaptation to circumstances, and thus it arises that the courtyard carries, not the explicit
interest of a particular period, but the very flavour of time. One only
becomes conscious of dates and epochs when looking at specific details,
such as the fine solid north minaret that contrasts with the elegance of
Kait Bey's later structure; or the delicious eighth-century treasure-
house on its Corinthian pillars; or, not last or least, the mosaics that
speak immediately of Byzantium. The latter are the wonder of the
mosque, and exhibit a magnificent sense of colour, design and fantasy.
The effectiveness with which gradations of colour impose and deter-
mine their form is astonishing. Imagination takes over where the
presentation ends, wonders at these gigantic trees and hurrying waters,
passes beneath the bridges, explores the towered palaces, and is held
and enchanted by the conventions of a perspective so romantic and so
far from naïve. Dating from the middle of the Umayyad period, they
were largely the creation of Byzantine workmen; but, with a compromise that was characteristically Syrian, it is the waters of the

Barada that the Byzantine buildings overlook and they are shadowed by the trees most typical of the Damascus Oasis. The mosque acquired a tremendous repute and sanctity in the Muslim world – no spider, it is said, weaves its web within the precincts – and one Arab geographer after another has left a description of the place as it appeared in its glory after the Umayyad Caliph Walid I had redecorated it at huge cost. It must indeed have created an effect of incredible richness in the days when its six hundred lamps hung each from its gold chain. Maqdisi, writing in the tenth century, thus describes the great courtyard:

'The whole area is paved with white marble. The walls of the mosque, for twice the height of a man, are faced with variegated marbles; and, above this, even to the ceiling, are mosaics of various colours and in gold, showing figures of trees and towns and beautiful inscriptions, all most exquisitely and finely worked. And rare are the trees and few the well-known towns, that will not be found figured on these walls! The capitals of the columns are covered with gold, and the vaulting above the arcades is everywhere ornamented with mosaic with arabesque designs.'

In addition to the Great Mosque, the Azem Palace and the Tekkiyeh, the traveller should make a point of not missing the new museum, the monuments of the Salhiyeh suburb, or the domed and vaulted Azem Khan which, built for the convenience of the eighteenth-century merchants, gives an impressive idea of the caravan traffic which still at that period brought immense wealth and repute to the town. The museum, a good building in itself, contains unexpected wealth: magnificent paintings from Dura Europos; a complete fourth century Jewish Synagogue, decadent but vastly entertaining; a necropolis from Palmyra with its typical and curious blend of classical and Iranian influences; a variety of first-class material dating from the Islamic period; and not least a strange and beautiful statue rather under life size whose stylistic overtones of India and the East bring home the wide interpenetrations of cultural influence which have always taken place on Syrian soil and which make the artistic remains of Syria so interesting. To all this has lately been added the impressive reconstruction of the façade of the Umayyad castle of El Heir west of Palmyra (not to be confused with the other Kasr el-Heir described in Chapter VI).

The suburb of Salhiyeh must be visited for two reasons. First, many of the pious foundations (oratories, mausolea, religious schools) which once swarmed on the lower slopes of Mount Kasyoun and, according to Arab legend, portended to that mountain the unique distinction of being spared the upheaval of the day of judgment, yet remain.[1] Second, the slopes of Kasyoun offer far and away the best general view of Damascus, a view moreover that will help the traveller to an understanding of the Damascus temper. He will do wisely to ponder on the general features and implications of the scene that from these slopes unfolds before him. On three sides bare desert hills enclose a wide shallow basin filled to a level line, as if vines and palms were the waters of a lake, by a sheet of green vegetation. On the fourth side, though there are no hills, there is the desert. Flat and interminable it stretches out to a horizon that marks only the first stage of a long unvaried waste that does not end with the Euphrates. Ringed by the desert and by desert hills, the town with its oasis of luxuriant green is clearly an island. Only the movement of the caravans across the seas of sand – a movement that has now almost ended – kept it for three thousand years in contact with much of the outer world. As one views this strangely insulated microcosm many things become clear. With empty spaces eastward and with little more than foot-hills to the south, the significance of the higher mountains to the west, which constitute a veritable barrier, becomes apparent. While the Mediterranean can only penetrate here with difficulty, from the deserts and to desert men the Oasis offers the first post of call; it is a goal to which sand tracks set. Damascus willy-nilly has been oriented towards the desert, and has been the home of desert enthusiasms. From Jauf and the Wadi Sirhan, from the whole plateau of Arabia, emotions flow into the Damascus Oasis, are charged there with new intensity and in due course ebb out again into the sands. The peculiar consequences of the town's geographical position have been intensified by its particular connection with Mecca. As the point of departure of the pilgrim caravan Damascus, the 'gate of the Ka'aba', long since acquired something of the nature of a sacred city. Such distinction, as seems to be usual, did not encourage habits of mental sobriety which might have been an antidote to desert enthusiasms and religious fantasies. Mecca and the sands may be said between them to have in considerable measure determined the historic temper of Damascus. It has often been a bitter and uncertain temper, breeding endemic faction. Riots, sudden and violent outbreaks – as swift and unforeseen as the razzia of the Bedouin tribes – have striated the town's history. When thousands perished in the massacres of 1860 it was no new thing. Time and again prosperity and well-being have been

[1] As do also in the adjacent streets the descendants of the Kurds whom Saladin brought to Salhiyeh in the twelfth century.

sacrificed, it would seem almost willingly, to the spirit of suspicion and unrest. When Aleppo in the seventeenth and eighteenth centuries was flourishing through the peaceful establishment of the agencies and merchants of the western trading nations, Damascus kept its gates closed. In the fifteenth century a distinguished French traveller, Bertrandon de la Brocquière, had his beaver hat knocked off for no better reason than that it was unfamiliar, and it is typical of the uneducated Damascenes' attitude to the non-Muslim world that a party of English travellers in 1697 should have had to enter the town surreptitiously by the gardens for fear the populace would take offence at seeing so many Europeans together. The temper of the town even in Lamartine's time was such that no stranger could visit it except in oriental costume: only those were tolerated who shared, or pretended to share, the traditions and outlook of the populace. Twice in the middle decades of the nineteenth century, in spite of the presence of the Turkish garrison, the mere news that the British Consul-General was coming from Beyrouth to visit the town provoked violent rioting. On one occasion the official in question had to turn back when already half-way across the mountains. Had Cyprus then been annexed, or had the British then been established in Egypt or Palestine, such a reaction might have argued a shrewd prescience. As it was, it simply represented the Damascene dislike of anyone or anything non-Muslim. The Oasis mentality leaves no room in its scheme of things for fundamentally divergent views and outlooks.

The Syrian Arab, belying the truth of romantic portraits, is a talkative creature. Not unnaturally so; in the company of others he compensates for the long silences of the desert, past and to come. In the tents the old topics are turned, re-turned, and worn threadbare. This propensity to talk receives a rich stimulus in the Oasis. But the lush and pleasant green and the intoxication of ever-present company is a severe test. The words sometimes tend to bear less and less relation to facts, the theories to grow more and more irresponsible, thought to be replaced by an emotional effervescence.[1] This, as it would do anywhere, provides a quick and permanent forcing ground for politics. Damascus is politics-ridden: and politics mean the café. In the *qahwa* from dawn to long after dark the threads are endlessly woven, the fancies and factions thrive and wane, or overnight take shape in sudden and premature action. Of these

[1] Exception must be made for a small but powerful minority of educated Damascenes who for thirty or forty years have had a clear and unwavering idea as to the meaning of Syrian nationalism and have usually taken the right steps to further it.

thousands of talkers only a handful know, or unfortunately are in a position to know, of the issues involved. Even as they discuss, the breath of their affections and fears raises storms as sudden and violent as the desert wind. It has been claimed that partial employment and the decline of the town's commerce since the days of the caravan trade are responsible for the political fever of Damascus. These may indeed play their part, but essentially the ague is geographically conditioned and of long persistence. If from time to time it has furthered the country's best interests – one might for instance cite occasions on which the Damascene fever, taking the form of xenophobia, has served a definitely useful purpose in tempering the too-ready pretensions and encroachments of the West – it has very often been the cause of prolonged unrest and instability.

Though Damascus has not often shown outstanding political sense, it has great political power. The hectic energy generated wherever a group of Damascenes meets drives the wheels of policy in places far afield. It is in a sense the political hub of Jordan, the Lebanon, Syria and the deserts beyond. Whether Damascus will retain this position is uncertain. It may continue to decline, as it has been doing these eighty years, relative to the seaboard. It is possible to argue that in its temper, its methods, its very means of livelihood, the town looks back not forward, and is bound up with things that have had their day. Westward the economic power of Beyrouth increases daily, while the Lebanon mountain barrier cuts off Damascus from the Mediterranean with cruel finality. (The transit to the coast takes over eleven hours by the present narrow gauge track.) The wider range of air travel necessitates no halt at the Oasis *en route* for Baghdad; even the pipe-lines avoid Damascus. The town's chief hope would seem to be the revival of trans-desert commerce by motor caravan. Recent developments have shown that such a trade is feasible, but it seems unlikely to assume important proportions.

For the traveller, however, removed from the town's politics and impervious to its prejudices, it is precisely the Damascene character and desert traditionalism which create its charm. Were it more progressive it would be less decorative, and an axiom – true of course only for the passing traveller – is here well illustrated: that a decaying town is more attractive than a growing one. To the more interesting parts of Damascus the vulgarity of the West has hardly penetrated: a medieval tradition of life and conduct persists unchanged. Should one of those fifteenth-century governors return whose tenure was even of the briefest, he would recognize the same types plying the same trades in the same

B

fashion; through the tangle of *suks*, though rebuilt and often sadly roofed with tin, he would pick his way without difficulty, finding many of the crafts he knew situated in their old streets. He would find baths his contemporaries frequented still in use, and see in the mosques at midday the same rows of figures bowing in unison to the ground. Entering those discreet private houses, whose façades are like prisons and their interiors miniature palaces, he would surprise the same dignified merchant class as represented the wealth of the city in his own day. Not least, he would still be fearful and puzzled by the import of sunset rumours, having had reason to know the unpredictable temper of the Damascus bazaars.

To the traveller, on the contrary, all these things come fresh, and he wanders round the old parts of the town in surprise and gratification. The cross-legged fortune-teller, the public scribe, the student of the Koran, the man of substance in the striped silk robes so typical of Damascus, the sherbet seller with his brass ewer and skirt of red and white – these and all the other types are as good as imagination painted them. So too are the crystallized fruits for which Damascus is famous, the luscious Turkish sweetmeats, and the great coral-coloured watermelons that melt in the mouth. For mornings on end one can eddy with the crowd out of one bazaar and into another, savouring the colour, sound and movement, straying beyond into courtyards and gardens, losing oneself through archways in *culs-de-sac*, empty and apparently forgotten. Symbolically enough the desert permeates it all. Down the *suks* swagger the young bloods and the great men of the tribes trying to look, and looking, as though they owned the place. Many of them are magnificent and their clothes enhance the impression: the floating rich *abayiehs*, in summer finer than gauze, and the wonderfully becoming desert headgear – the white *keffieh* – held with a gold or silver rope. With their brown parchment skin the women, hawk-nosed like the men, are almost as fine in their own way and form a striking contrast with the middle-class women of the town. The dress of the latter shows most unfortunately the influence of the West and must represent one of the most disastrous sartorial compromises yet evolved. The old white veil and the old dress have gone, to be replaced by a three-quarter length garment of black bombasine or similar stuff and a veil of the same colour that completely hides the face. This costume is often terminated at the lower end with boots or shoes of that sort to which a button-hook is the necessary complement. The Victorian feather 'boa' has more than once been observed setting off this curtained anonymity, though how these faded furbishings should have found their way to Damascus so late in the day is a question unanswered.

Many of the *suks* have been largely 'Manchesterized' as to their goods, but this useful and graceless merchandise has not changed their general atmosphere. It fits itself into, rather than imposes itself upon, the eastern background. There are, moreover, whole sections of the bazaars still purely native in character: such are those delightful streets where they sell bridles, harness and camel gear, and in fact most of the streets which cater for the practical needs of the Bedouin and supply the tools of local craft and husbandry. Here are to be found creditable workmanship, simplicity of form, and an unconscious good taste based upon tradition. The traveller who looks for more than this, however, will be disappointed. The exquisite craftsmanship which made the repute of Damascus wares has disappeared: the cunning glaziers and leatherworkers, the smiths who tempered the world-famous blades, no longer exist, and the rich inlay work, having lost its elegance and sense of design, thrives only as a tribute to modern taste. The silk weaving, recently revived, alone displays much of the old Damascene excellence, but even here the designs used, fortunately perhaps, are those which once attracted Byzantines and medieval Caliphs. It is generations since the sense of pattern evolved anything new. The general disappearance of the Oasis Art owes, however, nothing to the malign influence of the West. Over a century ago European travellers were already searching in vain for the jewellery, leather, glass and arms, which had once made Damascus famous. The decadence had indeed set in far earlier and, partly at any rate, dates back to 1400, when Tamerlane carried off the best artists in the town to his own capital at Samarkand.

Though works of art have more or less disappeared from the *suks* of Damascus, they have not altogether left the town. They still exist in some of those old private houses which, unpretentious and retired, have remained long unchanged, and are one of the most characteristic and delightful features of both Damascus and Aleppo. In such appropriate setting are to be found carved and painted ceilings, inlay that by some miracle manages to be complicated without being fussy, Damascus pottery that is elegant and decorative, and not least a quantity of later Turkish things which when not beautiful are at any rate audacious and amusing. Though the cheap silver-hilted daggers that the 'trade' turns out for visitors may be nauseating, in one such house you may see and handle blades made for the son of Saladin and the grandson of the meteoric Tamerlane. The romantic traveller Warburton a century ago found the English consul installed in one of these old Damascus houses. His description still applies. 'I entered', he says, 'from a dull street, by a low and unpretending portal . . . the small outer court, whence I passed into a garden, round three sides of which the apartments ranged. A little lake of crystal water lay enclosed by marble banks, and over-shadowed by beautiful weeping willows. Little fountains leaped and sparkled in all directions, and shook their loosened silver in the sun. . . . At one end of this court, or garden, was a lofty alcove, with a ceiling richly carved in gold and crimson fretwork. The walls were ornamented with arabesques, and a wide divan ran round the three sides of the apartment, which opened on the garden and its fountains. Next to this alcove was a beautiful drawing-room, with marble floor and arabesque roof, and carved niches and softened lighting falling on delicately painted walls. In the middle of the room was an alabaster basin, into which water fell from four fantastic little fountains.'

To know Damascus one must also know its Oasis – *El Ghouta* – to which it owes much of its charm and all its history. It is not difficult to know. Its fertile gardens invade the very town, and whole suburbs are cut off by green. This Oasis, that so urgently hems in the town, has obviously been a natural haven for men from the beginning of time. It is an amazing contrast to, and a grateful refuge from, the deserts; and the sun-baked Arabs in their enthusiasm place the site of Eden here. Muhammad, legend states, viewing it from the desert, was so struck with the beauty of the Oasis that he refused to visit it, not wishing to be deprived of the full joys of the heavenly Paradise by such a splendid anticipation. Though there is apparently little to support the Eden supposition, it was perhaps natural enough. Cupped in its bare hills, the fertility of the *Ghouta* makes a strong impression. With its poplars, sycamores and orchards, and its running water, it seems more like an immense informal garden than a source of crops and wealth. Vines luxuriantly twine themselves like garlands among the trees, and intimate paths run from orchard to orchard. Among the groves one comes across the whitewashed dome of a saint's tomb or an empty hut, used only at the time of harvest, which might elsewhere be a deserted summer-house. For the traveller the delight of it all is enhanced by the queerness of finding side by side the strange and the familiar: cacti growing under walnut-trees, apricot and pomegranate in flower together, palms and poplars shoulder to shoulder. The famous spring freshness of the *Ghouta* – a sudden brightness common to all desert places – changes in summer to a sheer weight of fruit, a richness that is almost oppressive. Here trees groan if ever they have groaned. The orchards seem weighted beyond endurance, and from the olives at the time of the great heats are pressed out tons of lukewarm oil.

This weight of fruit brings home to one with immediacy the fact that of course the *Ghouta* far from being a garden is a very old, and serious, agricultural enterprise.[1] The *fass*, the ancient instrument that replaces the spade and the mattock in this part of the world, has turned and re-turned this ground for thousands of years. The idyllic garden is a hive of activity. The vines, the vast swollen figs, the walnuts like cricket-balls, are the fortune of the villages that dot the Oasis. Every inch of ground is exploited; each olive grove is also a field of corn or barley, and clover crops by happy arrangement grow under apricot-trees. Strangely enough, however, there are a few waste spots that rise from the green industry of the orchards, dusty bald patches tenanted by goats and crumbling Muslim cemeteries. It is only when one realizes that these scars stand on higher ground that their significance becomes clear: they alone are not reached by the fertilizing waters of the Barada. They remain islands of desert and have so remained century after century, untouched by all the activity around them, getting and giving nothing.

The absolute dependence of this human and vegetable world on the Barada becomes dramatically plain as one moves eastward down the Oasis. There, as the reduced and parcelled water comes more and more sparingly, the garden-orchards progressively lose their richness, the huge walnut-trees that were like ships in sail grow stunted, the olives peter out, and the villages grow poor and few. Only acres of thin-soiled vines remain, where the peasants raise on stilts high wooden platforms with a roof of leaves and sit throughout the late summer, watching the solitary crop for thieves. At last even the vines give out and there is only short salty pasture and reeds. A great vague marsh here receives the last stagnant water of the Barada, spent and flaccid. In summer it dries out completely, but in winter harbours a great variety of duck that come flighting in over the Oasis. Beyond lies the desert, sloping away flat, endless and empty. Only here at the last blade of green may Damascus be said properly to end.

This eastern extremity of the Oasis has a considerable and rather sinister charm. The tired landscape resolves itself into washes of pale colour, extenuated greens and faded browns, against which wandering

---

[1] Some idea of its actual fertility may be conveyed by the fact that the apricot crop alone amounts annually to about 145,000 tons. J. A. Tower, *The Oasis of Damascus*, Beyrouth, 1935.

cattle, and here and there a solitary, dramatic tree, are sharply etched. The region conveys an extraordinary impression of being at the very end of the world. The richness, the vitality, the movement, have slowly failed. Here is the ultimate flicker of life, the last hopeless gesture before extinction. The one or two isolated villages, poor and malaria-ridden, that cling to the thin scant pasture, are worth visiting. They have a lost quality and one senses a tragic tenacity in these people who live and die with the drone of mosquitoes in their ears. Such are the semi-nomad men of Hedjaneh with their village full of horses and seluki gods, and, last outpost, the people of Harran el Awamid where the women are astonishingly beautiful – a beauty all the more striking at the world's end – and go in costumes of indigo blue and faded red. The Romans knew Harran el Awamid, though what can have brought them there is difficult to guess. Among the mud cottages rise three giant Corinthian pillars of black basalt. Enigmatic and impressive, they mark the farthest limit of the Oasis. There is nothing beyond.

North-east of Damascus and set in the arid hills there are two other places worth seeing: Sednaya and Malloula. Both are pockets of mountain Christians and their survival as such in this most Muslim part of the country typifies the way this faith throughout Syria has hung on, in out-of-the-way corners, where the pressure, and advantages, of conversion to the state religion were less immediate and persuasive. The drive to Sednaya is impressive. Passing on the northern fringe of the Oasis the little village of Berzeh, where legend says that Abraham was born, the road climbs through a gorge into the hills. The stream there is one of the rare tributaries that co-operate in the labours of the Barada, and on its way down to the Oasis it creates among the hills green orchards and walnut groves of its own. These in due course are left behind and the road emerges on a high bare plateau, walled on either side with steep mountain ridges. It is on the lower spurs of one of these ridges that the village and convent-citadel of Sednaya stand. Though now an out-of-the-way place, it had for centuries a European reputation as a centre of pilgrimage, and was much frequented by the Latins at the time of the Crusades. Maundrell in the seventeenth century made the detour to visit it and was more impressed by the 'most excellent' local wine than by the convent. The wine, a sickly sweet vintage, still exists, and there is still an annual pilgrimage to the village on 21st September. Justinian built and fortified the convent, though of the original work not much remains. For the traveller its chief interest lies in the icons preserved both in the church and in the miracle-working shrine of the Virgin – to which one must penetrate unshod – and in the magnificent views from the convent walls; and not least in the fact that its fortifications still serve a very real purpose, since the convent is in a state of perpetual siege. The defenders, the Greek-Orthodox nuns, never cease to work their infernal engines, and their barbed tongues lash the Greek-Catholic priest and his partisans below the walls. Operations above have long been directed by an unsavoury character who goes by the title – a little startling for one who moves among female votaries – of *le procureur*. Undaunted by a hail of vituperation and the dissemination of fearful propaganda, the Uniate besiegers continue to attack with unflagging zeal, mining and counter-mining, sapping at reputations, battering at the convent walls. Some two hundred years ago the Catholics lost the citadel to the Orthodox, and it is to be supposed that this state of siege has existed ever since. As the forces in the village are pretty evenly divided in respect of numbers, there is little reason to suppose that the end of the struggle is in sight. For the passing traveller who plays the role of the courted neutral, the war is not inconvenient and may well be instructive. He will note with detachment that such fratricidal sects and schisms have throughout history cursed and fatally weakened Syrian Christianity. He will realize that this pocket battle is no different from much that has gone before: only the intellectual grip has weakened and with it the moral fervour; the thunders of Athanasius are succeeded by the whispers of the *procureur*. Sednaya is an object-lesson in Syrian history.

Malloula, some fifteen miles north-east as the crow flies, is torn by no such dissensions. The Greek-Catholics have it their own way. But the village also provides a curious – and in this case a unique – link with Syrian history. In Malloula and the neighbourhood they still speak Aramaic and here alone lingers the tongue which in Persian times was the international medium of expression throughout Syria, Palestine and this part of the Near East. Jesus, it is to be presumed, was familiar with Aramaic, for by the first century A.D. Greek had only replaced it among the hellenized upper class, and many of the Fathers wrote and spoke it. Later, unable to withstand the competition of Arabic, the old tongue took to the hills and became inseparably associated with the Maronite faith and the liberal aspirations of the Lebanon Mountain. There in the fifteenth century it was still so common that Franciscan missionaries felt themselves obliged to learn it in order to fulfil their task. Since that date, however, its disappearance has been rapid. Malloula is a last stronghold.

It is indeed in just such a place that one would expect to find an anomalous survival. Off the road to anywhere, lost in the desert hills of the Anti-Lebanon, the village is built at the dead end of a deep rocky gorge. Plastered against the side of the ravine, the houses climb almost perpendicularly and one roof seems to overhang another. A stream, bursting from the heart of the mountain, fills the echoing gorge with greenness and the sound of water. Though there is little to the village except its dramatic concealment within the mountain, and its strange-tongued people, it has exceptional charm. Imagination, doubtless quite wrongly, finds a secret and hermetic spirit in the place, as though with an Aramaic dialect had survived unfamiliar beliefs and mysteries. The only outlet from the dead-end of the gorge is a tiny passage-like ravine with perpendicular sides. Cut out of the solid rock by the wear and tear of the water, it is in places hardly wide enough for two to walk abreast, and bears a close resemblance to the famous *Siq* passage at Petra. Slowly climbing, it emerges finally on the hills above. There the delightful little whitewashed monastery of Mar Sarkis with its Byzantine cupola stands, amid the remains of tombs of a yet earlier epoch, overlooking the Malloula gorge and the village itself. The view is startling enough. Houses, stream and poplars are far below, yet you could almost pitch a stone on to them. Hawks, of the sort which love such precipices, glide on the middle air below you and their shadows drift across the village roofs and gardens. With your bird's-eye view, you too know as much of the villagers, and as little, as do the hawks. The odd-tongued people beneath are revealed to you only in their comings and goings. Like hurrying ants, the small black bodies suddenly seem to pause for no apparent purpose or turn away down streets to right or left with perfect aimlessness. Stopping to speak to each other they appear to achieve communion without sound. Seeing them so, silenced yet still alive, one reflects that time will indeed stop their Aramaic speech as effectively as distance seems to do. Their words, the sounds they make in greeting, once the current coin of an Empire, are now intelligible only to a few scholars. They speak a doomed tongue that sooner or later will disappear even from Malloula.

Though Aleppo, like Damascus, derives its history and importance largely from its position and the deserts which stretch eastward from its gates, its temper and feeling are altogether different. Damascus, in spite of its role as a caravan city, has always been essentially a goal, a place complete in itself, the Eden towards which desert faces and aspirations set. Hence Damascus has always been a capital, the hub of Syrian Arab life. Aleppo, on the other hand, is and has been essentially a stage, though a large, permanent and important one, upon a road somewhere else: a useful junction, rather than the home and term of imagination and ambition. It has little water, no belt of green to set it off, nothing to draw thought there from the dryness east and south, none of the things that make the Damascus Oasis almost a staple ingredient of Arab poetry. Aleppo does not even announce a sharp change from the desert to the sown. Having a tolerable winter rainfall, its desert is hardly desert, and to the west in place of a defining and dramatic barrier of hills a rolling plain stretches coastward, fertile and proper for travel. It is this access to the coast, and its position in relation to the Euphrates, that have made Aleppo. Coming up the Euphrates from Mesopotamia you travel day after day more or less north-west until, at a point about fifty miles east of Aleppo, the river suddenly swings away north and curls back upon itself into the fastnesses of Kurdistan. It is at this point that you must leave the river if you wish to cut through by the nearest route to Antioch and the coast. Standing midway between the river and the sea, the fortune of Aleppo was assured from the day that the Seleucids made Antioch the third city in the civilized world. From that time it has remained the point to which Mediterranean mercantile influence could conveniently penetrate, and there, where the desert hesitantly ends and cultivation begins to get a grip, the commerce of east and west have for centuries mingled. Aleppo grew and flourished as an exchange counter, where the seaboard, and often the sea-borne, trader took over the desert traffic. It thrived upon the movement of goods, and looking constantly east and west was not self-contained. Though never a fixed point to which the imagination of the wandering Arab turned as to Damascus, it meant everything to the merchant. To Aleppo he came for wealth and there he stayed to get it, building, to suit his requirements, the great caravanserais which remain one of the most impressive things in the place. Thus while Damascus is the town of the Arab, Aleppo is the town of the merchant.

Merchants are serious men and have perpetually urgent matters to consider. Aleppo therefore lacks the heady irresponsible effervescence of Damascus. It has less politics and less fanaticism; it has also undoubtedly less gaiety. The people, like the unamenable barren slopes that surround the town, have a certain dourness. The stranger will sense in them something of the spirit of the country that lies northward: a restraint, a determination and grimness which are quite un-Arab. It is

* B

worth recalling that here is the latitude where Arabic ends, and where
Turkish and the rough dialects of the hinterland of Asia Minor are first
spoken. Neither the place nor the people are acquainted with oasis
relaxation and the splashing of fountains – the water supply even today
remains inadequate – and one remembers having heard of the paralysing
cold of Aleppo winters. As in the architecture of the uniform beehive
villages, so characteristic of the Aleppo region and so curious, there is no
extravagance of gesture, no waste of energy. It is significant that this
serious place should have preserved more conscientiously than anywhere
else in Syria the stone-cutting tradition of the Middles Ages. Bad houses
are rarely built in Aleppo. Again, the Aleppo *suks*, for all their atmosphere and colour, strike one as being functional. They exist to do
business, and not the haphazard business that spreads its shoddy web
for the tourist and the stranger. The long tradition of solid caravan
merchants is still alive in the town. That is why Aleppo remains
strikingly vital and why better than any other large town in Syria it has
managed to assimilate the West without loss of dignity. Here local
colour is not fake, because it is not an artificial survival from the past.
It is the product of a working economy and organization – an economy
which only yesterday was making fortunes and bringing merchants to
the town with the same intentions and with almost the same programme
as when Jacques Cœur visited Syria on an economic mission in the
fifteenth century. It is this genuine, this contemporary, nature of the
'past' which so often makes the traveller today prefer Aleppo among the
towns of Syria.

The Aleppo plains are dusty and they are usually either too cold or
too hot, circumstances which make doubly pleasurable the ritual of the
bath. Both at Aleppo and Damascus the hotels leave much to be desired,
but the old Turkish baths, which for centuries have been the goal of the
dusty caravaner and traveller on arriving from the deserts, are excellent.
It is not difficult to discover a good one, and having done so to visit it.
In Aleppo, for instance, there is a very comfortable seventeenth-century
bath a stone's throw from the modern quarter. It is typical of many
others. A low door with a fine carved lintel and inscription gives access
to the place. Entering, you find yourself in a large domed room. Around
its four sides, on a raised dais divided into cubicles by low partitions and
a wooden balustrade, couches are disposed. In the middle, goldfish
cruise in a stone basin and a fountain plays. Attendants, seemingly as
ancient as the place itself, take charge of you. Since there are many
baths in Aleppo and, with the arrival of modern plumbing, every year

fewer patrons, they do their best to please. The hot rooms within are also of the period. A central room covered by a cupola carried on eight arches, and pervaded by a soft subaqueous light from apertures filled with greenish glass, gives access to various lesser vaulted chambers. Here the hot water issues into stone basins whence it is swished over you, prone on the marble floor, in a huge copper ladle. Your attendant is extremely dextrous and quite inexorable. Frothing up his soap in a vast bowl of beaten copper, he scrubs and pummels you with the same efficiency that the factors of the Levant Company appreciated three hundred years ago. Back on your couch, relaxed and happy, an endless succession of towels minister to the comfort of a purged perspiring body, ending, when you are ready to drink your Turkish coffee and smoke your long bubbling *narghila*, in magnificent silk affairs. So swathed, reclining on your couch and inhaling the pungent Syrian tobacco, you may be permitted the licence of envisaging yourself back in the Aleppo of Seif-ad-Daula. The types certainly have not much changed. Some of the patrons come in straight from the desert, laying aside their embroidered belts and daggers, shaking off sandals and emerging from folds of clothing, *keffieh* and burnous, to enjoy a bath such as cannot recur often in the length of their year. Equally typical of that past are the fleshed Aleppo merchants, old *habitués*, and in certain of these establishments, the good-looking boys who still play their ambiguous role. There could be no more authentic introduction to the town.

Aleppo comes into history with the Hittites and in the fourteenth century B.C. was, with Carchemish, one of the twin capitals of Shubbiluliuma's aggressive kingdom. Sculpture of this period has turned up from time to time at the citadel and is now collected with the finds from other Hittite sites throughout Syria in the local museum. This, like the museums at Beyrouth and Damascus, is intelligently arranged and excellently kept. The Hittite collection is unique and various, comprising a considerable number of large pieces of statuary and sculpture. Rarity and variety, however, fail to make up for lack of aesthetic interest. Great as must be the historical and archaeological importance of this collection, it has little else to offer. Such a discovery is a disappointment. For so long the Hittites were an enigma and now relatively late so much has been discovered and written about them, that their works come as a sad anti-climax. For the archaeologist trying to reconstruct a civilization, or for the historian of art tracing the origins of the Assyrian style, it will inevitably mean a lot; not so for the mere traveller. The Hittite exhibits, which are mostly in black basalt, are

coarse, heavy, and unimaginative, rarely showing any sense of form
or design. The Hittites, one suspects, were a dull people. It is ironic
that the modern Turks, with a bold disregard for fact, have set them
up as their official ancestors. The Aleppo Museum, it should be added,
contains much besides its Hittite collection. There are some fine
Assyrian things, particularly two decorative warrior heads in mosaic,
and some admirable Sumerian statuary from Tel Harari, at once sensitive and powerful.

Under the Seleucids, Aleppo again came into prominence and, as
Beroea, played with its neighbour Chalcis (Kinessrin) an important part
in the economy of the kingdom. The Seleucids used almost exclusively
the northern trade route to the East and to the city of Seleucia, their
creation on the Tigris; Beroea was thus inevitably a trade stage on one
of the main routes between Antioch and the Euphrates. It seems
probable that in Roman times the general shifting of the east-west trade
to Palmyra and more southerly routes had an adverse effect on the
town's activity. At all events devastation by the Persians in A.D. 540
put an end to Beroea's importance. When the town rose to prominence
again in the tenth century the name Beroea had disappeared and it had
reverted to its old name of Haleb, of which Aleppo is the westernized
form. In the tenth century for a brief period the Hamdanid Dynasty
made Aleppo virtually independent of the Abbasid Caliphate and the
town under the first of the Hamdanids, Seif-ad-Daula, became the seat
of a brilliant court. This gifted prince, eminent as a soldier, was also a
poet and a judicious patron of the arts. While the wealth of the East
flowed into the town, he surrounded himself with talent. For the first
time since the coming of the Abbasids, Syria held up its head. In the
brief florescence of this liberal court, which entertained the sceptical
poet Mutanabbi, and Al-Farabi, the foremost Arab thinker before
Avicenna, Aleppo produced its counterpart to the earlier Umayyad
glory of Damascus. It was unfortunate for Seif-ad-Daula that at the
end of his reign his Byzantine opponent should have been the capable
Emperor Nicephorus Phocas. Successive Greek invasions gave the
dynasty no chance to get a secure footing and soon after the Emir's
death the brilliance passed away. Two hundred years later under El-
Malek-ez-Zaher, Saladin's son, the town experienced its last political
and artistic renaissance. From this, the Ayyubid period, date nearly all
the best buildings that still stand in Aleppo. Its sack by the Mongols in
the middle of the thirteenth century was a severe blow, and the prelude
to over six hundred years' existence as a mere provincial administrative

post, either in the uncertain dominions of the Egyptian Mamelukes or under the Turkish Empire. It remained, however, a vital economic centre. Its geographical position, at the point where the route to India via Baghdad was joined by the more northerly route into Persia via Diarbekr and Mossul, rendered political eclipse relatively unimportant. Caravan traffic had for so many centuries wound in and out of Aleppo along these routes that the habit was not easily lost. Whenever the security of the deserts permitted, merchandise from the East continued to arrive; indeed until yesterday Aleppo remained of the first importance as a trade counter. Nassiri Khosrau, the Persian traveller who visited the town as early as 1047, says that customs were then levied there on merchandise to and from the whole Middle East, and that merchants and traders from the surrounding lands resorted there. A Christian traveller at about the same time says that in the cloth bazaar alone goods to the value of 20,000 dinars changed hands daily. The gold value of this sum, quite apart from its purchasing value, represents today something like £35,000. Neither was the discovery of the Cape route to India as fatal as might have been expected. The Levant Company and the merchants of Marseilles and Venice, who established the town as the chief depot for European trade at the eastern end of the Mediterranean, maintained a very considerable activity. Even the opening of the Suez Canal was not quite as disastrous for Aleppo as for other caravan cities; the town could still tap the traffic of regions to the north and east which remained comparatively unaffected by the new developments. It was only with the break up of the Turkish Empire in 1918 and the erection of fatal trade barriers to the north and north-west that Aleppo changed its character. Until that date it miraculously remained what it had always been, a merchant town based on desert traffic – a town which only once or twice in its long history had put aside (for men like the Hittite kings, Seif-ad-Daula, and the son of Saladin) the respectable business of caravaning to fill more brilliant and, perhaps in the end, less useful roles.

The inhabitants of Aleppo are cursed with a bad reputation and a strange species of boil which leaves a deep scar to be seen on many faces. Both are equally undeserved. Though the locals have not the graces and the Arab gaiety of Damascenes, they are certainly pleasant and helpful to strangers. They seem a quiet people, properly concerned with their own affairs. A large minority of Armenian refugees from Turkey have, however, modified the flavour of certain areas of the town. They have set up their shops throughout the nineteenth-century quarter – whose

attractive balconies with their iron-work railings are characteristic –
and in the modern concrete sector, where, excellent craftsmen, they
seem to have obtained almost a monopoly of certain trades. These
naturally are not the quarters which will attract the traveller. Both the
interest and history of Aleppo lie in its *suks*. These are more authentic
and more impressive than those at Damascus since they have not
been rebuilt. Dating, in part at any rate, from the thirteenth century,
with Saracenic gateways and fine vaulted roofs, they have preserved the
spirit of the desert traffic. They form a compact homogeneous whole and
the queer effect of subterranean life in the warren of streets and passages
is accentuated when one realizes that goats and sheep are grazing above
on the grass-grown roofs. It is worth finding your way on to these.
deserted roofs, a queer empty expanse where the confused murmur from
the vaults below continually rises into the sun.

The way in which romantic writers have spoken of the markets of the
East for a hundred and fifty years finds its justification in the *suks* of
Aleppo. Here indeed exist that atmosphere and those contrasts, strange
to the eye yet familiar to the imagination, described in so many books:
the coloured glooms and the white shafts of sunlight, the desert faces
and the silks, the bearded men who sit cross-legged at scales weighing
out gold and silver, the ceaseless eddying movement and the doorways
into quiet courtyards, heaped merchandise, sherbet sellers, stone fretted
into arabesque, loathsome beggars, brilliance, dirt; and the whole scene
deriving unity from the complex ritual and technique of eastern purchase. Each craft in the traditional way is established in its own street,
and thus the stranger progresses from the leather workers to the smiths,
and so perhaps to those who make the famous gold thread of Aleppo or
to the merchants in silks and stuffs, or to the men who sell spices. Its
spice market long ago, before the discovery of the Cape route, was the
town's chief source of wealth. It is still exotic, bewildering a western
nose with curious scents. Beside many familiar things, rose-leaves and
camomile, cinnamon and saffron, coriander, cloves, aloes, and the rest,
there are puzzling eastern powders, Indian leaves of whose purpose one is
ignorant, strange roots, and even scented stones. The matter for all rare
aphrodisiacs, perfumes and poisons, seems to be canted up in unassuming sacks or crammed into innumerable commonplace jars. The
most active and interesting part of the *suks* today is not the spice
market, however, but the shops where you find everything useful that
the horse, the camel, the sheep or the goat, can possibly produce,
except milk: fine saddles and camel-hair blankets, water-skins, belts,

woollen *abeyiehs* and not least great sheepskin coats to be bought for a song. It is these shops that illustrate the essentially functional character of the Aleppo *suks*. Here the semi-nomads and the desert people still come to buy the things they want; here an eastern market still fulfils its proper purpose, not yet a peep-show into the past for tourists and travellers, not yet perverted to the supply of 'eastern' brass trays, bad leatherwork, worse inlay and fake antiques. Even the merchant's pimp has barely made his appearance in Aleppo, is less limpet-like and still preserves a vestige of humanity and shame.

As a natural corollary to their trade, the Aleppo merchants in the past put up their warehouses and fine private dwellings. A number of these still stand and are of great beauty and architectural interest. The warehouses, or *khans* as they are called, are well-proportioned, satisfying buildings and are almost always constructed on a single model which prevailed from Cairo to Constantinople. Built in college fashion round four sides of a quadrangle, they are entered by an archway similar to those which in our universities are guarded by the 'porter's lodge'. Designed usually to accommodate not only merchandise but a number of merchants, the upper storey is divided into separate living quarters, while the ground floor consists of a series of 'lock-ups' where each merchant could safely store his goods. The function of such buildings forced a symmetry upon the architect; the *ensemble* had its own inherent form, and all that he had to do was to add grace of detail in window mouldings or in a cornice. In some of the larger *khans* his problem was indeed more difficult. There were often considerable wall spaces to be dealt with, but windows, owing to the brilliant light of the East and the necessity of coolness in the torrid summer heats, had to be kept small. The ingenious reply to this difficulty is perhaps best seen in the Khan Wezir, the finest of the old caravanserais, where the small windows are set in wide but shallow bays. The decorative effect is admirable and was evidently so thought since it came to be widely used. It is difficult to exaggerate the charm of these *khans* and the silence and bright sunlight of their courtyards when entered from the bustling gloom of the covered *suks*. Many of them have acquired a grape-vine and perhaps a tree, and in the semidesertion of the twentieth century they live a spacious, lazy life. In one corner an Arab will be asleep on a pile of bales, under the vine you will hear the rattle of dice on a *tric-trac* board, and tethered to the wall a mule or a couple of donkeys will stand by the hour hugging a strip of shade and pawing intermittently on the cobbled floor.[1]

[1] For the old European *khans* see Chapter VIII below.

The private houses are less well known, but perhaps even more remarkable. The old Beit Aida in the Christian quarter, now used as an Armenian school and known as the Beit Gazali, is among the finest of them. Its design is typical: a series of rooms giving on to a courtyard whose salient feature is a high *liwan*. The roof of the *liwan* and two of the rooms (dated 1691 and 1737) are covered with exquisite paintings, for the most part arranged in panels. In the two rooms branches of flowers, bowls of fruit, scroll-work and Arabic inscriptions are combined with extraordinary elegance, and set off by medallions of arabesque in painted plaster. A stone's throw away is another house of the same period and of a not dissimilar plan. There the painted decoration is supplemented on the outside of the building by a fantastically carved stone cornice and panels set over the windows. A first impression, and perhaps the right one, is that the artist here was copying with amazing versatility and in a far more difficult medium the rococo woodwork of the West. Many people will find these houses more impressive than the Azem palaces at Damascus and Hama and they are certainly far superior to the Emir Bechir's fantasies at Beit-ed-Dine. The fact that they were built for Christians spared the architect the necessity of having to modify his plan to include separate female quarters. It becomes at once apparent how much domestic architecture in the East would gain if it did not have to provide for a *haremlek*. These and other houses, tucked away with cautious reticence to hide the owner's wealth from arbitrary authority, are a good indication of what the bustle of the *suks* once meant to the prosperous merchant in terms of elegance and luxurious comfort. To these people the plodding caravans brought, in fact, the architect, the carver and the painter.

The caravans inevitably, and in a similar roundabout way, brought the town its public monuments. Something of the simplicity of the desert perhaps entered into the style of the mosques, which, in common with north Syrian art generally, are characterized by an absence of fuss and undue ornament, and rely for their effects primarily on their sure sense of proportion and admirable freestone masonry. The Gami Halawiyeh is all that remains from the pre-Muslim period. Built by the Empress Helena it became the cathedral of Aleppo, and was maintained as such until the twelfth century when in reprisal for the Crusaders' violation of the Muslim sanctuaries outside the city walls – the Latins were for some time established only twenty miles from Aleppo – it was converted into a mosque. Its fine acanthus capitals, of the type known as 'windblown', date from the fifth or sixth centuries and are pure

examples of the Byzantine style, but are unfortunately terribly beplastered. (The mosque has a famous thirteenth-century *mihrab*, a work
of great virtuosity, that will hardly appeal to contemporary taste.)
Directly opposite the Gami Halawiyeh lies the Great Mosque. This is a
very early Muslim foundation but, with a fate characteristic of so many
Syrian monuments, it was three times destroyed between the tenth and
thirteenth centuries at the hands of the Byzantines, the Ismailis and the
Mongols. Though not in itself a particularly impressive building in its
present form, it has an agreeable spaciousness, and its worn stones
grow delightfully mellow in the rays of an evening sun, while its square
minaret is a thing of astonishing beauty, perhaps the loveliest of many
lovely things in Aleppo. The minaret has a further interest since, dating
from the eleventh century, it is almost the only important monument
which exists in Aleppo from the centuries between Helena's cathedral
and the buildings of the Ayyubids some seven hundred years later. Of
the early Muslim period nothing substantial remains for the traveller to
visit and the tenth-century works of Seif-ad-Daula have similarly disappeared. It is only from the middle of the twelfth century – the ruined
but lovely Gami-es-Shaibiyeh near the Antioch gate is dated 1150 –
that the splendours of Aleppo have survived in any quantity. The
town's great builder was the Ayyubid prince El Malek-ez-Zahir (1185–
1218), son of Saladin, and it was his reign and that of the immediately
succeeding rulers which gave Aleppo its present architectural character.
To recapture something of this period one must go to the south side of
the town where in the Firdausi quarter these Ayyubid princes established their court. The palaces are gone, but in the attractive desertion
of the area, amid fields of ancient carved tombstones, there stand in
semi-ruin mosques and mausoleums which indicate all that the quarter
must once have been. The finest of them and a building of exceptional
attraction is the Mosque of Paradise *El Firdaus* built by El Zahir's
widow. Today it stands among fig and olive orchards and the key must
be sought from a venerable *hadji* who guards the place. The mosque
courtyard is simple and elegant, and creates its impression of beauty
without the slightest effort. Down the *liwan* are pale rose-granite pillars;
a pomegranate, infinitely delicate, flowers against the stone, and a vine,
that must have been there a great many years, throws a dark net of
green out into the court. Not a sound flows in from the deserted tombs
and orchards to break the quiet. The *hadji*, to whom it is all so familiar
that he no longer sees it, has nothing to do day in and day out, and you
can enjoy the mosque at your own pace; and then return again. In the

surrounding quarter a morning may be spent among such silences and sights, entering ruined mausoleums, sharing with the goats the particular pleasure of straying among tombstones, and philosophically contemplating with the shade and support of an olive-tree the remains of twelfth- and thirteenth-century Aleppo.

All visits to this town begin or end with the citadel. From the Firdausi quarter you reach it by a complex of delightful small streets, passing the mausoleum of the last Mameluke governor who in 1516 betrayed the city to the Ottomans, and the Gami-el-Taouachi with its highly interesting and decorative façade. The traveller has heard so much of the Aleppo citadel that he has a right to be disappointed. It is a right that he will rarely wish to exercise. The dominating position of the curious *tell* on which the castle stands has always made it the focus and defence of the town. The Hittites and the Assyrians used it, as fragments found in the substructure of the castle have revealed, and even Abraham is said to have milked his cow upon the summit – a story which Nur-ed-Din evidently believed as he set up a mosque there in his honour in 1167 which is still to be seen. We are apparently not at liberty to believe another attractive story which attaches to the patriarch as dairyman, namely that Aleppo, Haleb as the natives call it, derives its name from *halib*, the Arabic for milk, in commemoration of his activities. The *tell* was a strong place in the Emperor Julian's time, but it was left to the Ayyubids and their successors, mainly in the thirteenth and fourteenth centuries, to transform it into the imposing medieval fortress that one visits today. The glory of the place is undoubtedly the great fortified gateway, once again largely the work of the indefatigable Malek-ez-Zahir. Perhaps the finest example of Saracenic military architecture, its conception is as audacious as it is architecturally impressive. Approached through a crenellated bastion and up a long ramp on arches, the main work is daringly set right on the side of the *glacis*. The entrance is so designed that the besieger, having forced the first gate, finds himself in a corridor with five separate twists or elbows, containing two further massive gates. As if such material obstruction were not in itself discouraging enough, the magnificent gate-archways carry sculptured dragons and lions whose magic influence was expected to prove an additional obstacle. When the defensive walls, now partly dismantled, presented an unbroken ring and the *glacis* around the castle was everywhere faced with stone to prevent the possibility of mining, it can well be imagined what a formidable problem the assault of such a stronghold presented. Within, the castle today is largely ruined, but the restored fifteenth-century throne room over the gateway is magnificent. With its well-proportioned windows and their metal-work grilles (probably of the Kait Bey period), and with just enough decoration to give it relief, it has great distinction. In the citadel one also should not miss the huge bricked vaults with fine barrel-roofing which call to mind the reservoirs at Resafa. An exploration of the citadel will end, and rightly, with the ascent of the square minaret, a shape of minaret so characteristic of Aleppo that in one's mind it always remains associated with the town. From the summit Aleppo, and in a sense its history, are unfolded. There, stretching eastwards, are the camel tracks and the endless expanses, and it is said that the Euphrates itself is sometimes visible from this spot on clear days. South goes the trade route to Damascus which once led on via Bosra and Petra to Egypt. West, where the cultivated green slowly deepens, lies Antioch across the hills, and the Mediterranean, and all that this has meant first in terms of Rome and Constantinople, then of Venice, Genoa, Pisa and lastly of Marseilles, Amsterdam and the worshipful English masters of the Levant Company. Aleppo's position brought caravans, and with them history and the invader. You look down to where the Crusader armies lay encamped near the present railway line, to the Antioch gate where the Muslims entered in the six-teenth year of the Hegira, and north to the Bab el Hadid whence the Mongols swept in with destruction. The past is all below you in these mosques and domes and narrow streets. The town, cupped among the bare plateaux around, is oddly sombre and grey for an eastern city and manages so to remain even in brilliant sunlight. No green relieves the houses, and to the north the cypresses of the Dervish convent of Abu Bakr stand out in solitary contrast. The merchant town has thriven on silk, not on cypress-trees, on ground spice, not on the scent of flowers. Looking down on this *entrepôt*, this warehouse where experts have handled goods for centuries and whose history is written in bills of lading, the sombre and serious note it strikes seems not inappropriate. Even in its stones Aleppo has taken the colour of merchandise. They reflect the dun bales and desert-travelled sacks that, labouring in on camel-back, made the place famous.

CHAPTER III

PHOENICIAN COAST

·❧·

NORTH, from the Palestinian frontier, mountains border the sea. On one side a blue Mediterranean; on the other sometimes foothills and sometimes peaks, but at all times a barrier. Between hills and sea runs a long strip of fertile land protected from the dry eastern winds and absorbing all the moisture of the sea breezes. This is Phoenicia. So narrow is this cultivable strip that here and there where mountain spurs come down, tumbling a cascade of rocks into the sea, it disappears altogether. On the other hand, wherever a river valley pushes back into the mountains, the green fertility creeps a mile or two inland. At such points, the luxuriance is almost oppressive. Rich plantations follow the winding river-course; bamboos and broad-leaved banana plants overhang the water. Exotic trees, which we in the West grow only for ornament, are there laden with fruit. Everything sprouts and burgeons, stirs in the fecund heat-haze. The air is warm and thick, obscuring distant views. The detail of the hills far above is blurred, making not quite real the very different life of shepherds and mountain villagers. Nassiri Khosrau, the Persian traveller, some nine hundred years ago, marvelled at the same generous earth, the same abundance wedged between sea and mountains. Each bay and scallop of the coast has its pleasant village, whose boats on one side and whose orchards on the other, alike creep up among the houses, showing how the people live. At easy stages there are taverns whose vine trellises stretch a tunnel of shade across the coast road. A good smell of *arak* and Turkish coffee greet the visitor, and in the arched coolness they hang up gigantic strings of bananas and set out panniers of tomatoes, oranges and rarer fruit.

It is a pleasant and desirable country, and so the Phoenicians found it when they first came there about three thousand B.C. (Herodotus once again seems to have been right when he says that Tyre was founded in 2759 B.C.). These Semites apparently came from the south, but whatever their origin their subsequent history was largely determined

40

by the geographical limitations of the coastal strip on which they settled. The soil in itself meant prosperity, to which the Phoenicians added enterprise and industry. Yet, as their wealth increased, their ambitions inevitably came up against that hopeless mountain wall behind them. So, cribbed between the peaks and the shore, territorial expansion was impossible. Imperial ideas, and the usual sequence of conquest and defeat, were not for them. Circumstances made them look outwards to the sea, and the sea meant trade. Thus was the particular destiny of the Phoenician towns forced upon them.

In the basement of the Beyrouth Museum, stretching almost from one end of the building to the other, lie side by side twenty-six heavy marble sarcophagi. The ends of these coffins are carved into the shape of heads which are quite evidently portraits, and may be presumed to represent the dead merchants of Sidon who long ago assumed these stone masks. The artistic influences to which the sculptors who carved the heads paid tribute were many, and the types which they attempted to portray also varied; yet there is something common to all these portraits – they reveal business men. There are no saints here, no conquerors, no poets. The determined chin, the cunning lip, the set of the eye, the shrewd features, these everywhere betray money. Interest is on the watch behind the deceptive immobility of stone: these men are traders. One, whose over-regular features are treated in the Greek manner, is betrayed by the slant of the nostrils: he had the monopoly of the murex fisheries, and juggled with prices. Another – see the tight jaw – controlled the timber forests on Sannine, made a good thing out of it, and kept his wages low. A third, in spite of Assyrian-dressed hair, reminiscent of warrior friezes, traded with Cadiz, knew war only over the scales and money-bags, engrossed and grew rich. All these men were wealthy. Company directors are buried in these sarcophagi.

They had the virtues of their calling. Money may have ruled them, but in so doing it certainly stimulated their shrewdness, their tenacity and their amazing enterprises. Their civilization may not have been inspiring, but it seems to have been at any rate practical and refreshingly free from fanatical ideologies. Self-interest and common sense, except in the matter of political disunity, was its keynote. Soldiering was obviously an imbecilic occupation that did not pay, and they accordingly used mercenaries. Their art, as might have been expected, they derived from their neighbours, but they possessed immense technical skill. This they employed to give realism and superficial vitality to the fashions they imported. Thus the hieratical and intensely stylized nature of Egyptian art meant little to these merchants, so while keeping the Egyptian framework and Egyptian motifs they naturalized them as far as they could. Figures and animals came to life, in the vulgar sense of the phrase, and art was brought a little closer to the practical business of living.

In religion also the Phoenicians were not innovators; their busy minds, though prepared to accept mysteries, did not easily invent them. Upon this count the great male and female principles, which they inherited as gods, became more and more local in nature and more and more confined in interest, until at last they seemed little more than municipal godlings presiding over maritime trade ventures. It was suitable also that these Phoenicians should have believed the creation of Tyre due to gods and demi-gods, who there invented all that was later to prove *useful* to the human race. Again take the alphabet, a convenience which the Phoenicians, if they did not actually invent, were largely responsible for making accessible to the Mediterranean peoples. How significant that they should have grasped the value of a thing so essentially practical, and exploited a device which made book-keeping easy and facilitated distant negotiations. The merchant nature of Phoenician society comes out clearly once again in the political constitution of the towns. Though each possessed its hereditary king, the office came to be divested of much of the mystical and ritualistic significance which it possessed elsewhere, and royalty worked in harness with an assembly chosen, characteristically, from among the *richest* merchants. In a wealthy trading community, big business had to be represented. Similarly the foreign policy of the Phoenician towns tended to subordinate allegiance or principle to commercial interest. When their alliances were unfortunate, they may reasonably be supposed to have had their origin in miscalculation rather than friendship. Along with such a business civilization went the comforts and conveniences that one would expect: they drank reputed wines and wore gay multi-coloured clothes (in contrast to the white-robed, priest-ridden Egyptians); their glass-work and jewellery were exquisite and famous; so too the embroidered stuffs of Tyre and Sidon, whose renown was such, Homer says, that Paris bought some to take back to his mother-in-law at Troy. Wealth created a demand for such things and Phoenician craftsmanship supplied it. The unheroic business man is never popular, and it is easy to decry such a civilization – in certain respects not very dissimilar to our own – but it is also unfair. These men may have been a little close across the counter – indeed they had a poor reputation for honesty – but they were hard-working, far-seeing, full of enterprise, and little cursed with irresponsible enthusiasms. Their pursuit of the profitable brought about neither famines nor massacres, and in their undertakings they spread the benefits of their practical outlook and their technical progress even beyond the Mediterranean. At home they must have evolved a society that, out of business hours, was relatively tolerant and easy-going, and – though unfortunately the town sites have been built over so often that little civil and domestic architecture remains, other than that excavated at Ras Shamra – they must have made the narrow strip between mountains and sea an animated, prosperous and comfortable place in which to live.

As the geographical position of Phoenicia determined the channel into which the energies of the people flowed, so did it account for their foreign relations. The tragedy of the country lay in its size: though wealthy, it was not large enough to stand alone. Thus the political history of the Phoenician towns lies in their attempts to maintain a precarious independence by playing off successive great powers one against the other. They usually failed to do so.

Egypt's need for timber had led to the opening of relations with Byblos before 3000 B.C., and, as excavations at Ras Shamra have shown, the link between Egypt and the Phoenician coast grew very close in the succeeding millennium. Tyre and Sidon come strongly into the historical picture with the Tel el Amarna letters which date in the main from about 1410–1360 B.C. These letters, discovered at Tel el Amarna in Egypt, brought to light the correspondence between the Phoenician princes and their Egyptian suzerains and show the state of affairs in the Phoenician coast towns when they were vassal states of the Eighteenth Dynasty. Three hundred years after the date of these letters, not only was Egypt in eclipse, but Assyria – the other big neighbour – had not finally settled her accounts with Babylon, and a unique opportunity presented itself. Phoenicia for a time was free. The centuries immediately after 1100 B.C. constitute the golden age of Tyre and Sidon.

This was the period of the enterprising Hiram, King of Tyre, with whom Solomon worked in such close co-operation, the period of the founding of Carthage (circa 814 B.C.), and that in which the Phoenician littoral fully developed its characteristically merchant civilization. The role of the Phoenicians was that of commercial intermediaries between East and West, and the wealth of both passed through their hands. Their prosperity largely depended on the maintenance of a brisk trade movement, and it thus became a primary problem for them to ensure a proper flow of commodities, and of the right sort of commodities at the

right time. This problem they sensibly and effectively solved by estab-
lishing counters east and west throughout the large trade basin which
during these fortunate centuries drained into the Phoenician littoral. It
is a mistake to regard their effort as a colonial one; they had not got the
population to colonize widely. (Carthage, created by a dissident minority
from Tyre as the result of a political upheaval, was an anomaly. It is
significant that the mother town could not support the loss of manpower
and began to decline soon after.) The Phoenician posts established
abroad were primarily trade missions. To Cadiz and Sardinia they came
to control the flow of ore; to Hama, Damascus and farther east, to keep
a finger on the pulse of the caravan traffic; and they went south to
Memphis to tap the wealth of the Nile and get the first pick of ivory and
gold-dust from Sennar. The resources of their own country were, of
course, also fully exploited. These had been the initial factor in the
growth of Phoenician prosperity and had provided the capital and
goods with which their first more ambitious enterprises were launched.
From the earliest times the timber on the Lebanon had been felled and
had provided an invaluable export. We hear of a large cargo being
shipped to Egypt about 2840 B.C. To this were added the murex
fisheries, a monopoly of the towns of Tyre and Sidon and the chief
source of the purple dye so prized by the Ancients. Lastly there were
glass-making and the Phoenician handicrafts.

Counters abroad and resources at home would have meant little
without an efficient marine. Here again fortune was kind to the Phoenicians at the beginning of the first millennium before Christ. The
Cretan naval power which had dominated the eastern Mediterranean
disappeared soon after the twelfth century with the eclipse of Minoan
civilization. The Phoenicians were not slow to seize their opportunity.
About 1500 B.C. they had not been able to find vessels enough to carry to
Egypt timber ordered by the Pharaoh, and transport had been provided
by the Cretans: five hundred years later their marine controlled the
Mediterranean. Phoenician vessels, trade-bound, studded the inner sea,
pushed down the west coast of Africa in search of new wealth, and came
to call at Cornish ports. Compassless, they steered by the Little Bear,
which the Greeks, in tribute to their maritime supremacy and skill,
came to know as the 'Phoenician Star'. Conscious of the vital importance of their sea communication, the Phoenicians stamped the galley
on their coins and transformed their inland deities into gods of the sea.
Even later when their independence had gone, their naval genius did
not desert them. A prince of Sidon was admiral of the Persian fleet, and

a Phoenician contingent fought with distinction against the Greeks at Salamis.

The Phoenician economy – home industries, trade counters abroad, and the indispensable linking marine – benefited over its neighbours by developing and exploiting the alphabet. Thanks to this ingenious device, writing became comparatively simple, a thing accessible not only to the scribe but to the ordinary man of affairs. The effective control of distant interests and intricate business thus was no longer a hopelessly complicated problem. Phoenician merchants and administrators, among the first to exploit the new technique, reaped a due profit. When others still often trusted to hieroglyphs, memory and word of mouth, they sent detailed written instructions a thousand miles.

There is, again in the Beyrouth Museum, a vast royal sarcophagus, and scrawled on its granite side an inscription. To the amateur eye it is perhaps just recognizably alphabetic, and here and there is a sign which might correspond to the primitive form of a Greek letter. It is, in fact, one of the earliest examples of advanced alphabetic writing. This Syrian tomb foreshadows half the future of man. Without these ragged signs we should hardly have preserved Homer, Shakespeare's plays might have been acted but not recorded, and even Gibbon may be said to have unwillingly set out from this religious monument. The tomb was actually the resting-place of Ahiram, King of Byblos, who died in the thirteenth century B.C., and the inscription reads: 'Itobaal, son of Ahiram, King of Jebail [Byblos], made this sarcophagus for Ahiram, his father, as his dwelling for eternity. And if a king among the kings, or a governor among the governors, raises war against Jebail and lays bare this sarcophagus, the sceptre of his power will be broken, the seat of his royalty will be overthrown, and peace will reign again in Jebail. As for his posterity they shall be cut off by the sword.' The warning proved in vain; the tomb had been uncovered and rifled, presumably by robbers, long before the archaeologists arrived. None the less these futile monitions might, not without reason, claim to be historically among the most important phrases recorded. They mark the beginning of a new era.

The origin of the alphabet is disputed. It may have been a Phoenician invention or it may have been derived from elsewhere. Sinaitic and hieratic Egyptian are among the rival parents claimed. (Disputed also is the honour of having first deciphered it: two eighteenth-century scholars, a Frenchman, and an Englishman by the name of Swinton, being here the rivals.) Whatever its origin, the 'Phoenician' alphabet (with its twenty-two letters, which included even vowels) possessed tremendous advantages over anything that had preceded it, and particularly over the cumbersome pictorial writing of earlier civilizations. The cuneiform and the hieroglyph, essentially expressing not sounds but things and ideas, were complex and inflexible. Written communication through such a medium would have remained laborious and stilted. There was no future in it. Whether the warrior nations of the time would have had the sense to grasp the full importance of the phonetic alphabet, or the interest to exploit it, is doubtful. Writing was for them the specialized work of a lower caste, the scribes. For the Phoenicians it was a different matter; their power and their civilization did not rest upon military exploits, but in account books. For them the alphabet was vital. They took it, shaped it, used it, and passed it on to the Greeks. So the alphabet reaches us today, and every written word remains in some sense a monument to the Phoenicians, a monument of a practical sort that they would have appreciated.

As the Phoenicians bustled about their business and the first millennium B.C. got well under way, the march of events on the Euphrates began to take a dangerous turn. Assyria having dealt with Babylon started to look west and south. Great powers were again stirring and the end of the happy interlude between military empires, that had meant independence for the coast towns, was merely a matter of time. The Bible tells how, as the eastern menace grew, Israel was torn between the alternatives of Assyria and Egypt, and backed the wrong power. The Phoenicians soon were in the same dilemma, and all their cunning in the tactic, which history so often imposed upon them, of playing off one military power against another, could not long delay the issue. In spite of tortuous intrigue and repeated revolts, by about 700 B.C. Phoenician independence had gone and the towns were Assyrian vassal states. Less than two hundred years later they moved into the Persian orbit, and Sidon revolting once again was burnt and forty thousand perished. Next, it was Alexander. This proved a more deadly conquest, for with it the hellenization of the country began. With the gradual substitution of Greek for the native language, the disappearance of the Phoenicians as a separate people was only a matter of time. The process was accelerated by the strong philhellenism of sections of the upper class. Thus the King of Sidon, who went over with his fleet to Ptolemy in 287 B.C., was proud to call himself Philocles. In spite of a brief spell of independence just before the Romans took over, when once again there was an interval with no great power dominating the coast, Phoenicia as a whole rapidly lost its identity. The Phoenicians had become Greeks and Phoenicia simply one of the composite parts of the Graeco-Roman world.

In spite of the geographical limitation on Phoenician military power, the story from the beginning might have been different had the various Phoenician towns been willing or able to co-operate. As it was they never achieved unity and never had the wit to see that only by standing together could they hope to stand at all. Sidon combined with the Assyrians against Tyre and similar treacheries were common in the history of the four major Phoenician towns. For this fatal disunity there were probably three main causes. First, poisonous commercial jealousies of long date; second, the political organization of the country into a number of petty local kingships, each based on one of the major ports, each claiming sovereignty over its neighbours, and each in turn striving at the propitious moment to impose its own hegemony on the others; third, once again geography. It was highly unfortunate that geographical advantages were so evenly distributed. The forces of nature did not operate in Phoenicia, as they have done in most other countries, to bring a particular town into a position of prominence. None of the ports was provided with a harbour of such outstanding excellence that it inevitably outstripped its rivals; none was so placed as to dominate an appreciably larger stretch of arable belt than did its neighbours; none was distinguished by particularly easy communications inland; none had the chance of immediate superiority that situation on a navigable river would have offered. Nature had been strictly and tragically impartial. Where there was no necessary superiority, competition was inevitable.

The four great Phoenician towns were Arvad, Byblos, Sidon, and Tyre. Of Tyre, foremost of these in the heyday of Phoenician independence, little remains. With its island fortress, on which the whole town came to be concentrated, it was a place of great strength, and its history is a series of long sieges. At the end of the eighth century B.C. it successfully sustained a decade of Assyrian blockade and assault. Some hundred and thirty years later Nebuchadnezzar vainly besieged it for half a generation. Two centuries after that Alexander, to reduce the city, joined it to the mainland by a vast causeway. No longer an island, Tyre fell, and the whole population were massacred or sold into slavery. The site, however, still remained formidable. Not long after, Antigonus sat before the walls fourteen months. So the tale goes on; one siege after another. At the time of the Crusades the place was still so strong that, as other coast towns fell, the Muslims flocked there, believing it impregnable. The Venetians, with the finest fleet of the time, had to be called in to reduce it.

Today it is not worth the taking. Djezzar Pasha in the eighteenth century removed most of the stone to rebuild Acre, the harbour long ago silted up, and sand has now invaded even the town. A wretched Armenian refugee-village hangs on its outskirts and the place itself has almost nothing to show for its past wealth. Ezekiel's curses have come home in full measure. Tyre's walls are indeed destroyed and her towers broken down, and the site become a fishing village, 'a place for the spreading of nets in the midst of the sea'. The prophet's tremendous attack on Phoenician civilization gives perhaps better than anything else a just idea of the economic splendour of the first of the coast towns in its heyday. Some of the imports, as listed by the prophet, indicate the variety of the Tyrian traffic: silver, iron, tin and lead from Spain; slaves and brass vessels from Cilicia and Ionia; horses and horsemen from Armenia; ivory and ebony from Edom; emeralds, embroidered work and fine linen from Syria; wheat, honey and oil from Palestine; wool and wine from Damascus; cassia from Dan; from Arabia sheep; from the Sabaeans spices, precious stones and gold. With exact insight Ezekiel also puts his finger on the moral weakness of this commercial civilization: 'Thou has corrupted thy wisdom by reason of thy brightness.' Material comfort obscured deeper values, and there followed commercial violence and 'iniquity of . . . traffic'. The whole indictment is a good summary of the dangers that beset a society based solely on trade and money.

Not only at Tyre, but almost everywhere up the coast, the domestic architecture of the Phoenicians has disappeared. The palaces, the warehouses, the municipal buildings, have all gone. Once again the geography of Phoenicia is largely responsible. On that narrow coastal strip every yard of each harbour site has been built over again and again. In such a confined area towns do not shift their ground; and the archaeologist cannot hope to find those deserted sites[1] which best preserve the past.

Sidon, on its elbow of land, has been built, and rebuilt, century after century, and the town not infrequently destroyed. Only the methods and degree of destruction have varied: the Assyrians knocked it down, the Persians burnt it, and the Saracens on two occasions razed the walls. Naturally enough little specifically Phoenician remains. Recent centuries, on the other hand, have been kind and Sidon has exceptional charm and the personality that towns with a long pedigree sometimes

---

[1] The buried town of Ugarit at Ras Shamra is a notable exception.

acquire. Thus, though the 'Mother of Tyre', as the town was often called, has strictly speaking disappeared, the imagination is not altogether disappointed. The place, as it should, reeks of the sea. Water laps against the houses, marine affairs invade the town, and boats are built almost in the streets. Standing on the harbour edge, the Phoenician past is not difficult to recall. Something tangible in fact still exists. The little port before one was the 'Closed Harbour' of the Ancients, closed by the same reef as protects it from the sea today, and though the Crusaders put up the ruined castle on the island, the building stands on the site of a columned temple, probably dedicated to the Phoenician Hercules. Only a few fishing vessels ride at anchor and the port has sanded up considerably since the seventeenth century when the Emir Fakr-ed-Din closed its main entrance to keep out the Turkish fleet; yet it is not impossible to imagine the crowded galleys there in Phoenician days and the noise and traffic of the harbour side. It was to this quiet basin that boats returned, after heaven knows how many difficult months at sea, with tin from Cornwall, or ivory from far down the coast of Africa. Here, too, arrived Egyptian works of art and Cretan culture, and the thought of the ancient world met and was fused in the first business civilization. Here daily the murex fishers brought in their catch, and near by, as vast heaps of murex shell reveal, the precious purple dye was extracted. The form of the harbours – for there are in fact two – has also preserved something typically Phoenician. Usually these merchants (as the Crusaders still did two thousand years later) simply beached their boats, and for their towns, as far as possible, chose sites having two beaches facing different points of the compass. One of these would be sheltered and accessible whichever way the wind was blowing. This convenience existed at Sidon. To the south of the town one may see the smaller 'Egyptian Harbour' which offered complete shelter when, owing to the north wind, it might have been difficult for incoming vessels to make the narrow mouth of the main harbour.

From the sun and sea, from the nets and children playing among the boats, you pass at a stride into small winding streets, cool and resonant. They are vaulted over, and with their arches, and their cobbles underfoot, are the characteristic feature of the town. It is a queer half-light in which you walk, broken here and there by vivid bars of sunlight from the harder, brighter world above. In spite of the hidden nature of the streets and their subterranean twistings, the smell of the sea persists, dominant, working its way even into the bazaars. The attraction of the latter is due not only to effects of chiaroscuro, but also to their modest

intimate character. They decently and effectively serve the needs of a
Muslim fishing town and its surrounding district. This is their function,
and pretending to nothing more they express the life of the place immediately and gracefully. To each trade is allotted, in medieval fashion,
its particular street. The carpenters inevitably, in a sea town, are many,
and there is an attractive street of cobblers in which the Sidonians – a
name by which the civilized world, and beyond, once referred not only
to the people of Sidon but to all the inhabitants of the Phoenician coast
– mend and sell shoes. The little fruit and vegetable street is filled to
overflowing from the town's almost fabulous gardens. Open to the sky,
but with a variety of awnings extending over the stalls, the street is a
moving tangle of shadow, sun and colour, and the fruits, heaped high
on trays or spilling out of wicker baskets, positively glow. Probably the
fine vaulting, the general air of good building and a certain style in the
streets – incidentally quite unsuspected from the main road which only
fringes the old town – all date from the time of Fakr-ed-Din. This
remarkable man, the last great figure Sidon knew, gave the town a
commercial renaissance in the seventeenth century, and for a time it was
again a thriving busy place and the port for Damascus. The Emir was a
shrewd man and it was part of his wisdom that he encouraged the merchants of the West and the trade they brought, and sheltered them as
far as possible from the fanatical persecutions to which they were elsewhere often subjected. It was in pursuance of this policy that he erected
the *Khan Fransawi*, or French Merchant Hostel, one of the most
delightful and interesting buildings anywhere on the coast. It has
survived intact and is a particularly good example, and typical in
style, of the buildings in which western merchants in the East lived and
conducted their business. With the decline of Sidon in the nineteenth
century the merchants went, but they have been succeeded by the
Sisters of St Joseph, for whom the old two-storeyed *khan*, set round a
quadrangle, makes an appropriately monastic setting. Each floor is
arcaded and these arches, once crammed with French merchandise,
have now taken on a devotional air. In the courtyard goldfish glitter in a
deep fountain-basin; there are pomegranates and oranges, and overhanging them two or three tall trees. There is the usual cloister-like
contrast of sun and shade, of cool scrubbed stone within and warm ochre
stone outside basking in the sun. The *khan* in a curious way is an intensi-
fication, though a silent and cloistral one, of all that is pleasantest in the
small Sidon streets among which it was planted. The twilight of arcades
or tunnelled streets, and an almost watery coolness – these, juxtaposed

to sudden vivid warmth and sunlight, are what one most remembers both of the lost Phoenician town and the *khan* of the seventeenth-century merchants.

It is atmosphere that constitutes the charm of Sidon almost exclusively. There is little actually to visit. The castle where St Louis stayed interests only archaeologists, and the Great Mosque hides its only decent feature, some old Corinthian capitals, under the usual layer of whitewash. One should not overlook, in this part of the world, the existence of a tolerable restaurant, where sitting on a balcony overlooking the harbour you can eat good fish. This is perhaps a course to be recommended before going to visit, in the drowsy heat of an afternoon, the gardens of the town. In ancient times there were two parts to Sidon – the port town and an inland town on the last spurs of the Lebanon; between them lay the gardens. Famous even then, they remain beautiful today. Fed by innumerable artificial runnels, taken off from the Nahr-el-Awali as it passes on its way to the sea, and nursed by the damp coast airs, the gardens epitomize, yet far outdo, all the luxuriance of the littoral fringe. Enclosed by high crumbling walls over which appear the heads of cypresses and palms, the gardens have an air of withdrawal, of having been shut in upon themselves for many centuries. They look intensely 'private' and are therefore irresistible. You knock on one of the large faded gates. Presently it creaks open and the guardian of the place lets you in. You wander on, preferably alone, into a world of green. The greater trees shadow the almonds and apricots, and these in turn look down on oranges and plants waist-high, and the sun filters down through them all to grass and water. The impression created is one of great age; even the saplings seem established, at home, heirs not newcomers. The paths seem old too; their earth settled, packed down long ago. The sense of time, that adds so much to a garden, is here almost tangible, and it is something of a mystery how leaves, re-created each spring, can be so heavily impregnated with the past. The harvest of these high-walled green enclosures is infinitely various and rich: oranges, bananas, lemons, guavas, mulberries, figs, apricots, peaches, almonds, melons, pomegranates, medlars. The fruits are unending. Half the charm of these gardens is that they are essentially for production, and so differ from the great southern gardens of Europe, or the formal wonders that Lenôtre designed. They are merchants' gardens, and the Phoenicians, who presumably first exploited them, carefully kept the balance sheet of profit and loss. In those days the gardens were perhaps less attractive than now; they were too neat and too well-run. Today they are unhurried,

and have that air, infinitely engaging in gardens, of running themselves, of being ungardenered. Yet though creepers spread and green
gates remain unpainted, the harvest continues to come in, almost automatically, though perhaps not with the exactly calculated foison which
it was once made to yield. The loss in volume is amply compensated, for
surely only by the lapse of time have these merchants' gardens come
to combine function and decoration, and grown in their old age rare
pleasaunces as well as orchards.

About two hundred kilometres north of Sidon lay the island town of
Arvad, northernmost of the Phoenician tetrarchy. Like Sidon it has its
own character and atmosphere, though only vestiges of the Phoenicians
remain. The town early acquired importance among the Phoenician
kingdoms, and founded satellite towns on the mainland known as the
'Daughters of Arvad'. It even extended its rule for a time as far inland
as Hama. When the Eighteenth Dynasty drew southern Phoenicia into
the Egyptian orbit, Arvad retained its independence, but it failed to
keep up with Tyre and Sidon in their heyday. Under the Seleucids, it
again came to the fore and, though only for a short while independent,
it continued to have first-class commercial importance until Roman
times. It was then displaced by Antaradus, the modern Tartûs.

It is from Tartûs that you hire a felucca to cross the three or four
kilometres to Arvad, or Ruad as it has come to be called. Early in
the morning there is often a misty gold haze on the water, distorting
shapes, blurring the horizon and confounding sea and sky. At some
indeterminate distance, the island of Arvad, catching the slanting sunlight, seems to float far above the water. There is rarely a wind at this
time of the morning and the sea is usually smooth, and heavy as blue
oil. Minutes go by, and in spite of oars to help the flapping sail the boat
hardly seems to advance. Though the mainland recedes, the unreal
island with its shining quays, its suggestion of towers and palaces, floats
away. The boatmen talk monotonously in an Arab patois; and the stillness, the early sun and the ineffective splash of the oars, induce a
drowsiness improper to the hour. In an imprecise world of haze, sun and
water, following the elusive island, you doze and nod in the stern. You
will at last look up to find the island quite near. For no particular reason
its flight has stopped, and with it the airy towers and palaces have
disappeared. There awaits you simply a fishing town crowded on a
little island eight hundred metres long. It is, however, as you soon
discover, a fishing town of special charm and interest. The island was
once a vast fortress encompassed with huge sea walls, and many of the

houses that come down to the water's edge are built into their ruins and give, by reason of the lighter stone of which they are constructed, an effect almost like inlay. The façade of the town – an alternation of umber houses and darker ruins – stretches like a ribbon edging the blue water. In front, a mole protects anything up to the thirty schooners that may lie at anchor. As your boat approaches, voices come echoing over the water, and with them the pleasant noise of hammers on timber. Ruad lives from the sea, and in the very streets that go down to the harbour they build up the skeletons of the schooners that enable them to run a coasting trade from Turkey to Egypt. Even the people are amphibian, and as you draw in, furling your sail, a shoal of naked brown bodies, the boys and the little girls of the town, come sporting round your boat.

Along the harbour front, among the drying nets, the cafés throw out rush-work awnings, and however early you may arrive the local seafarers, looking curiously unmarine in their baggy Turkish trousers, will be smoking their hookahs over coffee and talking of their trade. All the active life of the place is on this harbour front and there are no proper streets in the warren of the town that lies behind. The people are *Sunnis*, as you will guess seeing the veiled women creep in self-obliteration down the alleys, and hopelessly poor. It is the old story in Syria. All the wealth is in the hands of three or four families who own most of the schooners, exploit the fishermen and run the island in a degenerated feudal fashion. Yet the people retain their pride and self-respect. It is a pride that history justifies, for these *Ruadis*, men of Ruad, work what are probably the oldest shipbuilding yards in the world. Few such tiny harbours have played so great a role. As the Phoenician Arvad the island was, as we have seen, the centre of an important kingdom. Wholly girdled with cyclopean walls, and deriving its water-supply from fresh springs that rise in the sea itself, it was an impregnable fortress and warehouse. In the harbour was fitted out the expedition which served with distinction against the Greeks at Salamis, and later when Alexander hellenized the coast the wealth of the merchants adorned the town with every sort of splendour. Later again by over a thousand years, Ruad was the last stronghold of the Latin Kingdom and held out, garrisoned by the Templars, for eleven years after Acre had fallen. Lastly – and their part in this adventure the Ruadis have not forgotten – the island was seized from the Turks in 1914 by a single French vessel and for four years remained an isolated Allied outpost on the Turkish flank, whence the Ruadi sailors smuggled over supplies to the starving population on the mainland.

C

Of all this history there is little to show at Ruad today. It is the atmosphere and the harbour that must help the imagination to eke out the story, together with the remains of the Phoenician walls and, oddly enough, a liquor shop which also does duty as tobacconist and chemist. The shop lies just off the harbour. The owner, who knows French, speaks curiously of the world, but his interests, as one soon finds, are strictly subordinate to business. He is a merchant above all, and the chaffering Phoenician blood seems still to run in his veins. After you have bought his great yellow sponges, fresh as the divers bring them in from the sea, he produces a bag – odds and ends found in the ruins, blurred intaglios, and a few Phoenician coins. Coins stamped with the gods of Arvad: he lays them out on the palm of his hand, knowing you want them. He is informative; mildly discursive he talks of old things; yet all the time he is testing your temper, silently bartering, probing for a price. When you have finally bought them, you have paid too much. How could it have been otherwise? A man of Arvad handling Phoenician coin.

It was such counter-cunning that found the wealth to build the great sea walls. These, hewn in immense megalithic blocks, clearly indicate how formidable the *enceinte* must once have been, and on the west at one point they still rise nearly forty feet sheer from the sea. The size and solidity of these ruins leave no doubt as to the importance of the place and the obstinate energy of the builders. Of later date, there is a castle of the Crusaders, subsequently taken over and rebuilt, as was most of the town, by their Muslim successors. It is of no particular interest, but over the gateway is the Lusignan coat of arms – the Lion and the Palm – adapted in the pleasant malice of Saracen humour, or so the legend goes, by the addition of a chain firmly securing the royal beast to the palm over which he had presumed to rule. The Saracens were at liberty to put up such tokens of their victory, but the Muslim occupation in fact meant that the history of Ruad came to an end.

On the mainland facing their island, the men of Arvad founded one of their earliest settlements on the site now known as Amrit and marked by a series of ruins scattered across a mile and a half of ground. It seems queer country to have chosen. Salty, barren land, where a sluggish river twists out to the sea, it is good only for light grazing, and to breed malarial mosquitoes. It has, however, the charm of desolation and a pleasantly eerie grandeur in its strange ruins. There are three main things to see. First, as you come up the coast road, appears, some way off to your left, a sombre mausoleum. A great black cube, raised in cyclopean blocks and called by the Arabs for some reason the Tower of the Snails, it stands today inaccessible in the midst of a marshy pool. You approach it across barren undulating ground, the haunt of innumerable lizards, and covered with tall yellow-flowered thistles. In the evening the shepherd who pastures in the area leaves with his flock for the village that lies inland, and as the sun sets and the crickets abruptly fall silent, the place grows intensely lonely. In the quiet you become aware of the sinister hum of mosquitoes. A pair of Kitlitz plovers, that probably breed somewhere near, run with mincing steps away along the edge of the blackening pool. They are the only sign of life. No one knows who built the giant Phoenician cube or for whom its two funerary chambers were prepared, nor when the pyramid which crowned it came crashing down, where it still lies, in the pool below. The city that surrounded it has gone, but the savage black structure gains by standing alone and, as the light weakens, more and more dominates the desolation.

Farther north, and to the east of the main road, are two stone monuments equally strange, known as the Spindles. Both consist of pedestals (one of them rudely carved with four lions), which are surmounted by large monolithic cylinders, and these in turn are capped respectively by a pyramid and a half-circle. Standing on the top of a little ridge, and commanding an area honey-combed with shallow quarries whence the material for the Phoenician town was taken, these enigmatic pillars impress out of all proportion to their size. Phoenician art as it appears here and in the sinister Tower of the Snails is so unfamiliar, so utterly unconnected with anything the stranger has known in the West, that it arouses unusual emotions. Normal reactions to works of art and architecture would hardly include this curious awe, an almost frightened wonder, at the strange primeval beliefs of which these black stones are the visible tokens.

Yet farther north, just above the Nahr Amrit, lies a sanctuary which must once have been the focal point of all these ruins. It is a rectangular area cut, on three sides, out of the solid rock; a wall and gates once composed the fourth side, where nothing now separates the sanctuary from the fields. In the middle of the sacred area rises a mass of rock some ten feet high by eighteen feet square on which a tiny naos, with simple frieze and cornice, stands. The attraction of the site consists today in the fact that a spring, rising somewhere in the sanctuary, floods its floor to a considerable depth. As a result the cella rises like an island from lush watergrass, and the last light of the evening sky is reflected in this temple lake. In crevices of the smooth rock-walls bushes and flowers have rooted themselves and overhang the water. Where the Phoenician priests once trod, sedge-warblers chatter in clumps of reed, and as it darkens the bull-frogs set up a blasphemous sex chant.

The Amrit sanctuary is not only a lovely place at evening, but has much religious and historical importance. Where fanaticism does not destroy religious monuments, there is often good chance that reverence or superstition may preserve them. Thus, though the shops and palaces of this most merchant race have nearly all gone, by a curious irony their sanctuaries remain at Amrit, Byblos, Eshmun, and, in a later dress of Graeco-Roman stone, at the mountain sites of Hosn-es-Suleiman and the Springs of Adonis. To appreciate these places one must know at any rate something of Phoenician faith and practice.

The Phoenicians had at some point acquired the general religious conceptions of the Asiatic hinterland, involving the idea of the Great Mother and of her complement, the fecundating male god. Once settled on the coast their beliefs were naturally modified by a variety of contacts, most important among them being that of Egypt. Though in belief the Phoenicians were not innovators, in religious usage they apparently had something very positive to give many of their neighbours. Characteristically enough theirs was a practical gift; it was the scheme and layout of the Semitic sanctuary. This, as it was evolved by the Phoenicians, caught on in astonishing fashion, spread throughout Syria, and at last made its way to Rome on a metropolitan scale in the works of Apollodorus of Damascus. The form of the primitive Phoenician sanctuary was simple and its features uniform. It consisted of a large rectangular enclosure, sometimes cut in part from the solid rock, and it contained in its midst a *small* detached naos before which stood an altar and usually a sacred spring, or basin, or even a sacred tree. Apparently the earliest of these Syrian sanctuaries is that at Amrit; hence its unique interest. A more ruined but early example also exists at Eshmun, near Sidon. Once the essential plan of these sanctuaries has been grasped, they clarify much that would otherwise need explanation. When Amrit is accepted as the prototype, the heredity of its more illustrious children, such as the great Temple of Baal at Palmyra, or the lost Temple of Jupiter at Damascus, becomes evident. These, though on a far vaster scale, exhibited the same spacious *enceinte*, the same relatively small naos, and, exterior to the temple, the emplacement of the altar and the sacred basin for lustration. Something of Amrit even appears in the great court before the Temple of Jupiter at Baalbeck with its sacred altar and its two carved water-basins. It is curious to reflect that the latter with their tritons and nereids, and their cupids astride fabulous beasts, are simply the sophisticated descendants of the receptacles which held the waters of the natural spring in the sanctuary at Amrit.

The temple at Hosn-es-Suleiman marks an intermediate stage between the primitive sanctuaries and the great works such as the Temple of Baal into which they developed. Set on a site sacred to the Phoenicians from the earliest times, the temple at Hosn-es-Suleiman retained both the proportions and the exact form of the primitive sanctuaries, but rebuilt at a later period put on a Graeco-Roman dress. Situated in the wildest part of the Alawi Mountains, Hosn-es-Suleiman is certainly the most isolated of the Phoenician ruins. It is well worth visiting. You leave the coast at Tartûs on a bad road which very soon becomes horrible. In places you have to get out of the car and build up your track where, on the steep hillsides, the rain has washed it away. (All the roads in the interior of the Alawi country are unspeakable, and form a disagreeable contrast with the excellent mountain roads that the French engineered in the Lebanon.) As the crow flies it is not a long way, but it is difficult to average much more than ten kilometres an hour over the last twenty or thirty kilometres. It is possible and agreeable, if you like primitive local hospitality, to stop the night at Dreikich, rather over half-way. There is no inn, but the local sheik, head of the Shamsin tribe, when informed of your presence will wish to put you up. The hospitality of these mountain people towards strangers is warm, unfailing and almost embarrassing in its completeness. If a sheep is available it will be killed in your honour; and, after a night between rough but clean sheets under a vast eiderdown, you will be early regaled with eggs, *leban*, meat balls, Turkish coffee and fruit.

From Dreikich to the temple is a fine drive in spite of the stops and jolts. The sun will just be rising as you wind into hills which give the impression of a hopeless and inextricable tangle. It is surprising that the streams ever work their way out of such a maze. You, dipping into valleys and climbing hills, edging round shoulders and pulling over crests, have at any rate the sun and, in the far distance, the often reappearing sea to guide you. There are otherwise no landmarks, no dominating massif or deep-cut valley, no little village even, to lead you on in this wild jumble of hills and streams. Soil is sparse and the rocky country carries scrub, wild flowers and enough pasture for goats and a few mountain cattle. Where a rare cottage shelters under a hillside there is an isolated patch of cultivated land, usually maize, and in the steep valleys a trickle of bright green with perhaps a few scattered poplars follows the watercoursès. It is bare country but attractive, and as you get higher a new feature of strangeness and charm is added to the landscape: the sacred groves of the Nosairis. These dark clumps, usually of deciduous or evergreen oaks, not only come unexpectedly and with immense importance in a treeless country, but stand in unexpected places, not only in the sheltered cups where you would think they might have taken root, but on the very summits of the hills. Reverence for their antiquity has saved these groves from goats, Turks and the improvidence of the peasants. The Phoenicians worshipped such sacred trees, and their cult by the Nosairis, who have retained so many pagan beliefs, may be presumed to have survived from the day when Arvad and her 'daughters' popularized the worship of the grove. Today the groves house innumerable squirrels and sometimes the modest whitewashed tomb of a Nosairi saint. Shepherds – the only people you meet on these high hills – take the shade there and greet you as you pass.

The temple appears at last, set in a natural amphitheatre below a high grove-crowned crest. The mountain rises on three sides; on the fourth, where a spring bubbles from the rocks just outside the temple, the hillside, strung with dwarf poplars, drops away into the valley. All mountain sanctuaries are special; and this Semite shrine in the height and wilderness has something of the grandeur of places like Delphi and Bassae. North the tangled hills continue, south like a huge white cloud hang the Lebanon snows, and far out west is a streak of Phoenician sea. The sanctuary itself is typically Phoenician in layout, but built in the first and second centuries A.D. is Graeco-Roman in its detail. The large temenos constructed in massive grey stone – some of the blocks are over two metres long – is well preserved, but has been delightfully desecrated by the hillside vegetation. Flowers sprout from the masonry, bracken grows within and without and mulberry-trees shade the sacred area. From amid this nature, the naos rises laced with vine, a little Ionic temple, ruined but lovely. Before it stands the broken altar. At the four points of the compass, sculptured pylon gates with giant monolithic lintels give entry to the temple area. There, in stone, shine Phosphoros and Hesperos, the morning and the evening stars, eagles hold the messenger wand of Hermes, and Hellenic victories support a heavy cornice with the same nonchalance that they exhibit under Attic skies. Over the east gate an inscription tells how the people of the place with their own capital raised the temple to their local god. They forgot, however, to specify the name of the deity thus honoured. His importance seemed so evident that to name him was unnecessary. The omission has caused archaeologists some trouble, though the general character of the deity is certain enough: a local god, Baitocaicēan Baal, fused with one of the great gods. Today the Greek inscription, in exquisite simple lettering, beautifully proportioned to the area on which it is inscribed, is still clear. The traveller pauses in wonder before such precise enduring workmanship, and his eyes stray to a few hovels which invade a corner of the sanctuary. Inevitably the saddening but useless thought arises, as so often elsewhere in Syria, that this world ended with the Roman Empire. The reflection that so much good sense, good labour and good workmanship have in human history often been the prelude to such long and dreary sequels, is liable to make all effort seem pointless.

The Phoenician Olympus, on which Baitocaicēan Baal took his place, needs at this point a moment's consideration. It was a curious mountain where deities of the first rank stooped to do duty also as provincial gods. It is primarily important to realize that Baal, or Bel as the Assyrians had it, was both a god, and a generic title meaning 'lord'. Thus, though there was a specific Baal, there were also the particular baalim *of* Tyre, Sidon, Byblos, and so on. As the Phoenicians settling on the coast split up into jealously particularized municipalities, each town acquired its own god-protector, who combined universal qualities derived from the Great Gods of the hinterland with special functions as a local deity. Later a further complication arose, since these gods had somehow to be made to fit in with the Greek deities. Thus Melkart of Tyre came to be identified with Hercules, and Eshmun of Sidon with Aesculapius. There were also female gods, baalat. Byblos possessed such a one as its local protector: Astarte (known elsewhere as Ishtar, Ashtoreth, Atargatis), deriving from the great Mother Goddess and in due course assimilated to Venus-Aphrodite. As the personification of fecundity Astarte was in need of a male, and this need Adonis came to fill. So popular were their twin rites that Byblos and the surrounding region became the centre of an immense cult which in time coloured the religion and practice of the whole coast.

Though delightfully situated above the sea, and of interest as a religious site of great antiquity and long continuity, the more ancient parts of the sacred precincts at Byblos convey little to the amateur. The rows of *betyles*, those queer, seeming-phallic stones that the Phoenicians worshipped, are certainly most curious and raise unanswered questions, but, on the whole, it is difficult to get a coherent impression of the site in its present state of excavation. Imagination takes more kindly to the gorges of the Adonis River, and it is there rather than in

Byblos that the Astarte-Adonis legend comes best to life. The later
legend in outline is familiar to everyone. The young god, beloved of
Astarte, in spite of her warnings and premonitions, goes hunting, and is
killed by a wild boar. He descends in spirit to the underworld, whence
Proserpine refuses to let him go. Only after long supplications can
Astarte secure his release and triumphant return to the earth. The story
has various symbolic possibilities, but its implications as a nature saga
are clear enough, and it barely disguises, in the person of the young god,
the extinction of spring in the torrid Syrian summer, and the banish-
ment of green from the earth until autumn rains resurrect the seed and
the land blooms again. Adonis and Astarte are thus nature gods and
represent the twin principles which perpetually recreate a new life cycle.
The origins of the Adonis myth are apparently Sumerian (Thammuz =
Adonis), but its accretions are many and confusing. The word *Adon*
meant originally simply *lord*, and Adonis bears certain resemblances to
Eshmun of Sidon. On the other hand there are parallels between this
myth and the Isis-Osiris legend, and fusion of ideas would have been
very natural since Byblos was in particularly close relations with Egypt.
It will be recalled that it was to Byblos that the tides brought the body
of Osiris to rest, and that both stories involve the death of a young god,
his descent into the underworld and a mourning goddess who makes
resurrection possible. Further, Adonis first sprang from a tree, while
Osiris was released by Isis from a wooden pillar in the hall of the king's
palace at Byblos. The parallel is evidently close.

That the cult of Adonis should have centred near Byblos was probably
due to the geographical peculiarities of the Adonis River, which reaches
the sea a few miles to the south of the town. It is a remarkable stream.
Gushing with dramatic force from a grotto in the heights of the Lebanon,
it carves its way out to the coast through a series of spectacular gorges,
and at certain times of the year, owing to iron-ore deposits, runs bitter
red, discolouring the Mediterranean for miles about its mouth. The
mountains at the source, the haunt of the boar and the bear, were a
convenient place to suppose the death of the god, and the periodic
discoloration of the water, seeming to run red with his blood, appeared
to give a special plausibility to the supposition. Thus the Adonis valley
became a region specially sacred to the god, and the scene of a great
yearly pilgrimage to the Temple of Afka, raised in his honour at the
river's source.

The expedition to the temple must have been very moving to the
believers for whom the wild grandeur of the scenery had a sacred and

tragic significance. As they wound into the mountains, it was through the god's familiar hunting-grounds, and the setting of his divine love and death, that they passed. The route they followed cannot have been very different from that which the traveller takes today, for one of the stages at which their processions must have stopped – the ruins of *Shîr el Meidân* – lies only a stone's throw from the new road. Little remains of what was probably a subsidiary temple of the Adonis cult except an enclosure of weathered grey stones and some enigmatic carvings on the rocks near by. The setting none the less is superb. The ruins, which mark the half-way stage to Afka, stand on a small plateau three thousand feet above the river and look backward to the sea. It is a last glance, for beyond this point the mountains so hem and press the road that the sea is lost. As the road climbs on, the scenery grows even more spectacular. Screes of barren rock spill down the mountainsides. The strata of the gorge below twist into fantastic shapes and trees nod over the precipices. It finally becomes evident that the road can go no farther, for a huge wall of rock drops sheer from the mountain-tops and peremptorily blocks the valley gorge. From a cave at the base of this mountain wall the ice-cold Adonis River rushes out. The site is dramatic and grim enough, but, before plunging away into its gorge below, the river hesitates: sheltered under the mountain wall is a small oasis, unexpectedly green and idyllic. Its juniper and almond trees, flowers and sward, are set among precipices and eagles. It was here that Astarte saw Adonis for the first time, and here that, at their last meeting, she in vain tried to dissuade him from his fatal hunting expedition; here, too, that the memory of the god for centuries

> allured
> The Syrian damsels to lament his fate
> In amorous ditties all a summer's day,
> While smooth Adonis from his native rock
> Ran purple to the sea.

In this contrast of austerity and sweetness, of bare rock and green growth, the temple of the cult was placed. It lies so close to the source of the river that the spray of the water falling from the cave rises in a perpetual vapour on the air. The cyclopean masonry and the size of the precinct show what labours were expended on it in this inaccessible place. For so sacred a shrine only the best was good enough, and its builders in the Roman era even ferried rose granite across the sea from Egypt and dragged it up these mountain paths. It must have been in early summer at the Adonis festival that the temple was at its most

* C

splendid. At this season the images of the dead god were covered with anemones, which were said to have turned red from the blood of his fatal wound, and the women in lamentation chanted of his death and danced funerary dances. At this season they also set out those little pots, as Frazer describes, and planted seed which sprouted fruitlessly in the hot sun and withered prematurely, as the youthful promise of Adonis had done. When the Levant sun was scorching the hillsides and turning Phoenicia to a parched brown, there must have been great dramatic intensity in these festivals which celebrated the death of spring in the fate of Adonis and which, in the promise of his resurrection, foretold the autumn rain and the world turning green again.

The Afka temple is now no more than a ruin. Earthquakes have dealt cruelly with it, and they were in part anticipated by the Emperor Constantine, who sent troops to demolish the temple, deported the hierophants to Baalbeck, and cut the groves which today in part have grown again. The marked antagonism of so officially Christian an emperor was inevitable, for the sacred prostitution of both sexes was a practice inseparable from the cult of Astarte-Adonis. The twin principles of fertility were thought to be gratified, no less than the active participants, by this human symbolism which represented in a limited way the vast and universal processes of nature. This aspect of the Astarte-Adonis rites appears to have lingered in the Lebanon, in spite of official disapproval, under cognate forms, and would provide interesting local material for the anthropologist. Benjamin of Tudela in the twelfth century speaks of a very similar practice in the southern Lebanon. 'Once every year', he says, 'all men and women assemble and celebrate a festival, upon which occasion, after eating and drinking, they hold promiscuous intercourse.' Even to our own day, relics of the ancient rite are said to persist in the village of Juweiya in one of the wilder areas of the southern Lebanon. The men of the village exercise in the summer months the trade of itinerant tinkers. In their absence the women, young and old, give themselves readily to strangers, and *do not thereby lose any social caste*. Indeed their activity is regarded as a natural part of the village economy. At Afka, in spite of Constantine's efforts, the sacred rites appear to have continued until the fifth century, and even today the site is revered and frequented, though in more innocent fashion, by both the Christian and Shi'ite peasantry. Their superstition is the last reflection of the fervours which Adonis roused. In the gnarled fig which springs from the ruins there survives the type of the sacred tree the Phoenicians worshipped, and the local believers think to restore the sick to health by tying scraps of their clothing to its branches. Similarly when they light their lamps to the 'Lady of the Place' in the little alcove below, whether they envisage her as the Virgin, a saint, or goddess, it is really to Venus-Astarte that their homage is paid. She is the true lady of the place, and the lesser offerings today are payable to her and her lover, as were the greater when her temple flourished and when, all up this coast,

> To her bright image nightly by the moon
> Sidonian virgins paid their vows and songs.

CHAPTER IV

THE ROMAN PEACE

⸻ ·◌· ⸻

NOAH is reported to have settled with his flocks and herds in the Bk'aa valley. It was a wise choice if the patriarch had a taste for landscape and its atmosphere. There can be few more beautiful places in the world. Most people get their first view of the valley where the Beyrouth–Damascus road crawls over a pass in the Lebanon Mountains. Between the snow-capped ranges on either side, it appears to lie as smooth as velvet, a pastoral invitation. The valley runs so evenly up to the abrupt mountains, and the minute branch-valleys insinuate themselves so closely into the mountain flanks, that the total effect is one of natural upholstery. The width of rich alluvial earth is fitted into its rocky frame with pleasing precision.

The mountains that overlook the Bk'aa are very different from those on the Mediterranean side of the Lebanon. There the heights are exclamatory and picturesque, dramatic gorges carve and cut them, and peaks rise jagged, tier on tier. They are worn and fretted by millenniums of north-west wind and storm. Above the Bk'aa the mountains impress differently; they are quiet, sculptural and solemn. They watch rather than speak. In early spring their snows reach down to the valley, and where the snow melts crocuses push up. The soaked earth is everywhere a rich russet, across which creeps a film of green – at first almost imperceptible but growing daily brighter – the shoots of the Bk'aa corn. By midsummer the valley is burnt all shades of yellow-brown, carries thistles, sere grasses and indomitable wild hollyhocks, and wherever a spring breaks from the mountainside or water flows, the expanse blotches into a dark stain of green with birds, prospering vines and the grateful shade of trees. But to say so much, or so little, of the Bk'aa gives no idea of its quality. The traveller will often ask himself why the valley is exceptional, why, each time he sees it, the same feelings of wonder, almost of awe, should be evoked. Proportion must have a great deal to do with its effects. Should golden numbers and ideal ratios exist, they would certainly enter into the composition of this landscape, so perfectly are the width of the valley and the height of the mountains proportioned to each other. The guide-books call the Bk'aa a plain; it might alternatively be called a mountain valley. In fact, it is either too narrow or too wide to fit either of these descriptions. Escaping both the sprawling vagueness of a plain and the cupped closeness of a mountain valley, it is the miraculous complement to the hills that frame it, and manages to be, at the same time, boundless and intimate, great and small.

It is curious to reflect that methods of travel can modify anything so apparently objective as the qualities of a landscape, but what is enthralling by car may become intolerable on foot. Slow progress calls for variety of scene. Thus Gertrude Bell plodding down the length of the Bk'aa on horseback found it a 'most dreary valley'. For once one may be grateful for a car. The miracle of form and colour has no time to pall. The road from Beyrouth drops into the valley at Chtaura, a green and fertile oasis seized by the indefatigable Jesuits some eighty years ago from swarms of malarial mosquitoes. The hillside above the village is now strung with vineyards where they grow a very drinkable *vin rosé*, while a certain Monsieur Cortbawi bottles an *eau de vie de Marc* which on the edge of the Syrian desert seems extremely good. From Chtaura the valley runs due north, smooth between its mountain ranges, corn-covered, snow-covered, or tanned as the desert, according to season. Variety perhaps there is not much, except the light changing on the hills, the great swathes and gulfs of shadow that grow upon them at sunset, and the brief *Abendglüh* that crowns their winter summits. Driving north, one hardly realizes that the valley is slowly climbing, and it is almost with surprise that its watershed is reached. There, where the valley at its wildest and loneliest slips over an almost imperceptible divide to fall away north into the wide plain of Homs, the Orontes rises. Its rising is worthy of so famous a river; one that was the backbone of the Seleucid Empire, that created Antioch, and saw upon its banks some few miles north at Kadesh the destruction of the Hittite power. At the very foot of the Lebanon its waters, clear and cold and deep, flood in curious silence from beneath a ledge of rock. They hesitate for a moment in a wide pool, shadowed by a gigantic plane-tree, and then hurry away down a curling ravine followed by a thread of tamarisks and twisted willows. The ravine softens into a coomb as it works its way out from the last mountain spurs into the plain, and the river between rapids and boulders flattens into long rippling glides and deeper pools.

There are trout here that run large, till lately unsophisticated and undisturbed. Fishing in this deserted Syrian coomb seems a dream-like undertaking, familiar yet not quite real. When one has fished the evening rise until a fly is no longer visible and there is only a white glimmer on the water, the black mountain shapes appear to grow larger, to overhang the river and to threaten. It becomes presumptuous to follow a leisurely Anglo-Saxon pursuit in this ancient landscape.

This is the moment, as the moon rises, to climb from the river to that weird monument, the Tower of Hermel. Capping a rise of ground in the midst of a desolate expanse, it surveys the valley for many miles around. Though in the daytime it is the resort of shepherds who stray there for a little shade, when the sun has set it seems long deserted. As you walk around it, staring up in the moonlight, you have the impression of breaking many centuries' isolation, of bringing a perhaps unwelcome human contact to a thing which knew utterly different types of men, and that a long time ago. A pyramid surmounts its massive stonework, and carved upon the square tower are deer and weapons, a wounded boar that dies pierced with lances, and wolves that drag down a gigantic bull. No inscription helps to date this enigmatic memorial, and in spite of the use of the Ionian order, it certainly has little classical about it. It is not altogether unlike the ancient 'spindles' of Amrit and the effect on the traveller is much the same: an impression of contact with a civilization altogether strange, and because not understood both fascinating and disturbing. The most probable supposition seems to be that it was put up in the first or second centuries B.C. by some local princeling who had made himself independent in the interval of chaos before the Romans came. One might even play with the idea that its dramatic quality is linked with the date of its birth, and that it was the last purely Semitic monument to be erected in Western Syria. When these stones went up in the Bk'aa, Rome was at hand, and Syria, about to acquire that all-embracing civilization, could never be quite her primitive Semitic self again.

It is in the Bk'aa valley, half-way between Chtaura and the Tower of Hermel, that one can understand perhaps better than anywhere else in Syria the force and energy of the civilization which the Romans brought. One of the springs that rises at the foot of the Anti-Lebanon creates the oasis that has been famous for nearly two thousand years as the site of the Temples of Baalbeck. Baalbeck itself, as its name shows – the Baal of the Bk'aa – was an ancient religious site, but the vast ruins that remain today are a legacy of Roman rule. They were mainly raised in the second and third centuries A.D. when Baalbeck had become the Graeco-Roman town of Heliopolis, and the surrounding fields were owned by the descendants of those veterans whom Augustus settled there when he made a colony of the place. In typically elastic Graeco-Roman fashion, the new-comers took over the old gods and gave them new names and a classic veneer. A triad of gods, analogous to the triads favoured by the Phoenicians, presided over the sanctuaries. To the Heliopolitan Jupiter, doing duty for the Semitic Hadad, Venus cloaking Atargatis, and Mercury, perhaps disguising Adonis, the three major temples were raised. Jupiter was worshipped in the Great Temple, Venus in the so-called Temple of Bacchus, while Mercury's shrine, which has long since disappeared, lay perhaps somewhere in the gardens to the south-west. The tremendous wealth and popularity which the sanctuaries then enjoyed, the ruins still reveal. They are vast and give an impression of undertakings on a scale paralleled only in the temples of Upper Egypt. The stones of the *Trilithon* – perhaps the largest cut blocks in existence – are famous, but the giant proportions of the whole place are perhaps even better typified by the size of the stone slabs with which the Temple of Bacchus was once roofed: each one of these stone 'tiles' has an area of thirty square feet. Great wealth, great organization and a great cult could alone have achieved such a group of monuments. They are colossal, and have remained so in spite of the inroads of earthquakes, emperors and collectors. Constantine and Theodosius, with Christian fervour, started the destruction, and hardly more than a century ago, Lamartine, with a modesty exceptional for the times, made off with a mere camel load of good things. The destruction went on until a German archaeological expedition rescued the site in 1900.

There is little point in adding yet another description to what has been before so often and so enthusiastically described, yet it is perhaps worth while noting that the effect of Baalbeck is not by any means purely architectural. The temples are more impressive than the architecture strictly warrants, because the landscape, this amazing Bk'aa valley, sets them off. Weathered stone against blue distances, Corinthian columns against snow-covered mountains, such things are an essential part of Baalbeck. Largely conceived and monumental, buildings and valley are suited to one another; they are in proportion. The best place and time to appreciate the temple and its setting is at sunset from the terrace of the ruined tower in the south-west corner where a small fountain bubbles away to itself and the whole valley is unfolded. In winter the oasis is a network of bare branches finely etched in sharp air, and the trunks of the walnut-trees stand out a clear purple-grey against the dark reddish soil. In summer it is a sea of green, lush, bird-filled and shady. Beyond are the mountains, from which the snows never quite melt and which perpetually change their tone and colour, somehow always modifying and conditioning the feeling and atmosphere of Baalbeck itself. The interaction of nature and art which adds so much to the temples is almost equally striking in the Great Mosque. Situated at some distance to the north-east of the Propylea it is easily missed, but well worth visiting. Built from the spoil of the Roman sanctuaries, probably in the Mameluke period, and now itself ruined, its position gives it a particular charm. Its remains have been altogether incorporated into the rural economy of the oasis: corn grows between the pillars of its triple colonnade and fruit trees overshadow the Corinthian capitals.

Though one may adjust one's eye to the monumental scale of Baalbeck, and on successive evenings absorb its beauty, growing accustomed to the happy alliance of architecture and landscape, one will not cease to wonder at the sheer achievement of the Romans in creating this great pile of buildings, and at the civilization that flourished around them, here in the Semitic East and almost at the desert edge. One had always known of the extent of the Roman Empire, had known that its stone imprint was to be found on all the confines of the then civilized world. But it was mainly a book-knowledge, a thing understood intellectually. Here at Baalbeck, with tremendous force, the known becomes the felt, and history puts on flesh. Compelled by the Latin genius the Anti-Lebanon assumes the shape of the Seven Hills, and here in the Bk'aa *is* Rome. The transformation naturally was not accomplished in a day, and to understand Rome in Baalbeck and a whole epoch in the history of Syria, one must go back to Alexander the Great.

When the House of Seleucus succeeded in 312 B.C. to the large portion of Alexander's Empire that included Syria, the Greeks found themselves a tiny minority among their subject populations. If they were to rule it would have to be in part by persuasion rather than by force, by selling a superior culture rather than by the use of arms. Except where the monotheism of the Jews was concerned, they practised in matters of religion a wise and commendable tolerance. In civil affairs they did little to upset the old internal administration, preserving as administrative units the earlier Persian satrapies which the Greek *strategoi* ran with much the same powers as the satraps had enjoyed before them. Greek culture naturally could only be sold to the upper and middle class, who were informed enough to be snobbish about its prestige, and educated enough to appreciate all that it had to offer. The Greeks thus concentrated on the towns, and these became the backbone of hellenism in Syria. Furthermore, where towns did not exist, the Seleucids created them. It was a constant, though costly, feature of the Seleucid policy to reinforce the Greek element in their Empire by introducing settlers from Macedon and Greece, and founding colony-towns to receive them. From Asia Minor to Dura Europos on the Euphrates and the great Seleucia on the Tigris, such foundations served as effective centres of radiation for hellenistic culture and propaganda. The heart of the Empire, based on such newly founded cities, lay along the Orontes River. There arose Antioch, the administrative capital, and Apamea, the military base. The port of the kingdom, Seleucia, was at the river mouth, and Laodicea (Latakia) lay not far south. Unfortunately, except at Dura Europos which the archaeologists have uncovered, the remains of Seleucid architecture, above ground, are meagre. Apamea, however, should have much to tell when fully excavated. It is strange to think that the scanty ruins now visible there, some eighty miles north of Baalbeck, hide the site of a city that covered six hundred and fifteen acres, and had a population of a hundred and twenty thousand. The main street, colonnaded throughout its length, was nearly a mile long. The Aldershot of the Empire, Apamea housed the six hundred Imperial war elephants, and the now deserted slopes above the Orontes pastured the famous stud which supplied the Seleucid cavalry. Every Aldershot is not alike, and Apamea was also the seat of a Neo-Platonist school. Posidonius of Apamea was one of the most influential scholars and philosophers of the Ciceronian Age, and Numenius of Apamea was a capable champion of Hindoo thought in that period of fluid religious speculation before Christianity swept the country. Apamea's philosophical school, and a famous oracle situated there, made it one of the last strongholds of paganism, and in the period of militant Christianity the citizens called in the mountain peasants, with temporary success, to guard their shrines and temples.

Radiating from such Greek towns, hellenistic thought deeply influenced the upper sections of the population and laid the cultural foundations which Rome was later to use. Greek ideas penetrated wherever taxes were collected or the law administered; in fact, so deeply did the Greek legal system take root that it was still functioning after four hundred years of Roman rule. Further, the liberal spirit of hellenism gave an impetus to initiative and free inquiry, and came, after two centuries of absolute Persian domination, as an exciting novelty. Largely owing to the fact that Greek as the universal language of the Eastern Mediterranean was available to all inquisitive-minded people, ideas began to circulate more widely in the Syrian hinterland. An ever greater number of Syrians came to realize their individual and personal responsibility in matters of taste, belief and conduct. Previously speculation had been an activity confined to a few inhabitants of the Phoenician coast towns. Now many Syrians began to think, and thinking, they became a part of that wider classical cosmos which Alexander had envisaged when, in the words of an ancient author, he 'ordered all men to regard the world as their country . . . good men as their kin, and bad men as foreigners'. Educated Syrians now in fact became citizens of the world. With this new cosmopolitanism, the arts and sciences assumed greater prominence, and aesthetic and intellectual pursuits, in part owing to philhellene snobbery, became socially very much the 'right thing'. It is characteristic of the tolerant cosmopolitan life of the newly hellenized middle classes, that women should have acquired a fresh importance. The Greeks gave oriental women a role to play in society and showed them that they had a mind to play it with. Laodicea was named after Seleucus' mother, and Apamea after his Persian wife: where the Hellenes gave so strong a line, the native Syrians would not be slow to follow.

The wide dispersion of hellenistic influence through Syria eastwards is certain. It was felt in the art of the Han dynasty in China and, in the time of Crassus, Greek tragedies were acted at the Parthian Court across the Euphrates. The *depth* of its penetration is, however, disputable. That the Parthians were in no sense truly hellenized is painfully revealed by the fact that at one of these same performances – the *Bacchae* of Euripides – the Parthian conqueror allowed the head of the unfortunate Crassus to be used as a stage property. Such hellenization was evidently a veneer. In Syria the situation was more complicated. While the middle classes of the towns were considerably hellenized, and Greek for them replaced Aramaic, the country populations were hardly touched. Among the peasants Aramaic was still the current language, and along with it they kept their old outlook and their own local customs. The towns in fact were largely Greek, but the countryside wholly Semitic. The well-directed policy of urban colonization – which by a fatal irony spelt the doom of Greece and Macedon because it drained them of their best men – thus only secured a partial success, and conferred benefits only on parts of Syria. The Seleucids were too occupied in maintaining their frontiers against the Ptolemies and their eastern enemies, and too divided by dynastic quarrels, to transform Syria as thoroughly as they wished. It remained for the Romans, when the Seleucid dynasty rotted away, to assume the Greek mantle and continue the work they had begun.

When Pompey took over Syria officially in 64 B.C., Seleucid administration had broken down. The Bedouin were everywhere making inroads, the Nabateans from Petra controlled Damascus, and princelings, such as he who perhaps raised the desolate Tower of Hermel near the source of the Orontes, had established native principalities of their own. The Romans at once set about restoring order. In doing so, they introduced the most prosperous era in Syria's chequered history, gave her the *pax Romana*, and with it nearly three hundred years of unbroken quiet. Never was Syria so effectively ruled, and so populous. The numberless ruins in places now desert, and the olive presses abandoned in land untilled for hundreds of years, still indicate this Roman high-water mark. There is no need to enumerate the separate steps by which this prosperity was achieved. As elsewhere in the Roman Empire common sense and organization lay behind it. In the usual way, unruly tribes were pushed back, roads built, trade fostered, civil government organized, and above all a stable political framework ensured. It was the strategic position of Syria and the danger of Parthian invasion – in 51 B.C. the 'lean and hungry' Cassius only just succeeded in stemming the Parthian inroads, and a decade later they temporarily overran the whole country – that probably decided the emperors to make Syria an imperial province and keep it under their direct control. Four legions were apportioned to the province, and it was under the supreme command of the Syrian legate, an office which was perhaps the most sought after of all those in the imperial gift, and which was held for a time by Cicero's son.

The Romans were intelligent enough not to destroy what the Greeks had established. The new order was to be hellenistic in spirit, though administered with Roman resources and efficiency. The Greek towns were especially favoured and, at any rate to begin with, enjoyed a semi-autonomy; at the same time Greek was recognized as the official language, and the cult of hellenism was everywhere maintained. As a corollary there was no attempt made to teach Latin or to push Latin culture. The early Latin colonies formed by the settlement of veterans, such as those at Beyrouth and Baalbeck, remained islands in a Graeco-Semitic sea, and in time acquired a hellenistic tone and flavour. Even the Legions, which at first must have exerted a Romanizing influence on the garrison towns, as time passed came to be recruited locally, and though orders continued to be given in Latin, the troops themselves were no longer always Latin-speaking. Further, the number of Latin officials installed in civil posts was insignificant. In the hellenized cities the Empire found a competent and educated middle class suitable and willing to constitute a responsible bureaucracy. Lastly the Roman business men, the large-scale contractors, who everywhere made vast fortunes by following on the heels of the imperial armies, came to Syria in restricted numbers. The Syrian merchants were too sharp for them and Roman business kept away for the same reason that the Jews did in the nineteenth century.

Thus, in this Roman province, a knowledge of Greek was essential to preferment, and social and cultural life were predominantly hellenistic. This life is often criticized for its lack of idealism and spirituality; it is said to have preferred colour and shape to real substance. Such criticisms can only be made with fairness if the weight of the credit balance is fully acknowledged. Though evidently not the clearer cut civilization of earlier Greece, it represented a pure gain for the middle-class Syrian. The geographical position of Syria has conditioned its people to the easy acceptance of other cultures, and it would be untrue to maintain that their adjustment to the Graeco-Roman outlook was not far more fruitful than most of the adjustments which they have subsequently been compelled to make. It was certainly more satisfactory than that hurried adjustment to the West which has characterized the last fifty years of Syrian history. The life of the average well-to-do citizen in hellenized Syria was intelligent, stimulating and highly agreeable. With Greek education, he acquired poetics, rhetoric, music, mathematics and graduated finally into philosophy. There was the Greek theatre to appreciate, and in the evenings wine and music were pleasantly frequent. People cultivated their minds, their palates and their friends. Further, since the *pax Romana* happily left no other outlet for physical prowess, there was a great deal of sport. The rich hunted in a land where there was still an abundance of big game, and the common man patronized the athletic stadia, the chariot races (it was at Antioch that Ben Hur distinguished himself) and finally the gladiatorial contests which the Romans introduced here as elsewhere. These, cruel as they were, possibly provided an important safety-valve for a society which had fought its wars, and which did not usually satisfy its sadism in the persecution of minorities.

A more pertinent criticism of Graeco-Syrian society was that its culture, wealth and gaiety were paid for by an exploited peasantry. The Seleucids and later the Romans encouraged the property owners and the urban middle class and carried on the administration with their co-operation and active participation. The interests of the lower classes, particularly in the country, were disregarded. Most of the land was in the hands of town-dwellers, and the peasants, excluded from municipal citizenship and living at a bare subsistence level, had no choice but to work on these town-owned estates or on the great imperial and private *latifundia* scattered throughout the country. One must think of the grandeur of Baalbeck rising from the labours of an oppressed peasantry. Such a state of affairs was, however, usual in most parts of the Ancient World, and this substratum of misery was a factor underlying most of its great achievements. Throughout history the lot of the Syrian peasant has varied only in this, that under *intelligent* exploitation he has been relatively better off. In the earlier centuries Graeco-Roman economic organization was often pretty effective and the peasant in Syria probably benefited indirectly from the resultant increase in wealth. He must also ultimately have benefited from the vast release of capital occasioned by Alexander's conquests, when the hoarded treasure of the eastern potentates became available to the Greeks. In Ekbatana alone Alexander collected nearly forty million pounds' worth of coin and jewellery. Certainly the peasants of the upper Bk'aa cannot have been worse off in the heyday of Baalbeck than they have sometimes been in the twentieth century. Though rulers and dynasties have constantly changed in Syria, they have not much altered the status of the peasant, and today, for all his political rights, he is hardly more free than when he worked on the land of the Augustan veterans that lay about the Temple of Jupiter.

The visible tokens of Graeco-Roman Syria remain in the countless buildings strung from Jerash to Antioch and scattered from the Mediterranean westward to the Euphrates, buildings which have made Syria of special interest to the outside world. An architectural fever seized these Graeco-Semitic towns, and from the mountain-tops to the desert oases they expressed in stone their approval of the life and institutions which they had acquired. No aspect of that life and of these institutions seems to be missing in the ruins of Syria today: there are towns set out on the rectangular pattern, first introduced into Syria by the Seleucids, with parallel intersecting streets; innumerable baths, the prototype of the Muslim *hammams*; triumphal avenues; stadia; imposing villas; and not least the temples dedicated to their heterogeneous gods. It is into this architectural achievement that the great temples of Baalbeck fit. One could hardly wish for more monumental testimony to the energy of this classical Semitic state.

There are two important aspects of the *pax Romana* in Syria of which nothing has yet been said: security and trade. It is more particularly in connection with these that one thinks of the ruins in the Hauran and at Palmyra. These ruins, together with Baalbeck, include most that is worth seeing of the Graeco-Roman remains. Security had gone to pieces before the Romans entered Syria, and with it prosperity had disappeared, for in Syria the latter has always depended on the effective subjection or control of the desert tribes by the central power. Security the Romans proceeded to recreate. At first Syria proper was cloaked with a ring of vassalized buffer states, but as the Roman grip tightened these one by one were absorbed and *Provincia Syria* stretched ever farther into the deserts east and south. In due course the province came to be cemented by a network of Roman roads better than any that were to exist until the coming of the French. The famous *strata Diocletiana* linked the Euphrates valley near Raqqa with Damascus, and another great road eventually ran from Damascus right down to the Red Sea. A magnificent stretch of the ancient Aleppo–Antioch road, built in great blocks a yard thick and sometimes over two yards long, is still to be seen about forty kilometres from Aleppo on the Alexandretta road. The Emperor Julian marched down this road to his death on the Euphrates in the spring of 363 'when the skies were bright', as his historian says. It still gives one a most dramatic impression of the solidity of the great routes which once ensured the security of the country. East, the Euphrates was the ideal boundary for Roman Syria, and though it was by no means always held, nor held down its whole course through Syrian territory, it was always the objective. Southward no such natural frontier existed as a bulwark against nomadic incursions. There was only the hilly massif of the Hauran, known today as the Jebel Druze. At all periods an admirable retreat for the lawless, it offered on the other hand, if held by the forces of order, a useful vantage-point from which to dominate the southern deserts. It was inevitable that the Romans should wish to control it and only a matter of time until they did so. Trajan in A.D. 105 ordered its occupation, and after a short campaign it was annexed to the Empire to form the backbone of the new *Provincia Arabia*, with Nova Trajana, the present Bosra, as its capital.

It is easiest to approach the Jebel Druze southward from Damascus.

Except in spring, the road that runs endlessly out through the Hauran plain is dusty and drear in the extreme. The plain itself is thirsty, stony and unchanging, a dull yellow-brown. Once one of the great granaries of the Empire, it has lost much of its vitality and, in place of the rich crops it once yielded, the peasants in poor years garner only spare barley. Hermon on the west, that most imposing of mountains, does a great deal to compensate for the dreariness of the plain. Its huge mass has the inestimable advantage of rising quite detached from the valleys on either side, and its crest therefore, instead of being one peak among others, merely *primus inter pares*, rears its nine thousand feet in solitary supremacy. The view from the summit is probably the finest in Syria, and for many reasons it is worth undertaking the two days' excursion to climb it. Without ski the ascent is not conveniently made before May when the snows are melting. It should at all events be made from Arné on the east side, whence the climb is less laborious. A road winds up to the village of Arné at nearly four thousand feet and, from there, a mule may be found to carry camp-bed and provisions. Springs break from the mountainside, and above Arné the path climbs pleasantly to the sound of water, while the brown valley drops farther and farther below. The air is fresh and the hillside covered with creeping plants and aromatic shrubs. As one gets higher, even in late Syrian June, there are huge drifts and scarves of snow melting rather sadly in the sun, and a great variety of wild flowers rooting in the rocks at the snow's edge or spilling in slips of colour down the slopes. From the summit the whole of Syria seems spread below. South is the Jordan valley, and the Lake of Houlé where the chatter of innumerable waterfowl may be heard a mile from the water's edge; west across the intervening hills the Phoenician sea shines from Mount Carmel to Tyre; north is the Bk'aa and the two Lebanon ranges with great snow-capped Sannine, 'bearing on its shoulders the four seasons'; while east, where the Jebel Druze seems no more than a cluster of little hills, the Syrian desert stretches without limit. From the crowning crest the slopes of Hermon fall away in even folds and swathes, whose undulations carry the eye regularly down to the heat and shimmer of the valleys far below. The very smoothness and rotundity of the mountain's vast flanks, lapsing outward and earthward, add to the sense of bulk and solidity. It is not a haphazard mass of rocks and precipices forced and twisted up by some fortuitous convulsion, but a great shoulder of the earth climbing steadily into the sky, immense, and silent. A sense of the solemn and tremendous hangs about its bare solitary vastness. It has indeed from all time been considered a unique and magic mountain. Nimrod the mighty hunter made his home upon its slopes. It is the Baal-Hermon of the Bible and its summit has always been the site of sacred altars, while in the Graeco-Roman period its skirts were positively embroidered with temples. (There were two at Arné.) The ruins of the sanctuary which crown its summit today date from the Graeco-Roman period, but must have succeeded a more ancient temple. Sacrifices were still celebrated on the mountain-top when St Jerome visited Syria at the end of the fourth century, and presumably the pagan rites forlornly held out in this high stronghold as long as anywhere in the country.

There is no abrupt transition from the plain of the Hauran to the Jebel Druze. The landscape at first simply grows more inhospitable and more uninviting; the characteristic black basalt appears, running in savage stripes across the spare tillage, and tortured thorn trees struggle for a footing among the rocks. Yet all the time the road is imperceptibly but steadily rising, and the moment comes when the traveller looks back to find, rather to his surprise, that the body of the Hauran plain is well below him. He is in the Jebel. It is a sinister country, twisted, fretted and dry as a bone. Scrub oak and thorn, and yellowish undersize vines, straggle over the hillsides; the cattle are small and tough, and the pastures that elbow out a little space between the rocks are pathetically meagre. And everywhere is the harsh angry basalt. It dominates the landscape, and is in a sense the Jebel. Each one of its serried spiny ridges provides a natural defence which the marksmen during the Druze rebellion knew well how to utilize. It is not surprising that it should have cost the French two years' fighting and several thousand men to subdue the country. The bitterness of this wilderness, however, makes the two most important things in the Jebel stand out with vivid effect: the Roman past and the Druzes today. Though the latter had begun to establish themselves in the Jebel in the eighteenth century, it was not until the second half of the nineteenth that they came in any number, finding a refuge there after the massacre of the Lebanese Christians (for which they were factually if not altogether morally responsible). Worshippers of the heretical Caliph El Hakim, an enigmatic mixture of mystic and charlatan, sadist and reformer, the Druzes have been a religious minority for nearly a thousand years which has served to accentuate their natural characteristics. Their bare, unpretentious shrines scattered throughout the Jebel are the sanctuaries of a hermetic faith to which only initiates are admitted, and which, in spite of much research, still remains in part obscure to the outside world. Their

courage, bred in them by the mountains of the Lebanon from which they
fled, and even more their astonishing beauty, are the things which have
given the Druzes their reputation. They are notable fighters as the
French discovered and the Turks before them. Their reputation as
guerrillas seems to be of long standing, for Benjamin of Tudela in the
twelfth century says, 'they are subject to no king or prince . . . [and]
are so nimble in climbing hills and mountains, that nobody can successfully carry on war against them'. Unlike the Syrian Arab, they look you
straight between the eyes. The Druzes of Soueida in particular have
style stamped in their looks, their manners and their clothes. The poorest
appear chieftains. The women are unveiled, and among both men and
women not to be beautiful is the exception. Their looks and their blue
eyes long ago made the Westerners believe, with naïve vanity, that they
must be the descendants of the Crusaders, and the English traveller,
Sandys, in Shakespeare's day described them as 'the remainder of those
Frenchmen which were brought into these parts by Godfrey of Bullen'.
This ancestry appears to be fictitious. Some link with the Crusades
perhaps exists in the conical head-dress and wimple that the women
wear with such grace. It is very similar to that worn in Europe in the
fifteenth century and quite unlike anything found in Syria, though
whether the West borrowed from the East, or vice versa, remains
unsettled. The dresses that the Druze women wear are as becoming as
their wimples. They have tight waists, and full bell-skirts sweeping the
ground. The colours are magnificent – magentas, browns and greens.
The men are equally impressive, notable in carriage, in feature and in
colouring, with white turbans, ornamented belts and inlaid weapons.
They love to show off and strike a figure, and as they are great horsemen
there is a continual clatter of hooves up and down the streets of Soueida.
On the other hand they adapt themselves with difficulty to the com-
plexity and the co-operative demands of modern life which steadily
encroaches upon them. This adaptation after 1918 was not made more
easy by their unfortunate relations with the French administration and
the sad Druze rebellion to which these gave rise. However, since 1927
things in the Jebel have taken a far better turn. French administration
brought medical services, education and much-needed water, though
the last is not yet available in sufficient quantities. The Druzes as a
direct result have been steadily increasing in numbers and prosperity.

A century ago the Jebel was almost deserted, the inevitable result of
the long decadence that had settled upon the area since the day the
Byzantines left. Rome brought a civilization to the Hauran and when

its Byzantine successors were driven out, that civilization died, and life slowly ebbed away from these hills for a thousand years.

The ruins of the Roman past remain, preserved to some extent by the very depopulation and misery of the centuries that have intervened. Had an organized civilization been maintained in these hills, the mark of Rome would have been overlaid. No such civilization lingered on, and the ancient buildings have crumbled uncomprehended in the scruffy villages of these ragged basalt hills. Soueida, the new capital, is the best centre, indeed the only one, from which to explore the remains of the ancient Hauran. The modern town has no charm beyond its people; the new buildings, with the barracks and the administrative offices put up by the French, are extremely ugly, and the single inn where the traveller will perhaps be unfortunate enough to lodge is dirty and mosquito-ridden. Soueida, however, was once Dionysias and there is still the remains of a temple and basilica, and a great Roman reservoir even now filled with water – a gracious place at sunset. There is also an excellent museum where the sculpture and mosaics of the region have been assembled. The latter are very fine, extraordinarily well preserved, and achieve effects of form and colour (particularly in the case of the great mosaic floor with its medallions) curiously analogous to those obtained in still-life by Braque and other modern painters.

Though the whole Jebel is littered with antique remains, Kanouat, Chahba and Bosra are the sites most worth visiting. They are doubly impressive by reason of the withered inhospitable country in which they stand. Rome rises among hovels, and the ancient sites are honeycombed with the shapeless structures of the peasantry. It is a strange irony to find baths and theatres in such a country, or triumphal avenues down which a flock of ragged goats is driven, the sole traffic, at dawn and sunset. The Roman achievement here was only made possible by careful organization, and this in its turn depended upon security and water. Security was achieved not only by the garrisons, but by a regular Camel Corps, the *Meharistes* of antiquity, who kept in check the Bedouin of the surrounding deserts. The water problem was more complicated, since there were and are no natural springs in the Jebel, and a supply had to be assured by a complex system of reservoirs and aqueducts such as that which fed Chahba. The water system must have been effective. If one may judge from the frequency of the grape-vine motif among the existing ruins, it supplied not only the wants of the towns but a flourishing viniculture. The Jebel, however, was fortunate in receiving both organization and imperial favour. Son of a Hauran chief, Philip the

Arab succeeded to the purple in the middle of the third century, and during five years as God and Emperor reflected his glory on his native district. Chahba, the town of his birth, became Philipopolis. It was walled, embellished with two fine avenues flanked with colonnades and had a tetrapyle at their point of intersection. It received also villas, baths and a theatre. Of all this architecture much fortunately remains. To the Emperor's father, a notorious brigand posthumously deified, was dedicated the simple but attractive temple that until recently did duty as the village school. Bosra, which had already received the favours of the Severi, Philip raised, as the capital of his native province, to the rank of a metropolis. Its theatre, baths and market, its triumphal arch and the fine columns that still stand, attest its former importance. *Nova Trajana Bosra* had its own era, dating from Trajan's conquest, minted its own coinage, and even after the Islamic conquest, owing to its position on five intersecting routes, preserved a considerable importance until the fourteenth century.

Kanouat, though not apparently blessed with special imperial favour, is in its many ruins perhaps as impressive as the former sites. The bitterness of the country is there a little tempered by a meagre stream and a few fruit trees and birches that soften the hillsides. Except in the midday glare, the land that slopes away interminably into the Hauran plain takes on at Kanouat a certain mellow tone, and in the distance the basalt ridges and the bare fields show purple and yellow. Against this coloured distance and from among the trees of a little orchard rise the columns of an enchanting peripteral temple, dedicated in the second century to the sun god. Farther up the hill is a Byzantine basilica with fine carved decoration. A great mulberry-tree grows in the now roofless hall, and the east end has been converted into a whitewashed Druze sanctuary, empty but for the usual coffin-like box adorned with tatters of coloured rag. These sanctuaries commonly enshrine some sacred stone that obscurely links the worship of the Druze peasants with the Ka'aba at Mecca, and the rock under the great dome at Jerusalem. Contiguous to the basilica, and sharing a common wall, lies an older Roman temple, itself long since adapted to do service as a second Byzantine church. Farther east are some impressive vaulted cisterns and yet another ruined temple of considerable size, whose standing columns are remarkably pure in style. The whole village with its tortuous streets and the surrounding fields are indeed one maze of ruins. That a Byzantine basilica should here have encroached upon a Roman temple is symbolic of the architectural history of the Jebel, where the pagan gods were superseded by a flourishing Christian cult in the Byzantine period. Kanouat and Soueida were bishoprics, and Bosra the seat of an archbishop, and each had its Christian basilicas.

As the necessity for providing a bulwark against the tribes of the Nejd led to the Roman occupation and civilization of the Hauran, so Roman commercial policy led to the rise and greatness of Palmyra. The Romans realized, as the Phoenicians had done earlier, that the geographical position of Syria, a gate between East and West, made it admirably suited to the exchange of goods. Accordingly they did everything in their power, even allowing bilingualism in documents and business contracts, to encourage a flow of traffic. Though local industries, such as the weaving of linen, wool and silk flourished and the Emperors continued to exploit the Lebanese forests, commercial policy rightly concentrated on traffic. This had always determined the prosperity of Syria and was to do so until modern times. The flow of traffic through Central Syria depended on two things – the caravan routes inland, and the enterprise of the Syrian merchants of the coast who directed goods onwards to the West. The enterprise of the latter has throughout history been remarkable, and St Jerome in the fourth century noted that the Syrians had a tremendous appetite for business which drove them across the world in search of wealth (*permanet in Syris*, he says, *ingenitus negotiationis ardor, qui per totum mundum lucri cupiditate discurrunt*). The Phoenician maritime tradition had survived in the Graeco-Roman state and was only later to disappear with the growth of piracy. It provided the experience and the vessels that shipped the eastern goods to Rome and farther west. The Syrians have been called the middlemen of antiquity, and at this period filled a role that in the later Middle Ages was to fall to Venice. Their vessels went everywhere, and the cunning Syro-Phoenician banker and merchant was a familiar figure in all the markets of the West. The Latin Roman did not altogether care for the vulgar wealth and monopolizing efficiency of these people, and by the first century A.D. there was room for Juvenal's famous complaint about the Orontes encroaching on the Tiber: *Syrus in Tiberim defluxit Orontes*. The encroachment, however, continued. A Syrian Christian became bishop of Paris, and as late as the fifth century Syriac was spoken by an eastern community at Orleans.

The control of the caravan end of this Syrian traffic was a more delicate and difficult operation. Caravan traffic had, of course, existed in Syria from the earliest times, and Totmes III speaks of receiving lapis lazuli from Persia overland. On the whole, however, early traffic

had avoided crossing the Syrian desert and had preferred a northern
route following the Euphrates into tolerably watered country before
striking west to the coastal belt, while later Egyptian traffic under the
Ptolemies had taken the Arabian route south of Syria through Petra to
Lower Mesopotamia. Before the introduction of the camel from Bactria
and Arabia somewhere about 1000 B.C., the most northerly of the
Syrian routes had been the only one possible, since no other pack
animal could normally be relied upon to make the desert crossing. The
Seleucids, both on account of the northern position of their capital at
Antioch and because they wished to keep their trade well out of the way
of the Ptolemies, had maintained the same route in use. The Romans
had no such strategic reasons for favouring the northerly route, while
their practical sense appreciated the shortness of the central desert route
that halved the distance to Mesopotamia. Thus it only needed organization, and the acquiescence of the Parthians on the Euphrates, to establish the caravan routes of Central Syria. Organization Rome never
lacked, and when it became evident that the Parthians could not be
crushed, Augustus decided to come to terms. A compromise was arrived
at – and was on the whole honoured – by which both parties agreed to
call a truce and to foster for their mutual advantage the caravan trade
across the no man's land which lay between them.

There are limits even to the distances which a camel can go without
water, and the essential preliminary to the organization of the trans-
Syrian desert routes was the provision of wells. Mention has already
been made of the Roman roads in Syria. Those that linked the Euphrates to the coast were strengthened with forts and provided, at
intervals of twenty-four miles, with wells. It was typical of the Roman
thoroughness that these should have been sunk with absolute regularity
regardless of the depth which had to be dug before water was found.
To protect the caravans themselves the desert was patrolled by the
Roman Camel Corps, and in addition a regular convoy system was
evolved. Strabo says that these huge trade columns, trekking across the
desert, sometimes two and three thousand camel strong, were like
armies on the march. Considerably more capital was needed to launch
these great enterprises than the average merchant could find, and it was
provided by the Empire banking system in which the Syrians played a
notable part. In the coast towns bankers would guarantee a 50 per cent
return on money invested in one of the Mesopotamia-bound ventures.
General political stability, local security, water and capital: Rome
provided them all and the fantastic florescence of the Syrian caravan

trade became possible, indeed almost inevitable. The focus of this trade, as everyone knows, was Palmyra. From the caravan city ran three major roads eastward to the Euphrates: the northernmost to Raqqa, the next to Circesium at the junction of the Euphrates and the Khabur, and the third to Hit. The last was the chief route to Mesopotamia, and the care which the Romans lavished in wells and fortification on its two hundred and ninety-five miles has preserved for it among the Arabs the name of *Darb el Kufri*, or Road of the Unbelievers. Westward from Palmyra another group of roads led to Egypt via Bosra and Petra, and to the coast via Damascus, Homs, or Hama. Palmyra was geographically the centre and key of the Roman caravan traffic, and it is to Palmyra that one must go to get a notion of the wealth and civilization to which this traffic gave birth.

The first Europeans to 'discover' the fabulous site were Englishmen who visited it from Aleppo in 1678 and 1691. One of them left an account of the second adventurous expedition, but it was not until 1751 that the ruins were properly described and then by another Englishman, Wood, who published careful drawings.[1] Until recent times visitors continued to be few and far between. The last Baedeker (1912) informs travellers that the trip out and back takes nine days and that an armed escort is usually necessary. It was not in fact until the late nineteen-twenties when motor transport opened up the desert that the trip to Palmyra became at all usual. Today one gets there from Damascus in a long afternoon and in a few hours driving safely covers the desert track along which others for so many centuries have plodded on camels. The drive, like most desert driving, is monotonous but beautiful. There are one or two villages near the desert edge with the usual halo of green vegetation and dusty threshing floors. Each depends on some spring or well that alone makes life possible, and the traveller reflects that, in this arid country, villages do not, as with us, produce gardens; on the contrary ft is the garden, the fortuitous patch of green in the wastes, that inevitably draws to it the dwellers and the houses. Beyond the last village, the track pulls out into the unbroken steppe. Bare hills, outcropping rock, a width of plain, and a spare vegetation of feathery grass, asphodels and low aromatic plants: this is the general impression that the country gives, an impression modified by the feeling, not altogether wrong, that the whole thing is at a slight slant and that the

---

[1] His *Ruins of Palmyra* (London, 1753) is an extraordinary achievement, and remains a valuable work, though executed under the greatest difficulties and before the advent of strict archaeology.

landscape is gently tilted towards the Euphrates three hundred miles due east. The desert world is in pastel shades. The butterflies that inconsequently zigzag across interminable space have faded in the white sun, and even the larks which rise beside the track have taken on protective desert colouring. Only the Griffon vultures, the sole patrol today along hundreds of miles of peaceful desert route, appear out of tone, black and enormous. After some time the desert vegetation begins to be rather more generous and soon nomad tents appear. They are heralded by grazing camels, at first in little parties, then by scores, then in hundreds, and finally the whole desert as far as the eye can see is covered by the grazing herds. The area between Damascus and Palmyra is one of the main pasturing grounds of the Rualla Bedouin and there are sometimes tens of thousands of camels gathered there. The herdsmen in the glaring sun, muffled up to the eyes as all Arabs are, watch you pass with the greatest indifference. Not so their wonderful seluki dogs who come flashing after the car in impotent rage and who must have appeared formidable enough to earlier non-mechanized travellers.

As the traveller approaches Palmyra the Bedouin tents again disappear and in a fitting solitude he emerges from a shallow valley above the ruins of the city. Nothing can express the strangeness of these temples, colonnades, tombs and arches, silent and deserted under the desert sun. Next the ruins lies the vivid green oasis of Palmyra and an inconsequential Bedouin village: beyond extends to the horizon a vast even desert across which the caravan routes once stretched eastward. Here, as everywhere in Syria, things are best seen in the tempered light of dawn or sunset and one should try to time arrival for the late afternoon. From the Valley of the Tombs with its sombre towers, the track leads down to what was once the main artery of the city, the great colonnaded avenue that runs east and west. Some hundred and fifty of the original columns are still standing and the weathered stone in the evening light takes on an apricot glow. From the fourfold arch, or tetrapyle, at the very centre of the town, whose granite columns came the long way from Egypt, the best impression of the unity of the ruins is perhaps to be obtained. A whole city lies around with its temples and its caravanserais; even the emplacement of its shops, and the pedestals on which its statues stood, remain. With the intrepid Englishmen who reached Palmyra in the seventeenth century, you are tempted to ask 'whether any city in the world could have challenged precedence of this in its glory'. The impression of stepping into the life of the past is

received at Palmyra in a far more real way than is possible when contemplating elsewhere single monuments however considerable or well
preserved they may be. Such is the wealth and extent of the ruins that
statues still lie where they have fallen and wandering round the ruins one
may stumble on a Graeco-Roman torso half buried in the sand and enjoy
something of the sense of discovery that belonged to the earlier travellers. It is this very sand and the hundred miles that separate Palmyra
from the nearest town, which have preserved the ruins. When Palmyra
failed, the town had no successor, and the sand yearly drifting into the
oasis buried the past. It is not always a kind preserver, however, and
when the wind blows it scurrying down the avenues, it licks, rough as
emery-paper, round the bases of the pillars, and aids the curious
chemical process which, in the deserts, everywhere gnaws away the
monuments a foot or so above the ground. A curious feature of the place
at evening are the 'indignant desert birds'; the pin-tailed sand grouse
then come in from the desert in thousands to water, and with their high
complaining note sweep flighting over the ruins.

The Great Temple of Bel dominates the city and rightly, since if
Palmyra was the hub of the caravan trade it was also an important
religious centre. The sanctuary is a queer mixture, for while the pillars
and the outer wall that enclose it are clearly Graeco-Roman (they
apparently date from the second century A.D.), the narrow, oblong cella
in the middle, with its odd proportions (dating from the reign of
Augustus) is, apart from its decoration, quite unclassical and links up
with the earlier Semitic sanctuaries. Evidently the architects wished to
preserve the shape and emplacement of an older holy site. What makes
the temple impressive today is its size and the empty echoing spaces of
the courtyard. It is solemn, yet also pathetic, for the place has few of
those qualities of proportion and symmetry by which a building continues to live in its own right even when its functional life has ended.
The Assyrian god was expensively templed and commanded the faith
and energies of all these deserts, and now only disjunct monumental
masonry remains. Climbing to the top of the cella, and sitting there,
with the swifts that haunt the place wheeling and screaming in the sky
above, it is possible to appreciate the strangeness of Corinthian columns
against the massed green of the oasis, or against the greying reaches of
the desert. The contrast between the latter, the undifferentiated and
limitless, and the willed thing, the stone worked and raised by human
effort, comes home very strongly, increasing the sense of pathos that the
temple court inspires. Of the many contrasts in time and space that

I A Beyrouth *Suk*

2   Damascus from the air, showing the Great Mosque

3   The courtyard of the Great Mosque, Damascus

4   The 'besieged' Convent at Sednaya

5   18th century stonework at Aleppo

6   The Aleppo Citadel (the Saracen Gate)

7 The Harbour at Sidon

8 The Island of Ruad

9   Baalbeck

10   The Mosque at Baalbeck

11   The approach to Palmyra

12   Palmyra at sunset

13   Palmyra : sand and acanthus

14   The Euphrates from the desert escarpment

15   Resafa from the air

The curious pockmarkings have been made by Beduin digging for treasure

16   Resafa: the North gate

Palmyra provokes, this – the juxtaposition of the differentiated human act and the undifferentiated sands – is everywhere the most striking.

If the traveller wishes to pass an untroubled night, it is wiser to sleep out, either under the stars or with a tent pitched in the orchards. In any case a mosquito net is essential. The acrid but not unpleasantly sulphurous water of the big spring which feeds the oasis provides a welcome evening plunge. The French turned it into a swimming-pool, as the Romans apparently did before them. After the traveller has dined beside his own tent, inelegantly but at least cleanly, he will have time, looking out to the ruins under the stars, to consider all he has seen and to ponder on the strange chances which combined to create for a brief century or two this desert florescence.

Though Assyrian documents speak of Palmyra, under its Semitic name of Tadmor, before the first millennium B.C., it was still no more than a prosperous oasis village when Marc Antony made a raid on the place. Though its rise was eventually swift, its greatness was brief, and its serious history falls within the first three centuries of imperial rule. Roman trade policy created it, and when in its grandeur it presumed to forget the origin of its wealth and success Rome destroyed it. Its sudden rise dates from about the beginning of our era when as the result of an understanding between the Romans and the Parthians it became a trade depot, tacitly understood to be exempt from Parthian incursions and enjoying imperial protection. It was not, however, until the beginning of the second century A.D., when Trajan broke the power of Petra, incorporating it into *Provincia Arabia*, and the more precarious southern route from Petra into Lower Mesopotamia declined, that Palmyra acquired its undisputed pre-eminence. This pre-eminence was further increased when Rome gained control of Dura Europos in A.D. 164. This fortress town on the Euphrates, whose size and importance extensive excavations have revealed, guarded the flank of the main caravan route to Hit. The Dura garrison, exercising on the formal parade ground that is still to be identified, ensured that an ever-increasing flow of wealth passed unmolested to swell the mushroom importance of Palmyra. By about A.D. 200 the latter was honoured with the title of a Roman colony. Not long after, the family who were both to create a Palmyrene empire and bring about the city's downfall appeared upon the political scene in the person of a certain Odenath, who was executed for rebellion. Rebellious ambition was in the family blood, and found in the vast and sudden wealth of the foremost Palmyrenes a fatal stimulus. The dead man's son boldly styled himself 'Prince of Palmyra', and that prince's

D

son was the great Odenath. The last had further increased the family power and received the title of consul, when events occurred that seemed to favour Palmyrene independence. The Sassanians irrupted into the Empire, Dura Europos was lost and the legions were defeated. Odenath, evidently a general of exceptional abilities, stepped into the breach, drove back the Persians and saved Syria. His power was immense, and a grateful but no doubt apprehensive Rome granted him the titles of *dux* and *imperator*. Rome was perhaps surprised to discover that in return the imperial suzerainty continued to be respected at any rate in name. At this point Odenath was unfortunately murdered, and his widow, the romantic but less cautious Zenobia, proclaimed the independence of Palmyra in the name of her young son Vaballath, 'King of Kings'. A Roman expedition was defeated, Egypt and Asia Minor invaded, and overnight a merchant Empire appeared stretching from the Nile to the Caucasus.[1]

Of this Empire the Queen was the ruler and the driving force. She seems to have been a remarkable woman and to deserve the aura of sentiment which attaches to her memory. Gibbon thus describes her: 'She claimed her descent from the Macedonian kings of Egypt, equalled in beauty her ancestor Cleopatra, and far surpassed that princess in chastity and valour. Zenobia was esteemed the most lovely as well as the most heroic of her sex. She was of dark complexion (for in speaking of a lady these trifles become important). Her teeth were of a pearly whiteness, and her large black eyes sparkled with uncommon fire, tempered by the most attractive sweetness. Her voice was strong and harmonious. Her manly understanding was strengthened and adorned by study. She was not ignorant of the Latin tongue, but possessed in equal perfection the Greek, the Syriac and Egyptian languages. She had drawn up for her own use an epitome of oriental history, and familiarly compared the beauties of Homer and Plato under the tuition of the sublime Longinus.' When it is understood that Zenobia was also a huntress of big game, a military tactician, and so tough that she would march for miles on foot at the head of her troops, it is difficult to grudge her the splendid title, which she herself assumed, of 'Queen of the East'. It is curious to contemplate what might have been the future of her caravan-sinewed enterprise, had Zenobia not been unfortunate enough after A.D. 270 to come up against an emperor of Aurelian's mettle. As it

[1] Apparently even the Queen's name emphasized the commercial structure of the Empire, for *Zenobia*, it has been claimed, was a hellenization of the Arab *Bath-Zabbai*, meaning 'daughter of a merchant'. See E. S. Bouchier, *Syria as a Roman Province*.

was the Palmyrene armies were twice defeated in the field, and the city besieged and taken. Zenobia herself was captured on the banks of the Euphrates, having penetrated the Roman lines at Palmyra in a vain attempt to get through to Persia and obtain Sassanid help. The sequel for the queen was the humiliation of participating in Aurelian's Roman triumph, though it seems that her chains were of gold and her eventual asylum a villa on the Tiber. For Palmyra the real end came in the following year when, as the result of a further rising and the murder of the Roman garrison, Aurelian hurried back to raze the city walls and destroy the water supply. Palmyra's grandeur was over. Though the town retained a certain commercial importance in the Byzantine period, and Justinian, with an eye always to the outskirts of his Empire, tried to rehabilitate it, a renaissance was made impossible by reasons more vital than its political downfall. The caravan trade slumped in the fourth and fifth centuries and, as the Byzantine hold on the central parts of the desert became progressively more precarious, the old northern trade route came once again into favour. Palmyra, folded in its deserts, was less and less frequented, and lapsed again into insignificance. There remained water, palms and ruins.

To form an impression of the caravan city in its heyday, before the Sassanians troubled the Euphrates or Zenobia broke with Rome, is not altogether easy. The ruins stand deserted and much has gone of the original splendour, while the caravan routes, which were the city's *raison d'être* and the arteries that carried its life blood, are untrodden and known only to the Bedouin and the archaeologist. It is difficult to understand that the Palmyrene gods of these ruined sanctuaries had also their temples in Rome, that a Palmyrene flotilla was stationed on the Lower Euphrates and watched the Persian Gulf, and that this shrunken city had its trade counters southward to Egypt and westward to Gaul and Spain. At Seleucia on the Tigris Palmyra's caravans met the convoys from Persia and the Chinese frontiers, loading silks and jade; at Babylon, where they had a counter by A.D. 24, they freighted the Indian traffic – muslins, spices, ebony, ivory, pearls and precious stones. The tariff dues payable on goods entering Palmyra in A.D. 137 have been preserved and indicate how this stream of traffic brought wealth not only to the merchant venturers but to the city itself. Its temples and its colonnades were virtually borne on the backs of camels. The private tombs in their number and their ostentation show well enough how at the same time the individual prospered and how fortunes were built on desert sand. Nor was it only merchants who became wealthy, for beside them grew up the finance of traffic. Palmyra became the centre of caravan banking and the manipulators of money sat still in the Oasis, made calculations, lent coin and died richer than they had ever dreamt. Emperors visited the Oasis in state – Hadrian and the Syro-phil Alexander Severus; and their retinues were perhaps a little supercilious about the manners of self-made business men, and not a little envious of their wealth. Their sense of aristocratic superiority, however, can hardly have been publicly aired in a town where traffic carried so little stigma that even the lesser gods stooped to take an interest in business. The deities Arsu and Azizu rode on camels and were sometimes so depicted by the Palmyrenes, and their beneficent powers were exercised wherever the camels of business men ferried saleable goods. In its every aspect Palmyra was a caravan town and the desert routes dominated not only the economic life of its inhabitants but all their values. Thus in the ruins archaeologists have found an inscription gratefully carved, not to a hero or to a general who had gained victories, but simply to one who had protected and furthered the caravan traffic: to a citizen in fact who, directly, had brought added wealth to Palmyra. On the heels of wealth followed art and intellect. Though the ruins still reveal much of the first, one must attempt when looking at the weathered stone to envisage the lavish colour, the paintings and the mosaics (the paintings from Dura Europos in the Damascus Museum and the mosaics at Soueida will help in a general way), and the precious and semi-precious metals, such as were employed for the gilt bronze capitals of the Corinthian colonnade round the cella in the Great Temple of Bel. Of the typically Palmyrene statues that decorated the town there are numbers both in the Palmyra Museum and elsewhere. It is significant of the fact that the rich also liked to import works of art from abroad that in the tariff list of A.D. 137 there is a special duty mentioned on the import of bronze statues and busts. Lastly this city of wealth had in its great days a brief but brilliant intellectual life. Longinus, whose work On the Sublime still figures among the 'set books' of English University curricula, was one of Zenobia's political advisers, and Paul of Samosata, the famous and heretical bishop of Antioch, was among the number of distinguished men who thronged her court.

The civilization of Palmyra was frankly commercial, and in its every aspect just such a curious mixture as one might expect in a caravan town. Its hybrid nature was symbolized in the early days of its prosperity by the intermediate political situation which it held as a buffer between Parthia and Rome, subject to the influence of both states. Such a political situation could hardly be permanent and, as the power of the Empire increased, its administrative grip tightened and the city was dragged more and more into the Roman orbit. Yet though her great men might become Roman citizens or even be admitted to the aristocracy of Rome, and though a Roman governor and garrison were installed in the Oasis and Palmyrene archers were recruited to serve as auxiliaries with the Legions, local and Parthian influences remained vital and vigorous. Though the political constitution of the city was outwardly Graeco-Roman, comprising a Senate, and officers with the familiar names of *strategus* and *archon*, municipal authority remained largely in the hands of four prominent families, whose princes held classical titles which barely disguised the older Semitic tribal organization. Again, though local deities might obtain Roman names, they were content still on occasion to be portrayed in Parthian costume. A fondness for Parthian costume was also shown by the inhabitants. Intellectually the best society might be hellenized and the ideas of Greece and Rome pass as common coin, but in matters of dress and furniture the East remained in Palmyra. Persia spoke in the rugs, carpets and divans of the houses, and in the jewellery and robes of the women. The same mixture existed in race and language. Thus, though Aramaic was the language of the people, it worked comfortably enough in harness with Greek and Latin, and many inscriptions exist in all three tongues. It was among the rich and the intellectuals that people were effectively hellenized; elsewhere classical influences remained a veneer upon a population still Semitic and oriental. Even among the rich themselves, the extent of their wealth and the unique nature of their city probably developed feelings of antagonistic independence towards the classical world whose civilization they had adopted for their own purposes. Their feelings were perhaps not very unlike those of the rich Syrians today who, while piling up their fortunes with western methods and machines, and avidly following the fashions of the West, none the less resent western pretensions.

The curiously mixed administrative, cultural and linguistic life of Palmyra gives the necessary clue to the nature of Palmyrene art. A visit to the ruins inevitably suggests a number of questions concerning their 'style', questions of a sort which perhaps first arose, though less urgently, when one visited Baalbeck. The style of Palmyra, like its civilization, is a blend. Evidently the general flavour is Graeco-Roman and the Corinthian order is almost monotonous in its ubiquity. But the more the traveller sees of Palmyrene art the more conscious will he become of a substratum wholly non-classical. Even at a first glance the weird tomb towers, the oblong cella of the Great Temple and the sculptured figures announce something quite unfamiliar to the West. In Palmyra's art, as in its civilization, East and West meet, and beneath the classical lie Aramean, Persian, and yet other influences. Experts find Babylon in the temples and houses; Syria and Anatolia in the sculpture; Persia in wall paintings, stuffs, implements and furniture; and in the sombre tomb towers, elegant yet severe, a stylistic enigma that apparently neither Greek nor Semitic influences altogether explain. As a general rule, Palmyrene art, like the Oasis society, becomes more Aramean as it becomes more popular. As a general rule also, the twentieth-century traveller will prefer Palmyrene art when it remains purely decorative and attempts as little representation as possible. Decoration and representation may be contrasted, conveniently and to the detriment of the latter, in the sculptured frieze around the gateway of the Great Temple cella. The statues of Palmyra on the other hand are particularly interesting in showing clearly and strongly the Semitic-oriental substratum of Palmyrene taste. Though the beards are worn in the Roman fashion, the shape of the eyes and the arrangement of the hair is purely oriental. Oriental, too, is the solemn frontality of gods and merchants, and the preoccupation with detail. The control of classic modelling and the vigour and simplification of classic rhythm have disappeared. The drapery is stilted and gauche. It is easy, as was once the fashion, to be over critical of Palmyrene art. Clearly enough it is not what is commonly termed a 'pure' style. There is no reason indeed that it should be. As Gertrude Bell, speaking of Baalbeck where is celebrated a less mixed marriage of East and West, so rightly points out, to those interested in the past there is neither clean nor unclean, and all the works of the human imagination fall into their appointed place, directing and illuminating the understanding of the observer. Many of the Palmyrene heads are both striking as portraiture and a pleasure to look at. Though the sculpture has lost the elegance of Greece and not yet acquired the astringent beauty of Byzance – it stands in a sense midway between the two – it aptly expresses the nature of the civilization which gave it birth. These heavy-headed men and women, whose busts have been found mainly in the tombs, are indeed what is most communicative in Palmyrene art. There are few 'beauties' and no swan-necks; the heads, symbolically enough, are screwed on tightly. The large almond-shaped eyes, the full cheeks, the heavy noses and the direct unambiguous stare, show an unintrospective people, whose poetry was in their caravans, not in their thoughts, and whose imagination found sufficient outlet in planning uncertain ventures and following, in the mind's eye, the dusty progress of their goods from one desert station to another. The busts show also the confidence and determination which their originals must have undoubtedly possessed, and perhaps in many of the tight mouths appears a Semitic cruelty, not disadvantageous in the cut-throat competition of caravan trafficking. The range of portraits is, however, large and the types vary. There appear, wearing a cylindrical headgear, not unlike the *tarbush* of Egypt, successful merchants who are a generation removed from chaffering, and with Roman civilization have acquired a bland comfortable air and the easy manner of the great social world of Rome. In their stiff head-draperies, the competent matrons, set, responsible and provident, emerge as another salient type. They evidently do not underrate the new position and security which wealth has brought to the daughters of women who once moved with tents and knew little more oasis comfort than their beasts. They are perhaps the note on which to leave Palmyra. Nothing in this civilization was more extraordinary than the existence of these solemn, bejewelled matrons, with the implicit background of linen-cupboards, keys and domestic and social routine, who flourished for a few generations with the inhospitable sand blowing about the doors of their orderly houses.

The splendours of Baalbeck and Palmyra, and the Roman remains in the decayed Hauran, show in themselves the tremendous importance of Syria in the imperial scheme. The Syrian Legions had created Vespasian emperor as early as A.D. 69, and they performed the same welcome office for Avidius Cassius a century later. Not long after, the Syrians themselves acquired the purple. Septimus Severus married a Syrian of Homs and his grandson Elagabulus, a Syrian in manners and upbringing, and a gourmet and profligate by taste, succeeded to the Empire much to the scandal of respectable Romans. He was followed by Philip the Arab, whose elevation, as we have shown, brought signal good fortune to his native village of Chahba. Such Syrian eminence was at the expense of Italy, and was naturally galling to the Romans. It was presumably one of the latter who inscribed on the rocks of Sinai the heartfelt complaint: *Cessent Syri ante Latinos Romanos*. The protest, however, was vain. Though Syrian emperors were an interlude, history awaited Byzantium. A century after the destruction of Zenobia's empire, what had once been the Roman east was ruled from the Bosphorus.

CHAPTER V

A RIVER AND BYZANTIUM

———————————— ◁◇▷ ————————————

No traveller ever came upon the Euphrates unexpectedly. Its appearance, in space and geographically, may be sudden; but, whether achieved in camel stages or motor-hours, it will long have been the goal to which thought and expectation moved through the deserts. From the mountains of the Anti-Lebanon where cultivation ends, the imagination, as Gertrude Bell so rightly says, is 'tributary to the Euphrates'. It is without competition, the solitary feature to which all tracks lead when the last green outpost has been left behind. And the name resounds; association would lend it drama in a far less dramatic situation. When at last, probably hot and dusty, the traveller looks down to the river from the barren escarpment which, horizon to horizon, hangs upon its western flank, it is, and it is not, as imagination had pictured it. There indeed is a muddy-brown river, a great river heavy with silt, winding through interminable deserts, a volume of moving water in a treeless expanse; yet in spite of so dominating the wastes, of being the thing welcomed and waited for, the centre of thought – and of all life too upon its banks – it is unspeakably mournful. Despair is latent in every prospect of this river, and the words of Pascal have more than once been recalled upon its banks: *Les fleuves de Babylone coulent, et tombent, et entrainent. . . . O Sainte Sion, ou tout est stable, ou rien ne tombe.*

A sense of sadness and futility is perhaps in part prompted by the fact – serious enough to anyone familiar with this desert country – that the power of the river is largely running to waste. Unlike the Nile's, its progress is limitedly beneficent. It should march, not through dust, but through a belt of green and every drop be lifted to the deserts by creaking water-wheels. At one time much water was so diverted, and on the east bank a number of canals led off the water into cultivated areas. But nearly all these ancient works lapsed into disuse centuries ago and in Syria have only reappeared recently as archaeological

92

discoveries. The Euphrates, again less happy than the Nile, has almost always been a frontier and has suffered accordingly. It is indeed the classic example of a frontier and clearly typifies all that a boundary means. Most other great rivers, which conveniently exist to set a limit to national security or presumption, have a vigorous life of their own. Their political function is secondary. The Middle Euphrates as it runs through Syria is in a different case. Its intrinsic nature – the river itself, the few poor village-towns upon its banks and the poorer Bedouin and semi-nomads who squat in its winding valley – has for centuries at a time been overshadowed by its political importance as a frontier. If one cares to believe in a dialectic of East and West – which superficially goes a long way to explaining the history of Syria – it was along this line that the opposed forces came to grips until the Muslim conquest, and particularly in those nine hundred years, the most fruitful in Syrian history, which intervened between the expedition of Alexander and the defeat of the Emperor Heraclius. Down to this river, this natural no man's land, have marched a procession of great men, and the isolation, the absence of common humdrum life, throw them into prominence. They cast long historical shadows, as dramatic as any solitary object in these deserts at sunset: Xenophon and the Ten Thousand; Crassus whose eagles turned ominously back from the ford at Thapsacus; the apostate emperor going to his death; Trajan battering through to Ctesiphon; and Belisarius – only a century before Islam swept the frontier away – with his knack of victory.

The problem of consolidation, of how the West was actually to intrench itself along this watery line, was naturally of the first importance, and one emperor after another gave his attention to the question. Wisely the Romans and their successors, in very modern fashion, adopted a system of defence in depth. There was no attempt to construct an actual line with ditch and mound, such as protected parts of the Rhine and Danube frontiers. The Roman *limes* on the Euphrates consisted merely of a number of strong points created at positions of strategic importance. Such were Zeugma where the northerly traffic crossed the river; Sura near the ford at Thapsacus; Callinicum which we know as Raqqa; Circesium at the junction of the Khabur and the Euphrates (a transit point for Palmyra traffic); and lastly Dura Europos and Halebiyah whose extensive ruins are so well preserved. These and other major strong points were linked by lesser 'stations' whose sites today are marked only by faint earth mounds or the few mud huts of an Arab village. They must have been dreary posts, a grim exile at the best, and

* D

it is curious to think of their garrisons overlooking the mournful river, year in and year out, in order that gold might flow into Rome and the authorities constitute over a hundred and fifty public holidays and keep a third of the inhabitants on public charity, with free meals, games and triumphs. These strong points and stations formed the *limes exterior*; behind them lay the *limes interior* based on an inner series of defences which included Hama, Homs and Palmyra. Inner and outer defences were linked by an efficient system of communications which allowed for the rapid concentration of troops and knit the whole scheme into one easily controlled unit. Of this disposition we know from the writers of the time, such as the geographer Ptolemy, the author of the *Itinerary* published in the reign of the Emperor Antoninus Caracalla, and the *Peutinger Table*. It is significant of all that has since intervened, that these – the standard road-guides of the period as they might almost be called – have now to be laboriously collated by the archaeologist to establish what was once common knowledge. Thus towns of whose existence no actual trace remains are again given a local habitation, and routes that were imperial highways make a tentative reappearance on scholars' maps. It is a queer situation: as though Baedeker should outlast the autostradas, and railway time-tables survive the places they once served.

The perfect organization of the caravan routes, that in the heyday of Palmyra led a stream of traffic up to the Euphrates and across, has already been noted. Even after Aurelian had wreaked his vengeance on the city, Diocletian continued to improve the frontier camps and the lines of communication between the river and the seaboard. A hundred and fifty years later the wells and blockhouses, situated at convenient journey-stages that made the desert transits possible, were still fulfilling their purpose. In the fifth century an abbot, travelling from the Euphrates to Egypt, put up at these desert forts in his progress westward, he and his companions receiving all they needed and enjoying the hospitality of the tribunes and their men. It is fair to suppose that there as elsewhere the boredom of outpost life made strangers welcome. In the deserts southwards from Palmyra, the wastes of the *Provincia Arabia*, security was always less certain and less effectively organized. This vast indeterminate area continued to be a problem long after Trajan's annexation and we hear of Decius, nearly a century and a half after this event, importing lions from Africa and letting them loose in the southern deserts to discomfort the unruly Bedouin tribes.

The Byzantines took over the desert responsibilities of the Romans, and they left in the Middle Euphrates at least one tremendous ruin, Halebiyah. It is the greatest of the Byzantine frontier forts, as Dura Europos is the greatest of the Graeco-Roman ones. The point of departure for Halebiyah is Deir-ez-Zor, where the traveller coming from Palmyra and Damascus will probably strike the Euphrates. Apart from the cafés on the river's edge which at sunset have their gaiety and charm, the only attractions at Deir-ez-Zor are the modern carpets made by the inmates of the town prison, and the possibility of going on a hawking expedition. The Bedouin of the region are among the few tribes which still practise the intricate and fascinating pursuit of hawking for gazelle.

The road from Deir-ez-Zor to Halebiyah leads northward along the escarpment above the river, through painfully accidented country, climbing in and out of the many ravines that cut their way down to the Euphrates valley. In one such ravine a tablet marks the spot where two French officers were held up and murdered by brigands in 1925: a memorial of a sort calculated to give the traveller a pleasant sense of adventure in a country where there is now perfect security. He will possibly enjoy a similar stimulus on noting that many of the Bedouin are armed. The inhabitants of the Euphrates valley did as a matter of fact bear for hundreds of years an evil reputation as robbers and assassins and were said to have all the cunning of the Bedouin without their sense of responsibility towards strangers. All this however is now old history. The traveller watches the views, not the road. The Euphrates dominates the scene. Though the winding river-bed appears flat, the lugubrious brown waters actually move fast. The river swirls along through the wastes. Islands covered with thickets of tamarisk, and innumerable mud shoals like giant crocodiles, split and parcel up the hurrying water. Often the river is divided into two or three streams, and in addition it forms lagoons where the annual spring floods have spilt over its proper banks. These lagoons where the clouded water has time to settle are surprisingly blue – the river itself is so uniformly thick and muddied – and are frequented by numbers of birds, among them the white-winged Black Tern which in defiance of proverbial wisdom prefers to fish in clear waters. Cultivation follows the Euphrates, and varies in width from a precarious pasture snatched out of the desert to wide bays of corn enclosed between the escarpment and the river. Villages are rare and the inhabitants few; the Bedouin live in tents and the semi-nomads build with reeds like birds, their huts barely distinguishable in fields of sedge. They catch fish, stalk the lumbering geese, raise a little water to irrigate their fields, and pasture their sheep along the river-banks. A strip of green, inset among rocks and sand, is their life and livelihood, while the wealth of the river hurries away southward.

About sixty kilometres north of Deir-ez-Zor the desert hills approach the river on both sides and the Euphrates for a considerable distance surges through narrows between bald grey-black rocks. In this defile the western hills at one point for a moment recede and on the semicircle of open ground, so created between hills and river, stand the ruins of Halebiyah. To reach them the traveller must leave the Deir–Raqqa road and for several kilometres follow a track that is *just* possible for wheeled traffic. In places it seems as though a car could never pick its way through the basalt boulders, at others as though there were simply not the requisite space to squeeze a chassis between the hillside and the river. It can be done, however, and the track eventually debouches on even ground before the ruins.

Some time in the middle of the sixth century A.D. two men from Constantinople set out for this spot upon the Euphrates to rebuild the fortifications that were already ruined at that date. They were the architects John of Byzance and Isidore of Milo, the latter a nephew of the famous architect of Santa Sophia which had gone up only a few years before. Halebiyah as it stands today, from the foundations up, dates mainly from their rebuilding. The castle, or perhaps more correctly the fortified area, is a long triangle having its shortest side facing the river. Here, where the wall abuts directly on the water, mammoth blocks of stone were used and a protective mole built out into the river to shield the base of the fortifications from the gnawing action of the current. From the river front the other two walls of the fortress-ride inland and climb to meet, some quarter of a mile away, upon a steep knoll. Here, almost within bowshot of the desert escarpment to the west, and at the apex of the triangular fortifications, lay the main strongwork. From its ruins there is an impressive and striking view over the fortress area, with the river washing its eastern wall and the gorge between desert hills drawing away north and south. What at first appears curious is the emptiness of the great triangle within the walls. It lacks those endless mounds and hummocks which at Palmyra, Resafa and elsewhere denote the remains of the ordinary humble life of the place, shops and the houses of artisans and merchants. The explanation is that Halebiyah on the frontier was first and foremost a fortified camp and in so far as it had a civil life it was only the casual life that the presence of a garrison attracts. People were stationed at Halebiyah; they did not live there, at the very end of things, if they could avoid it.

Halebiyah's hold on history, since based on strategic rather than trade considerations, was precarious. When the frontier went and the Euphrates no longer divided east and west, Halebiyah had a future only as a ruin. It first entered history as Zenobia, a name that commemorated its foundation (about A.D. 266–70) by the Palmyrene Queen in the years of glory just preceding her defeat by Aurelian. Nothing remains of the Palmyrene period except the tombs outside the present walls to the north. To what extent the Romans subsequently maintained it, appears to be uncertain. It was at all events in no state of defence by A.D. 540 when Khosroes I swept down on the fortress and the inmates fled westward at the news of his approach. Justinian not long after, sensing the strength of the position, included Halebiyah in his extensive programme of military fortification and dispatched – as Procopius tells – those architects of whom we have spoken to build the grey gypsum walls that still surprise one in the wilderness. Apart from the strongwork where the constructions of the Byzantines have been superseded by Arab building, and certain sectors of the south wall where brickwork has replaced the original stone of the upper courses and tells of later repairs, the fortifications are those of Justinian's architects. The walls of moderate thickness with their square flanking towers are characteristic of Byzantine military architecture. Similarly the Governor's Palace, or whatever the three-storey structure may be that projects from the north wall, is also of Justinian's building, as are apparently the two basilicas in the centre of the grass-grown area within the walls. Unfortunately the latter are now so sadly ruined as to be almost unrecognizable to the lay eye. The fine gates in the north and south walls also date from the same period and were once the termini of an arcaded avenue which ran right across the fortress area and of which the merest vestiges remain.

Justinian's garrison town lasted only half a century, for in 610 the Persians came again and the troops of Khosroes II captured and devastated it. After this date there is no further news of the place. Its probable fate is not uncertain. With the coming of Islam in the next century the borders of Byzantium were rolled right back from the Middle Euphrates, and Halebiyah, no longer a frontier key, lost all significance. The remains of Arab workmanship show that the walls were patched and the strongwork at the summit of the fortress rebuilt at some time after the Persian devastation, but this is all. Nothing else emerges from the medieval twilight, and it is improbable that its Arab occupation was more than temporary or that throughout the succeeding centuries there was much activity in the Byzantine ruins. The place was forgotten and even the original name of Zenobia was so far lost as to be carried across the river and conferred on the ruins of Zalebiyah, a kilometre or two downstream. The charm of the Greek fortress, however, remains, perhaps has even increased with time and desertion. A pair of foxes that live in the ruins are now the only inhabitants, and even the sheik's tomb outside the south gate appears to be unvisited. The unbroken silence, the sombre grey walls, the Euphrates sucking and dragging at their feet as it swirls through the defile, and the bald hills, *regardant* as heraldry might term them, combine to create a particularly insistent atmosphere. Halebiyah is in fact one of those confusing places which demand a careful examination of conscience, since as the traveller leaves the ruins he is hardly sure whether the impression that remains is due to the original Byzantine achievement or to the dramatic desolation in which the ruins stand.

Farther north and west the value of the Byzantine or Christian achievement in Syria admits of no such doubts. The magnificent Christian town of Resafa actually lies only some eighty desert kilometres west of Halebiyah, though to get there it is necessary to make a considerable detour, following the Euphrates up to Raqqa and then turning south again through the desert. Somewhere between Deir-ez-Zor and Resafa, if Halebiyah and Raqqa are to be visited on the way, the traveller will have to pitch camp for the night since the native inn at Raqqa is impossible. There can be no more impressive place to do so than on the banks of the Euphrates. The wind which often blows downstream drops at sunset and is succeeded by a comprehensive hush. Even the tall feathery-headed reeds cease to scrape and sway. As the far bank grows indistinct, the river assumes Amazonian proportions. Beside it the traveller and his chattels seem incidental and insignificant; his fire in the gathering darkness flickers by permission, a mere candle. From under his mosquito-net he will hear duck calling on the water and the disembodied and disturbing night-conversation of birds. Even in his sleep he will not altogether lose consciousness of the river swirling past, the brown, melancholy, wasted Euphrates.

Resafa lies some forty kilometres south of Raqqa, on the desert plateau, if a grassy undulating plain may be called desert. The ruins of the ancient town, standing within its rectangular walls, are visible for miles in every direction. Built of a peculiar light gypsum, it shines, almost glitters, in the sun as though it were a town of mica or glass. From a distance it appears a complete place, undespoiled and unbroken, and though you know that it has been deserted for centuries, the silence as you drive up to the walls and past the gates is unexpected. Here was once a whole city, where now only hawks wheel and adders bask among the stones. At most there may be three or four black tents of the 'Aneza tribe, pitched outside the walls. The Bedouin come for water and find little enough. There is a single well which far below ground yields a meagre brackish supply. Having lowered his waterskin, an Arab attaches the rope to the pommel of his saddle and canters away a full hundred and fifty yards before the scant load reaches ground level. With such provision for a few days they refresh themselves and their flocks, and then move on.

Resafa first enters history in the Assyrian period; and the Assyrians probably turned it into a military camp in the ninth century B.C. Its position as time went on inevitably gave it local importance: first, it lay on the caravan route from Damascus northward via Palmyra to Raqqa and the ford of the Euphrates at Thapsacus (when this route became a Roman road, Resafa was the last station before the Euphrates was reached); second, the desert escarpment due east of Resafa approaches at places within a few feet of the Euphrates and caravans coming up the west bank of the river in flood time were obliged to turn inland south of Resafa, whence emerging on the plateau they made for the settlement. Two caravan routes thus converged there, and the place for centuries played a respectable but not outstanding part in the caravan traffic from which it drew a livelihood. Its development was, however, hindered by lack of water, since it never possessed natural resources other than those inadequate wells which the Bedouin still use. Its role would probably always have been a modest one had it not been for the chance that led a saint and martyr to his death there early in the fourth century.

Somewhere about A.D. 305 a certain Sergius, commander of the Imperial Palace guard, convicted as a Christian, arrived at Resafa in the most pitiable state. He had been driven by his guards on foot from the Euphrates in shoes lined with sharp nails. On arrival he was condemned to death and decapitated, having had his lips bored through to receive the rope by which he was led out to execution. The death of Sergius, or Saint Sergius as he soon became, made a deep impression. His fame spread rapidly, and with the end of Roman persecution a cult arose at the place of his martyrdom and burial. Resafa in his honour changed its name to Sergiopolis and therewith embarked on fame and a period of immense prosperity as the centre of his pilgrimage. Though faith might create a town such as Resafa became, its maintenance without proper water supplies demanded the exact organization that only a highly developed material civilization could supply. Byzantium stepped in to supplement Christian fervour.

Sergius had died outside the north gate and there fifteen bishops at some time unknown set up a first church over his grave. This was followed in the early fifth century by the building of a great basilica and monastery inside the walls in the south-east corner of the town. Three hundred pounds weight of gold were spent on this church, a fact of which the Nestorian Bishop of Hierapolis bitterly complained to the Empress Eudochia when the Patriarch of Antioch removed Sergiopolis from his heretical jurisdiction soon after. The basilica in due course became a cathedral and finally by A.D. 550 the seat of a metropolitan with four bishoprics under him. These lay to the south of Sergiopolis and one of them is believed to have been Zenobia (Halebiyah).

As a centre of faith and superstition the power and repute of Sergiopolis rapidly increased and St Sergius himself acquired that local pre-eminence which in due course was to make him the patron saint of Syria.[1] Anastasius thought it worth while to remove the martyr's tomb to Constantinople; the Arabs of Palmyrena, with a bold disregard for ethical implications, carried icons of the saint on their freebooting raids; and the rich showered gifts on his shrine. This wealth and fame brought its inevitable and unenviable reward. Khosroes I in 540 sent word from the Euphrates to the Bishop of Sergiopolis ordering him to ransom twelve thousand captives taken by the Persians at Sura for two hundred pounds of gold. Candidius the Bishop, unable to raise the money, was left no alternative but to offer a promissory note and pledge the treasures of the saint and his own reputation as security. Of the twelve thousand captives which he was supposed to receive in return, the majority did not survive their treatment at the hands of their illustrious captor, and the bishop at the end of two years found himself unable to meet his obligations. Khosroes not content with the treasures of Sergiopolis – including a magnificent cross presented to the shrine by Justinian and Theodora – decided to seize the town. Treachery having failed, the king 'boiling with anger' as Procopius phrases it, sent a force of six thousand to take the city by assault or siege. The place, though at the time sadly under-garrisoned, repulsed initial attacks. Its effective resistance was due to the fortified walls which Justinian had perhaps just restored. A siege, however, disheartened the defenders almost to

[1] St George, martyred in the reign of Diocletian, holds second place in Syrian favour. Oddly enough the Syrian doctors, Cosmas and Damian, whose joint martyrdom the Italian Renaissance painters were so fond of portraying, are less esteemed in their own country than in Europe.

the point of capitulation, when it was learnt that the Persians had only two days' water supply remaining. The city held out and the Persian forces were compelled to withdraw, having accomplished nothing. Half a century later Khosroes II treated the city differently. He showed a proper respect for the saint and dutifully returned the famous cross extorted by Khosroes I. When his Christian wife conceived a son, it is said by the express intervention of the saint, he sent further presents to swell the metropolitan's treasury.

With the Arab conquest the place did not at once lose its importance and when the Umayyad Caliph, Al-Hisham, established his residence outside Resafa-Sergiopolis, olive-trees and artificial ponds still relieved what is today the unbroken landscape of the steppe. But decay was inevitable; only careful Byzantine organization had maintained a city in this waterless place, and when Byzantium failed, drought was sooner or later bound to prevail. The arrangements for water supply in Byzantine times were remarkable and elaborate. A large reservoir to the west of the town collected the winter rains and the supply was thence led over the walls by an aqueduct to the profound vaulted reservoirs in the south-west corner of the town which still exist in an admirable state of preservation. A supply of water sufficient for two years was apparently available, though at the end of a particularly dry period the reserves sometimes gave out. Then an ant-like procession of slaves and donkeys plied between the town and the nearest point on the Euphrates bringing in essential supplies, until the winter rains again filled the cisterns.

By the ninth century the town had seriously declined. There were only a few shops and most of the inhabitants had reverted to pastoral occupations. Indeed, it was said that they only hung on out of a traditional devotion to the place. Even so, Justinian's walls remained in good repair and a wondering traveller two hundred years later said they provided hardly less efficient fortification than the Caliph's palace at Baghdad. Enough vitality persisted within the shell that the walls encompassed to effect the restoration of the Great Basilica in 1093 (it had perhaps been destroyed by earthquake earlier), and the medieval geographer Yaqût said the monastery, even in his time, remained one of the wonders of the world for its architecture and beauty. But the town had no future; in the twelfth century we learn that there were neither grain, cattle, comforts nor commerce at Sergiopolis. The few inhabitants lived, as they had done before Byzantium brought fame to the place, off a diminished caravan traffic and trade with the Bedouin.

It is interesting to know that these people apparently remained Christian, a touching tribute to the agonies of their saint a thousand years earlier. To this finished history the Mongol invasions came simply as a postscript. When Hulagu's hordes broke into the town in 1247 it was already dead; since then it has remained empty for over five centuries.

This very desertion has preserved it. Though the great ditch, which in typical Byzantine fashion ringed the town, has long ago been filled with sand, the walls with their round corner towers and square flanking towers along the curtain stand almost entire and enclose a rectangular area of between thirty and forty acres once packed with buildings. The scheme of the place is typical of those planned Greek towns which the Seleucids founded throughout Syria and which, favoured by the Romans, continued to be built until Muslim times. Laid out with geometric regularity and in a spirit unoriental, the town was divided by two large intersecting avenues. The four quarters so created were neatly subdivided, as far as was practical, by smaller parallel intersecting streets. At the termini of the four avenues stood the main gates of the town, facing the four points of the compass. The central avenue that ran from the north to the south gate was apparently, and according to custom, arcaded. In such towns all was, in principle, orderly and according to plan, though it is true that at Sergiopolis the exigencies of faith in the form of churches rather cut up the symmetry, and the late date of the buildings – they were mainly put up in the fifth or sixth centuries – meant that the classic sense of proportion had to compromise with religious interests.

On the north side of the town the little church *extra muros* is on the site of an ancient cemetery and probably marks the place of St Sergius's martyrdom and burial. If so it was presumably there that the fifteen bishops, at some early date, raised his first tomb-church. The present building, as is shown by an inscription over the apsidal windows, dates from the time of the ruler Al-Mundir who flourished in the second half of the sixth century. He was one of those semi-independent Ghassanid princes who did good work for the Byzantines in guarding Palmyrena and their desert provinces from the incursions of the tribes east and south. Though in detail the church is mediocre, except for the capitals with their rustic acanthus design, it is well preserved and gives a pleasing impression of solidity and proportion. Architecturally it is something of a rarity for it belongs to the non-basilican type of building, characterized by a central dome, which was unusual in the early churches of Northern Syria.

In the town itself the North Gate, the Martyry, and the Basilica of Saint Sergius are all important. They probably date mainly from the late fifth or early sixth century, but the last differs very much in style from the other two. In the North Gate and the Martyry the carving is exceedingly rich and shows classical decorative influence far more strongly than the Basilica. Its sophistication speaks of the art of a capital and it is indeed similar to the work at Kalat Seman and other ruined Christian villages in the orbit of Antioch (*see pages 105 et seq.*). The decoration of the Basilica is on the other hand extremely simple. It might be termed provincial work and is said to have affinities with the frontier art of Christianity across the Euphrates and in Mesopotamia.

The North Gateway, with its frieze of grapes and vine leaves and its acanthus capitals, is certainly one of the finest Byzantine remains in Syria. An interesting point is that such triple gateways elsewhere have two lateral gates for pedestrians and a central gate for wheeled vehicles, but at Sergiopolis the central gate was made hardly larger than the others since nothing more formidable than camel traffic was ever likely to enter this desert town. The decoration of the Martyry, like that of the North Gateway, is fine where it has been preserved (as in the south apse). The plan of the church, unfortunately very ruined, is also remarkable, for it seems to represent a transition between the long basilican type of church and the domed circular church associated with Byzantium, of which, as we have seen, an example stands outside the town walls. A rectangular nave terminates conservatively enough in an apse, but the sides of the nave itself swell out at a certain point into semicircular bays which recall the 'central' domed type of building. It was to the Martyry that the saint's body was transported from the original church *extra muros* and there that it probably rested for some time.

The Basilica in the south-east corner of the town is better preserved than the Martyry and is a large church. It consists of a narthex, two side aisles, and a nave terminating in a semicircular apse, whose vault takes the shape of a conch shell – a motif so common throughout the classical and Byzantine remains in Syria, and so pleasing. Like the Martyry, and indeed like all the Byzantine churches in North Syria, the Basilica had a wooden roof. Though Christian tradition attributed the church to Constantine and spoke of the mosaics with which he had adorned it, the Basilica as it stands today mainly dates from about the beginning of the sixth century. It received considerable, and none too fortunate, additions about 1093, when it was repaired following an earthquake which had occurred a few years earlier. The great arches of the nave, as may still be seen, were half-filled with rather shoddy masonry, and the piers reinforced by rose-coloured columns with capitals of crystallized lime-stone. The latter appear out of place, but have an interesting history as they originally stood, twenty-two of them, in the Martyry. The smaller church presumably was so ruined by the earthquake as to be thought beyond repair and they were thus transported to the Basilica. With them came the migrant body of the saint who there found a third resting-place. The ornament of the Basilica is unimpressive, but this hardly detracts from its effect. It is a great ruin. The nave and aisles, moreover, are not empty. The birds have converted the church-shell into a huge aviary, since it provides the only spacious shade in the dead town. Birds sit and watch the stranger from the clerestory and the capitals; there is an intermittent coming and going, a weaving and swerving between the arches, a fluttering out of sunlight into shade. The aviary is particularly favoured by rollers with their blue-green plumage and weird metallic voices, by numberless wild pigeons and by hawks which somehow manage to live on terms with the other birds.

Outside in the blinding sunlight the walled town is little but a maze of grass-grown mounds and fragmentary ruins. The alignment of most of the streets has long since disappeared and it is by no means easy to find one's way about. It is all deeply silent and deserted. In Palmyrene Syria the traveller soon discovers that the desertion and silence of its ruins are incalculably greater than the merely natural wildness and emptiness of the deserts which surround them. The desolation of these ancient sites is suffocating.

By contrast to the ruin of the town, the huge subterranean reservoirs with their fine brick-vaulted roofs remain intact. Though all the masonry above ground – the conduits and the aqueduct which brought in the water across the walls – has long ago disappeared, these impressive great cisterns still look as though they would hold the town's supply for siege or drought as effectively as in the sixth century. It is appropriate that this should be so, for upon their proper functioning depended the very existence of Sergiopolis. They serve to emphasize that remarkable Byzantine organization which alone enabled faith to build and maintain the town. North-west, beyond Aleppo, where one deserted Christian site of the Byzantine period succeeds another, and the waterless hills are full of ruined bishops' palaces, and inns, and aqueducts, the same thought comes home again and again: how admirable in spite of failing resources, of the Persians, and of the wearying quarrels of ecclesiastics, was the organization of the Byzantine world.

The majority of the Christian remains which provide such striking testimony to the civilization which flourished in Byzantine Syria from the fourth century until the invasion of the Arabs in the seventh are not easily accessible. The ruins of Rouheia, Serdjilla, the magnificent church of Qalbloze, the domestic architecture of El Bara, though all situated within striking distance of Aleppo, are not served by any road. They are also in such rough and rocky terrain that it is impossible to approach them – as a desert site like Resafa may be approached – by simply driving across-country. Foot or mule-back are the only alternatives. Fortunately this does not apply to Kalat Seman, the most important and impressive of all these sites. Kalat Seman, like Resafa, was populated by faith, but the fortunes and progress of its founder-saint were even more extraordinary, if less sad, than those of the martyr St Sergius. Simeon Stylites, who was later to make the reputation of the site that is known as Kalat Seman, early showed an aptitude for the maceration and asceticism that he later brought to so high a pitch. At the age of sixteen he retired to a monastery. There he wore a spiked girdle that drew blood, and digging a trench in the monastery garden he buried himself up to the chin and so passed the summer months. His next austerity was to wall himself up throughout Lent. That his fellow monks had not yet taken his true measure seems evident from the fact that they put themselves to the trouble of passing in six loaves to him. They were found uneaten when he emerged from his fast and confinement. It was apparently in A.D. 423, to escape the crowds which his sanctity already attracted to his solitary cell at Telannisus (now Deir Seman), that he took up his station near by, at Kalat Seman, upon a first modest pillar some ten feet high. From this he graduated, in due course, to a sixty-foot column on the top of which he remained for thirty years. The column was composed of three drums to symbolize the Trinity and its top was encircled by a brief parapet, presumably to stop the saint falling off. Such a danger was further reduced by the chain and iron collar which encircled his neck.

In this elevated station, where his private necessities and religious exercises were equally public, St Simeon passed his time in prayer and fasting. An exact spectator who attempted to tell the number of the saint's daily prostrations, having reached one thousand two hundred and forty-four, lost count. He received the eucharist once a week from a brother monk who brought it up on a ladder, and he twice daily preached to the crowds who assembled to hear him. Thus, through the bitter cold of North Syrian winters and the broiling summer heats, he lived on from year to year, a miracle of endurance and the cynosure of an Empire. When the progress of an ulcered foot threatened his life, the Emperor Theodosius sent a personal letter and a deputation of bishops begging him to descend to earth and receive treatment. The saint, however, had his own nostrums, and a forty days' fast restored him to health. When politely writing to refuse the Emperor's request, he added some pointed advice on imperial administration and indeed, as his reputation grew, he became generous with counsel and admonition to churchmen and emperors, emerging as a powerful champion of orthodoxy. It was through his direct intervention that a humane edict restoring their synagogues to the unfortunate Jews was cancelled. By the middle of the century his fame was immense and the number of miracles that he was reported to have performed enormous. The roads that led to the beautiful corner of the foot-hills where his pillar stood were crowded with pilgrims, and a sea of curious and devout faces daily gazed up at the extraordinary hermit. People even came from Britain to see and consult him. In July 459 when news got about that the saint was dying, a vast concourse from all parts gathered on the hills to hear his last words. His body was later transported in great pomp by the Patriarch to Antioch and buried in a church specially built for the purpose. His monk's hood, a relic of consequence, went to the Emperor Leo at Constantinople.

There is no doubt about the truth of the main outlines of the Simeon story, since his biographer, Theodoret of Tyre, was his contemporary and friend. Though commonly regarded as the first stylite, St Simeon's practice seems to have been anticipated in a mild form by the pagans and the saint's column had its prototype in the pillars associated with heathen temples. Thus there had been a column in the Temple of Atargatis at Hierapolis, north-east of Aleppo, which was ascended once yearly. A priest remained on top of the column for seven days offering up prayers for the well-being of the district and for such suppliants as brought offerings and demanded his intercession. St Simeon's example, however, gave the stylite idea tremendous publicity in the Christian world. The results of his elevation were immediate, and ascetics upon their pillars were soon to be found dotted all over Northern Syria and farther afield. Children were not spared the infection and Simeon Stylites the Younger mounted his first pillar at so early an age that, as Evagrius says, 'he even cast his teeth in that situation'. Four miles outside Constantinople the Elder Simeon's disciple, Daniel Stylites, was a sight for twenty years and from his pillar wielded considerable power, while at Beyrouth a stylite exhorted and influenced the university students. An ascetic tried to mount a pillar in Gaul; but the movement was not sympathetic to western tastes and his bishop brought him down again and demolished his monument. The attractions of a position which demanded such ascetic discipline, and at the same time made sanctity apparent, continued to operate in the East for a long time and St Simeon's successors lasted in Syria until the eleventh century and in Georgia apparently until the early nineteenth.

The road from Aleppo to Kalat Seman crosses at first a rolling plain with outcrops of rock; though in detail insignificant, the landscape as a whole is effective. The hills to the west lapse into washes of blue against which in early summer the maize provides a foreground of deep, almost aqueous green. The earth, which east of Aleppo is a bitter grey, here turns a brilliant red, like beef, and in some places is almost purple-black, seeming very fertile. From time to time one passes the characteristic villages of the Aleppo district built often on 'tells', with their tidy clusters of conical beehive huts. One of them, Terib, was for nearly twenty years the most easterly stronghold of the Crusaders in this part of Syria. The women's costume throughout the district is magnificent, and they stand at the village wells in dresses of Prussian blue and deep cherry red. About forty kilometres out, the road for some way runs beside its Roman predecessor (still in an admirable state of preservation), and then turns off into the hills for St Simeon. The character of the country now changes. There are stones everywhere, and the peasants till only a few cleared patches of red earth, and cultivate a few small olive-trees and fewer vines. Permanent poverty; but the traveller can afford to see only the sunshine, the showers of goldfinches over the rocks and the continually changing views as the road works up into the hills.

In this austere country, on a bare rocky spur, Kalat Seman is situated. A short steep climb takes you from the road to the ruins. In the sacred precincts small black cattle graze, and apricot- and fig-trees grow among blocks of fallen stone and fragments of acanthus carving. Across the rough turf where once was a vast courtyard you approach the basilica. The proportions and lavish decoration of the south, and main, entrance are splendid, but the size and beauty of the whole church are not at once evident. Only inside, when you have made your way to the centre of the church, is its magnificence apparent. You are, as a matter of fact, in the largest remaining Christian monument that antedates the tenth- and eleventh-century cathedrals of the West, and perhaps in the finest building put up between the Roman monuments of the second century and the creation of Santa Sophia in the sixth.[1]

The design of the building is unique and was dictated by the wish to incorporate the saint's pillar as the central point of interest. Where you had thought to find one basilica there are actually four, arranged in the shape of a cross and facing roughly to the four points of the compass. At the centre of the cross is an open octagon where rose the sixty-foot pillar, whose base is still visible. The detail is as fine as the proportions: monolithic pillars, magnificent Corinthian capitals (some of them with that treatment of acanthus which gives a 'wind-blown' effect, and is sometimes said to have originated in these Syrian churches) and scrolls and bands of carved decoration of such beauty that the traveller comes to search hungrily for a mere foot or two of such work where it lies scattered among the innumerable Christian ruins of these hills. Only the eastern basilica with its triple apse, whose fantastically luxuriant decorations are well preserved, was strictly speaking used as a church. It was separated from the other three, which served simply as *promenoirs* for the crowds which flocked to see the sacred pillar. Though rustics even brought their cattle to enjoy the benign influence of the place, women were excluded and might only catch a glimpse through the doorways, a rule which would evidently have met with the saint's approval, since he had in his lifetime allowed no woman, not even his mother, to approach within the circle of stones which surrounded the base of his pillar. For the traveller, solitary among the ruins, it is curious to think of the rapt crowds, shoulder to shoulder, making the circuit of this extraordinary relic, and of all the life and devotion which once built and filled the place, and which have now ebbed away. By A.D. 560, when the historian Evagrius visited the church (less than a century after St Simeon's death) and left a description of the site, miracles were already 'well authenticated', and he himself repeatedly saw a large and brilliant star shooting along the balustrade to the left of the saint's pillar. Others more fortunate even saw 'a resemblance of the saint's face flitting about here and there, with a long beard and wearing a tiara'.

Though the church of St Simeon is in its plan unique, the east basilica, or church proper, presents close affinities to many other churches in Northern Syria, and among them – as the traveller will probably notice – to the basilica of St Sergius at Resafa. It therefore provides a convenient starting-point for a brief inquiry into the

[1] St Simeon's basilica covers an area considerably greater than Wells or Lichfield cathedrals.

characteristics of the Christian architecture which sprang up all over these hills from the fourth to the seventh centuries A.D. Wishing to build themselves places of Christian worship, the Syrians might well have developed something on the lines of the temple cella with which they were familiar, had not such buildings been too small to house the communal services which the new rite involved. An alternative presented itself in the Roman basilica or hall of justice, and it was from this prototype that their churches evolved. The evolution was determined by two main factors: native Syrian originality and the needs of Christian worship. Starting in the fourth century from a hellenistic model, the Syrians went on to produce an indigenous architecture which progressively moved away from its classic original, until the Persian and Arab invaders put an end to their building activity.

The country provided them with quantities of good limestone, and the architects therefore had no occasion to use brick.[1] Their buildings are of stone, and of stone in such large blocks and so well fitted that no material was needed to bind it. Among the scores of Byzantine cities which dot the North Syrian hills there is hardly a scrap of mortar to be found. Though the buildings have weathered to a sombre grey, and have lost something of their finish, it is well to remember that they first went up a dazzling white.

The general type of basilica these architects developed differs very little throughout Northern Syria. It is characterized by a long central nave, separated from two side aisles by rows of columns (or sometimes piers). These columns carry round arches, often of considerable span, which rest directly on the capitals of the columns without the interposition of an abacus. The columns themselves are always monolithic, and the capitals show every variety of adaptation from the classic orders, though Corinthianesque types predominate. Immediately above the arches of the nave is a true clerestory (i.e. the outer walls of the side aisles are only one storey high). The windows in the clerestory and elsewhere are either rectangular or round-headed, though in the latter case they are seldom truly arched and simply have the lintel above the window-opening cut in semicircular shape (a form known as an arcuated lintel). Above the clerestory windows project the corbels which carried the roof (when it was not, as at St Simeon and some of the later churches, carried on a second order of small pillars rising between the clerestory

---

[1] Eastward at Resafa gypsum takes the place of limestone. There are only two brick churches in Syria – Kasr ibn Wardan, and Anderin – both built by the Emperor Justinian.

windows). The roof itself was pent-shaped and always made of wood. Eusebius describes a Syrian fourth-century church roofed with cedar from the Lebanon. These wooden roofs, with the tiles that overlay them, have inevitably disappeared, and the churches now stand in their scores open to the sky.

The east end of such churches was provided with an apsidal sanctuary covered by a half-dome (often in the form of a conch-shell). From the exterior of the church this apse was usually invisible, being concealed in a deep wall. It was flanked by two chambers, nearly always rectangular (the triple apses at St Simeon and the Martyry at Resafa are exceptional), the one used as a sacristy, and the other for the oblation before the litany. A woodwork screen separated the sanctuary from the nave, and another, somewhere in the body of the church, separated the male and female congregations. Woodwork screens, fitted into the windows, filtered the Syrian sunlight. None of these wooden accessories have survived. For decoration these basilicas relied primarily on carved stone, which the native masons knew so well how to handle, and which survive in their harmonious friezes and scroll-work, and in their deep-cut acanthus capitals. As an indigenous style developed and confidence grew greater, this stone decoration became more lavish and more various. The comparatively sparing decoration of the fourth-century basilicas gave place in the next two hundred years to long bands of intricate stone carving flowing on from one window to another, to fluted columns, and finally to more complicated fronts with elaborate cornices. Kalat Seman, probably built during the last half of the fifth century, in the generation after the saint's death, shows all these features. It is noteworthy, however, that as ornament increases the sense of construction does not weaken. Mouldings and decorations are rightly used to emphasize important lines or to link salient constructional features. The North Syrian builders, though they became artists, remained masons.

In addition to their characteristic basilican churches the North Syrians also built a simple type of chapel, a plain oblong building without pillars or aisles. It has been compared to a house with the interior walls removed and a sanctuary added at one end. Such chapels sometimes possessed an exterior colonnade or portico along the front where the main doorway was situated. They also on occasion built, but far more rarely, the domed type of church, such as elsewhere became characteristic of Byzance. A church of this type exists as we have seen outside the walls at Resafa, and the so-called baptistery at Kalat Seman provides another example. Such domed churches, without aisles, were in

Syria the speciality of the Jebel Druze in the south where, owing to a shortage of timber for roofing, domes and vaulting became the rule. Important early examples, antedating Santa Sophia, exist there at Bosra and Ezraa.

The rarity of the 'central' domed type of church in Northern Syria indicates the difference in the conceptions of architecture which prevailed at Byzantium and Antioch, a difference which Antioch, jealous to preserve its ecclesiastical independence, was probably not anxious to minimize. As we have seen, Northern Syria avoided the dome, whereas the Byzantines made it the outstanding feature of their buildings. The Byzantines again built largely in brick and then covered the substructure with a marvellous veneer of marble and mosaic; in Northern Syria, though mosaic floors certainly existed in some places (fragments of such floors remain at Kalat Seman and in one of the churches at Deir Seman), the builders envisaged a church as a thing in stone and relied on this same stone, when carved, for their primary decoration.[1] The comparative freedom of this North Syrian architecture from Byzantine influences is only less interesting than its manifold connections with the Romanesque architecture of the West. Romanesque architecture appears to take over where these Syrian churches end, and that they did exert some actual influence on the West seems probable. The same reliance in each place on stone and stone carving provides an obvious technical similarity; but at Kalat Seman there are two things which seem to forecast the West in even more striking fashion. They are the exterior of the apse of the east basilica with its two rows of superposed columns, now alas much mutilated, which might surely be transported to France without feeling out of place; and the façade of the south basilica, which seems in general plan only to want two flanking towers to take up its station, though not perhaps with the same ease as the nearby apse, in some French cathedral town.

In many of these North Syrian churches, particularly the earlier ones, the main entrance, provided with a porch or portico, was not as might be expected through the west end, but in one of the lateral aisles, most often on the south side. At Kalat Seman a special reason accounted for the fact that the main entrance was on the south. The spur of hill on which the buildings stand was not wide enough to carry the full breadth of the church and the extremity of the west basilica had thus to be built

[1] The resistance to Byzantine influences appears again in the fact that the basketwork capital, so characteristic of Byzance, does not appear in Northern Syria.

out over the valley on a substructure. This meant that the church could
not be entered from the west. The very narrowness of the spur, however,
gave the architects the opportunity of building a terrace along the west
side of the south basilica from which the pilgrims could enjoy the great
views which there unfold, identifying for each other as visitors will,
whether pious or profane, the salient features of the landscape: the
valley of the Afrin spread out below, the mass of Kurd Dagh beyond,
and farther still the Amanus range. South-west they would have pointed
out the Lake of Antioch and have explained how the capital, obscured
by the foot-hills, lay beyond. Directly to the south they saw, almost at
their feet, Deir Seman and, beyond it, Refadi and Fedri, adjacent
Christian villages; farther off stretched the tangled Gebel Barisha along
whose slopes towns and basilicas succeeded one another in almost
endless procession. The terrace has fallen but the views remain. Indeed,
much of the charm of Kalat Seman lies in the fact that at every point the
eye moves off from the grey stone of the basilicas and the detail of
carved leaf into vistas and blue mountains.

The drama of the site can only be realized on exploring the precincts
more fully. To the south-east of the basilica lies the monastery to which
it was attached, whose size and importance can still be guessed from the
extent of the ruins and the remains of a huge three-storey building;
directly south is the church known as the Baptistery. These buildings,
together with the basilica itself, stand on a long promontory; on three
sides the land falls away precipitously, on the fourth, its shortest side,
the promontory is attached to the mass of hill behind. The conformation
is immediately reminiscent of those sites nearer to the coast which the
builders of the Crusades were to choose for their fortresses six hundred
and fifty years later. It was not only a dramatic vantage-point that the
saint selected but, as his successors discovered, a highly defensible one.
Presumably it was only with the troubles of the sixth century that the
saint's shrine and its wealth needed and acquired fortification. A fortified
wall, much of which remains, was run across the promontory north of the
basilica, cutting it off from the hill behind, and flanking walls enclosed
it. It thus became to all intents and purposes a castle. As such its subsequent history is uncertain. The Byzantines were in control of it in A.D.
985, for in that year Sa'ad ad-Daula, the Hamdanid Prince of Aleppo
and successor to the more famous Seif ad-Daula, besieged the place for
three days, took it, sacked it, and killed the monks or sold them into
slavery. It is from its use as a strong place that the present Arab
name, Kalat Seman, the Castle of Simeon, derives. The memory of

the saint on his pillar has been merged with that of later military operations.

The way down to the village-town of Telanissus, now Deir Seman, is by the *via sacra* where the pilgrims once climbed to the saint's basilica. Nothing remains of the *via sacra* except a tottering triumphal arch; the path today stumbles down the hillside among boulders and scattered olive-trees. The ruins of Deir Seman are extensive and of peculiar nature, since the town was the Lourdes or Loreto of the period. The place grew as a religious centre with the express duty of catering for the pilgrim traffic, and to this end possessed a number of basilicas, convents and hotels. Two of the last are dated A.D. 479 and it must have been at about that time, twenty years after the saint's death, that the town began to be recognized as an established pilgrimage resort, providing suitable accommodation. The number and diversity of the remains are at first confusing. The general impression which emerges as one picks one's way – not always easily – about the ruins is one of wealth and architectural competence. The money was there, as the three-storeyed hotels and fragments of mosaic floor amply prove, and the architects were available to translate money into numbers of dignified stone buildings.

Though built for a special purpose, the domestic architecture employed at Deir Seman is not different in kind from that found in the other dead Christian towns of this part of Syria. Like the basilicas, the private houses are distinguished for the excellence of their dressed masonry, and no mortar was used in laying the courses. Even the stables and out-houses were built with the same care, in large well-finished blocks of stone. The houses, like the basilicas, were covered with pent-shaped wooden roofs, and had their upper floors in wood. On the other hand they did not feature the round Roman arch which appears in the churches, but preserved the more essentially Greek habit of surmounting columns or pillars with a straight architrave or entablature. The usual plan was to build these houses on a courtyard, which was often colon-naded. In true oriental fashion the façade of the house towards the street was left severely alone, and all ornament was reserved for the front that looked on the courtyard. At first the windows were square and undecorated, but by the fifth and sixth centuries the architects were using mouldings and had evolved double windows separated by a small pillar or a mullion. The staircase to the upper floor, or floors, was an exterior one, and usually rose from the courtyard. In the latter was situated the well. The inhabitants of these dead villages and towns were very conscious of their faith and its newly won recognition and again and again over the door lintels appear a cross, a Christian monogram, or a pious inscription such as the one that some well-contented householder caused to be carved over his door at El-Bara: 'Thou hast put gladness in my heart. With the fruit of the corn and the vine and the olive, we have increased in peace.' The inscriptions in the earlier buildings are mainly Greek, and though Syriac [1] in the fifth and sixth centuries grows more common, it does not altogether supplant the official language.

Though the existence of Deir and Kalat Seman is in part explained by faith and the life of their extraordinary saint, something different is needed to account for the other towns of the region, whose ruins proclaim the high level of wealth and civilization which once existed there. Over a hundred of these ruined sites remain and in the Gebel Barisha, south of Kalat Seman, there are, within a radius of some few miles, no less than forty-two ancient towns and villages (of which only fourteen are now inhabited, by indigent peasants). The explanation of this architecture and of these once thriving communities is to be sought in two causes, local and general. The ruins themselves provide internal evidence to show why this landscape, now barren and boulder-ridden, came to support a flourishing society. The remains of hundreds of wine and olive presses prove that the country must once have been patterned with vineyards and olive orchards. Oak, pine, cedar and cypress grew upon the slopes, and an earth now scrawny and unprofitable was once rich and fertile. The local wine and olive industries were evidently well organized, as in some places there are found groups of presses for communal use. Ready markets existed in the cities of Antioch and Apamea. The decline from wealth and fertility to the starvation crops which the country now yields is only in small measure due to a lack of similar markets and of intelligent organization in succeeding centuries. The great trouble has been deforestation. This had probably already set in during the Christian period, for immense quantities of timber must have been used in building all these wooden-roofed towns. After the Persian and Arab conquests, and in the disorder of the ensuing centuries (when the country was a frontier between both Byzantines and Muslims, and Crusaders and Muslims) much further damage was done. The Turks completed the devastation. The penalty of deforestation was soil erosion, and ultimately change of climate. Nothing remained to hold the soil, and year after year it was carried away by the winter rain. Inch by inch

[1] Syriac is the name given to the local Syrian tongue in Christian times, as opposed to the older and slightly different Aramaic which was superseded by Greek.

the boulders appeared which are now so characteristic of the country; grass became rock. Exact testimony to the extent of this tragic process is to be found in the ruined villages where – in spite of the debris of centuries – the ground floors of the houses are often well above the present level of the streets.

Antioch, as we have said, was the market for the produce of these towns, but it almost certainly contributed to their growth in an even more direct way. The capital possessed in the fourth century a population that must have been somewhere near a million.[1] It is reasonable to suppose that the well-to-do at Antioch, as elsewhere, enjoyed their country houses and escaped the severe summer heat by going up into the hills. (As the crow flies Gebel Barisha is a bare thirty miles from Antioch.) Only the supposition that this whole region enjoyed the patronage of a rich summer clientele will account for the existence in out-of-the-way villages of large and imposing villas, and of so many baths – the first of necessities for the luxurious Antiocenes. Wealth thus came into the hill country not only through its agricultural exports, but with its summer traffic from the capital. Vines flourished, government officials and wealthy contractors enjoyed the air and the views, and the architects, luckily for posterity, had their hands full.

These things explain much of the economics of the dead towns and indicate how they came to be working propositions. The picture, however, remains incomplete without reference to the forces which conditioned the form of the towns, and the ideas and the outlook of the people who lived there.

A significant fact about the towns is that nearly all of them were unwalled. Byzantine security made such defences superfluous. Even the dreary see-saw of the Persian wars along the frontier, where neither side could hope to hold the territory they ravaged, cannot have meant much to the tempo of life in these hill towns. They thrived on peace; when that disappeared, the towns quickly decayed and soon became not worth the walling. Peace is thus the essential background. In the foreground two forces loomed large, so large that in the minds of the inhabitants they may well have obscured all else, the Byzantine Empire and the Christian faith. Though a number of ecclesiastical historians record the affairs of the church in this period, there is little material for civil and administrative history in Syria. The general trend of this history, however, is clear enough and may be summed up in the process known as Byzantinization.

---

[1] John Chrysostom says there were 200,000 men, exclusive of women, children, slaves and the inhabitants of the suburbs.

At the time that most of the dead cities of Syria were being built, that is from the fourth century onward, the level of culture was declining. This was due to the decreasing influence of the old leisured class with classical and pagan background, and also to the effect of measures such as the extension of citizenship. The deterioration in the Mediterranean economy was even worse. In the early days of the Empire economic arrangements had worked fairly well. *Laissez-faire* was operative and, on the whole, the free flow of goods and labour had created much wealth and considerable general prosperity. In due course problems had arisen, some of which – instability and rise in prices, difficulties in distribution of goods and labour – are familiar in the twentieth century. Byzantium determined to put this right, and from the fourth century we watch the evolution of a drastic government control. Imperial edicts attempted to govern production and prices. Tariffs were multiplied, and labour was controlled: change of profession became illegal; in the country the *coloni*, the unfortunate tenant farmers, found themselves fixed by law to the land they hired; in the towns the burdensome and unsalaried tenure of public office became obligatory. Everywhere freedom gave place to compulsion. As the governmental octopus increased its administrative hold on capital and provinces, the old municipal institutions decayed and a ruined middle class gave pride of place to the petty official. Syria was governed from a Greek Whitehall.

Whether such a grim solution, involving the deterioration of provincial life, was necessary, it is difficult to tell; the Syrians certainly did not like it. On the other hand this centralized bureaucracy was amazingly efficient and extended the natural term of the Eastern Empire for many centuries. When the hill towns of Syria were at the height of their prosperity, Byzantium must have seemed the most stable, powerful and permanent force that they could envisage, and most of the inhabitants probably believed, with a famous contemporary geographer, that the Empire would 'remain unconquered till the final conflagration'.

The only object that loomed as large to the Syrians as the Byzantine Empire was the Church of Christ. Syria, where a natural aptitude for religious belief had previously expressed itself in the rise of innumerable cults, took to Christianity early and with devotion. It is believed that the symbol of the cross arose in Syria, and it will be recalled that the name Christian was first applied in Antioch to the followers of Christ. With Rome and Alexandria, Antioch was one of the three great sees of the early Church, antedating Jerusalem and Constantinople. It came to be regarded as the peculiar stronghold of the literal interpretation of the

Gospel, by contrast with Alexandria where a more allegorical approach was favoured. Eminent among the great churchmen of Antioch was the most eloquent preacher of the early Church, John Chrysostom, the 'golden-tongued'. The people of the hill towns, when they visited the nearby capital, must certainly have heard him inveighing against the wealth and morals of the rich. After the long period of trial and persecution which the faith had undergone before its official recognition by Constantine, it might have been supposed that these ardent Christians would have settled down to the tranquil and deserved enjoyment of their communion. Such was far from the case. A mischievous spirit did not permit the Church to remain at peace. The determination with which they had resisted imperial persecution, they now showed in disputing the tenets of their own faith. They were, as Gibbon unkindly but justly says, 'more solicitous to explore the nature, than to practise the laws, of their founder'. In Syria, as elsewhere in the East, the promulgation or the persecution of heresies was the fierce interest of churchmen. From the day that Constantine made Christianity the state religion until the coming of the Arabs, sectarianism racked the country. The Arian, Nestorian, Jacobite and Monothelite heresies were no more than the outstanding quarrels in three centuries of dogged metaphysical dispute. No article of faith escaped the closest scrutiny, and the ingenious temper of the time bred, and detected, heresies with disastrous ease. This unfortunate ingenuity was frequently accompanied by fanatical violence. At Ephesus the Patriarch of Alexandria kicked and trampled the Patriarch of Constantinople; at Apamea, just south of the hill towns, three hundred and fifty orthodox monks were murdered; even Jerusalem was sacked in the interests of heretical belief.

The violence of religious controversy, in Syria as elsewhere, acquired much of its driving power from purely secular causes. To understand why these people, particularly in the fifth century, killed each other over the splitting of a hair, when they might have been enjoying the pleasant country houses that were then in process of building, it is necessary to consider the relations of Church and State in the Byzantine Empire. In the first centuries of the Christian era, the shrewder emperors had realized the danger which the new belief presented to the unity of the Empire, and it is roughly true to say that the better the Emperor, *qua* ruler, the more determined was his persecution of his Christian subjects. By the fourth century, however, it had become clear that persecution was useless and that the duality of religious faith and political allegiance could not be resolved by this method. Constantine

E

wisely determined to control the force that he could not destroy, and made Christianity the state religion. From that moment, at any rate in the East, the autonomy of the Church was at an end. The Patriarch of Constantinople, less fortunate than his distant brother in Rome, lived in the shadow of the imperial palace. Ecclesiastical policy became in ever greater measure the policy of the court, and ecclesiastical affairs an important department of civil administration. Even in matters of dogma imperial interference became common and patriarchs found themselves accepting a blunt palace ruling on points of the subtlest metaphysical consequence. By the time of Justinian things had gone so far that they could hardly go farther, and the principle was openly asserted that doctrinal decisions could be made by imperial edict. Orthodoxy became a prerequisite for admission into the state service, and heretics with certain exceptions were not admitted to citizenship, could not tesify in the law courts or inherit property. Idiosyncrasies of religious opinion were everywhere suppressed and towns were razed to the ground in the name of conformity. This assimilation of religious to civil administration certainly had its advantages and the long-term efficiency of the Byzantine bureaucracy was partly due to it. The price, however, was out of all proportion, since every fresh heresy became a rallying point for latent opposition to the civil regime, and nationalist and separatist movements were incalculably strengthened in being able to enlist religious enthusiasm.

The ill success of the policy was particularly evident in Syria. There, from the fifth century until the Arab conquest, the relations of Church and State, as reflected in the Monophysite heresy, were the constant preoccupation of the people. The heresy itself concerned the nature of Christ, the Monophysites maintaining that this nature was single and that no separation existed between the Saviour's divine and human elements. It was not a problem about which laymen would ordinarily have bothered their heads and some conciliatory formula in more normal times would have been readily discoverable. As it was, the heresy was handled with extraordinary lack of tact, and became everywhere a focus for anti-imperial sentiments. The Church in Egypt, with more violence than dignity, supported the heresy almost to a man, and it was owing to the pressure of the Egyptian delegates who packed the Second Council of Ephesus that the Monophysite belief was for a time imposed on the Orthodox Church. The manner of its imposition may be judged from the language in which the conciliar decision was couched. 'May those', it was proclaimed, 'who divide Christ be divided with the sword, may they be hewn in pieces, may they be burnt alive.' Byzantium quite evidently could not allow doctrine to be dictated by a group of turbulent and schismatic Egyptian bishops. Accordingly the Emperor with great pomp invoked the Council of Chalcedon and, significantly enough, reserved the seats of honour, not for the great churchmen, but for twenty officers of senatorial or consular rank. The Council in A.D. 451 reversed the decisions of the Second Ephesus Council and solemnly branded the Monophysites as heretics. Unfortunately Chalcedon, far from resolving the matter, simply stiffened heretical opposition. Egypt *en bloc* refused to accept the findings of the Council, and in Syria and elsewhere separatist elements rallied, in due course, strongly to the anathematized doctrine. A serious schism had in fact been created. Of this the emperors were soon only too aware, and in frantic efforts to repair the damage alternated between repression and compromise. Neither course was successful.

In Syria the heresy did not have the same initial support as in Egypt, but a body of heretical opinion, seconded by national sentiment, steadily grew. We have seen that St Simeon from his pillar, some time before 459, threw his weight on to the orthodox side. It was not long before the Monophysites realized the propaganda value of his elevated station and in due course there was to be seen the strange spectacle on these Syrian hills of rival stylites, each declaiming on behalf of his own dogma. With the accession at the end of the fifth century of the Emperor Anastasius, who favoured the Monophysites and nearly lost his Empire in the imbroglio of religious controversy, heresy received a tremendous impetus and with the great Severus as Monophysite Patriarch of Antioch swept the country. The Emperor Justin, and his successor Justinian, introduced a characteristically drastic reversal of policy. In the imperial purge, Severus escaped to Egypt, but his right-hand man, less fortunate, was suffocated; fifty-four bishops were expelled from their sees; and eight hundred eastern ecclesiastics were thrown into prison. It looked indeed for a time as though in Syria resistance had been stamped out. It might have been but for an extraordinary man, Jacobus Bardaeus, from whom the Monophysites today derive their alternative name of 'Jacobites'. Secretly ordained by one of the heretical bishops in a Constantinople prison, he returned to Syria and rallied the unorthodox. Travelling secretly from place to place, he is said to have ordained as many as eighty thousand priests. His work was well done. In spite of Justinian's displeasure, large parts of the country remained devoted to the Monophysite dogma. Shortly before the Arab conquest the Emperor

Heraclius, painfully aware of the extent to which religious schism was weakening the Empire, made a final bid to reconcile the Monophysite and the Orthodox parties in a compromise. He propounded the Mono-thelite doctrine, which while recognizing the dual nature of Christ credited him with a single will. Appealing to less impassioned adversaries he might have been successful. Indeed, for a moment it appeared that he was to be so, for Syria half-heartedly accepted the compromise, whence later came the Maronite church (*see pages 184 et seq.*). Rome, however, refused to be tempted, and the Emperor who had so signally beaten the Persians was foiled by the niceties of ecclesiastical doctrine and ultimately succeeded only in initiating one heresy more.

These questions which now seem so academic were of vital importance to the pilgrims who thronged Kalat Seman, and to the inhabitants of the villages and towns whose ruins are scattered over the neighbouring hills. The religious problem was the first and absorbing question of the time, and the Erastian attitude of the imperial government was ultimately to be fraught with disastrous consequences. The repressions and legislations of Justinian meant that every Jacobite was in some sense outside the law and hostile to the Empire and its organization. Thus on the approach of the Arab forces in A.D. 636 the Christian heretics with shortsighted spleen made no attempt to defend the Empire. How ill they acted the ruins of these hill towns can witness. Heraclius was beaten on the River Yarmak and Syria fell at once into Muslim hands.

CHAPTER VI

BEDOUIN AND DESERT PALACES

— ⟨∘⟩ —

T HE larger part of Syria is desert or desertic steppe, and the unculti-
vated extends from the Anti-Lebanon Mountains to the Euphrates
and beyond. Aleppo, Hama, Homs, Damascus – such towns stand
with their backs to nothing, and the noise of their *suks* is lost in an
immense silence. This silence has throughout history modified the life
led on the settled lands.

The Syrian desert is a continuation of the Great Arabian Desert, and
on the southern boundaries of Syrian territory it is extremely desolate.
Farther north it begins to change its character owing to slightly increased rainfall – a change that first is noticeable in the Palmyra area –
and desert gives place to steppe, carrying a certain amount of vegetation. This northern desert, known as Palmyrena, forms a rough isosceles
triangle with its apex at Aleppo. The Euphrates on the east, and the
limits of settled cultivation on the west, constitute its sides, and its base,
some two hundred and fifty miles long, extends from Damascus to the
Euphrates. It is to this northern or Palmyrene desert that the interests
of the traveller will usually take him. Its altitude, tempering the
summer heat, and its greater rainfall have from early times, and in
selected places, allowed enterprising people to graft towns and civilizations upon sand and steppe. Though the civilizations have gone, the
buildings and mechanical apparatus remain – baths, aqueducts, temples
and fortifications. It is into this desert steppe that the traveller must go
to find, not only Palmyra and Resafa, but certain other sites of which
we shall speak in due course.

The area is really a great plateau, standing in the main at between
two and three thousand feet, but tilted at a slight angle and sloping
down towards the Euphrates valley. The sparse winter rainfall is just
enough to provide light grazing over certain areas, and, for a brief period
in the spring, the whole land blossoms with flowers. At this moment the
settled dwellers along the desert edge, the people for instance of Hama,

or Deir-ez-Zor, celebrate a spring festival to which they invite their
friends. Pitching their tents some way out in the flowering desert, they
eat tremendous meals at which whole sheep are roasted, and spend the
convivial day in song and music. It is for many of these people a
reversion, in comfortable and idyllic form, to the life their ancestors
led as wandering Bedouin. This desert paradise lasts, however, only
a few weeks. Under the hot sun, the colour fades from the green and
the blossoms wither. The gay show is literally consumed, leaves and
stalks shrivel, and the life of the plants withdraws underground. Yet
even in the depth of summer the Palmyrene desert is not altogether
barren. Sere feathery grasses, spinous plants, the aromatic *artemisia
herba-alba*, commonest of the Syrian dwarf shrubs, and the purple-
headed *onopordons*, hold out through the long heats and film the desert
surface with dun greyish green.

This is not the place to describe the various beauty and atmosphere
of the desert. It has been described by those who have spent long
months in it, on camel back from dawn to sunset. The fluid lines, the
delicate subtleties of tone, the silence that floods in like a wave behind
speech, the vast spaces that dramatize and then obliterate human
gestures, the sense of solitude and yet of not being alone (because somehow there is always a presence behind you), and lastly the effects of
light – varying from the colourless white of noon to the changing
kaleidoscopes of sunrise and sunset – all these have been reported, and
are true, of the desert. The quality of the light is perhaps worth empha-
sizing afresh, since in the desert – as often elsewhere in Syria – it is of
prime importance and makes or mars landscapes more decisively than
it does in the West. The light, together with the extraordinary clarity
of the atmosphere, accounts also for the strange deceptions of the desert.
Time and again, driving across the Palmyrene steppe, one sees with no
small surprise, or thinks one sees, a good-sized house in the distance. As
the car approaches, it shrinks progressively from house to shack, from
shack to Bedouin tent, from tent to crouching figures, and one surveys
at last nothing but a small bush. A further important point about the
desert is that, in a landscape where features are rare, single objects
assume a disproportionate importance. Even a bush, if seen by a water-
hole or used as a vantage-point by some watching hawk, may well
acquire a place among the essential images into which the memory of a
day's desert driving is later condensed. The same may be said of the rare
and solitary tree, stunted and unexplained, that reappears from time
to time in the deserts, of a camel's white skeleton, or indeed of any

object – as opposed to general effects of light and colour – to which the
eye is drawn. Anything with a certain inherent drama, such as the ruins
of an older civilization, or the charred and twisted metal of that aeroplane which lies – and seems always to have lain – on the long reach
from Palmyra to Deir-ez-Zor, becomes unforgettable. Thus it happens,
oddly enough, that one may retain more concrete images of a day's
progress through the desert, than of, say, a day's drive down to Cornwall
or across the north of France. The same thing is true in a lesser degree of
effects of vegetation in most parts of Syria. As objects set in great
spaces are invested with unusual importance, so, in an arid country,
gardens and green trees appear doubly lush and pleasing. In a land
where everything becomes sun-baked in summer and luxuriance is
extremely relative, points of perpetual greenery such as the *Ghouta*
round Damascus, or the headwaters of the Orontes, acquire a special
significance. Time and again in Syria, when one asks oneself why some
scene seems so 'right', so important or poetic, the answer lies in its
relationship to its environment.

It would, however, be a mistake to imagine that the Palmyrene desert
is always monotonous. Great stretches of featureless sand nowhere
exist. Not only is it steppe rather than desert, but it is a steppe landscape of considerable physical variety.

At times the Palmyrene plateau is intersected by sudden abrupt rifts
or straddled by bare bold ranges of hills – spines of rock and shale
scoured by wind and winter rain, without a blade of green. More often it
undulates away, interminable, its grey-green modulating into a purple
distance. Again there are areas reminiscent of the plains of the Middle
West of America, though instead of rich corn there is only a sea of spare
dried grasses. From horizon to horizon in such areas the surface is
sometimes wonderfully smooth, and it is exhilarating to drive a car at
speed across it. The absence of road or limiting boundary gives a feeling
of freedom, such as one rarely finds off snow or water. The grasses part
before the wheels as water parts before a keel, and across that shallow
rustling sea you can turn your prow in any direction, master of all points
of the compass. Even the gazelle are not more mobile than you, and are
easily outstripped on this smooth ground. Such driving demands a quick
eye, for the desert steppe may change suddenly and unpredictably, and
all at once you find yourself among boulders or ridges of sand. There are
indeed large stretches of this desert so broken, rocky and scarred with
wadis as to be quite untraversable by car. This is a fact that should be
borne in mind if one leaves the few tyre-beaten tracks. In planning a

cross-country itinerary allowance must be made for very bad going and perhaps a twenty-mile detour around impossibly accidented terrain. Such expeditions into the blue are not to be undertaken in a single motor-car. Two cars with proper water supply, desert equipment, ropes, spares and so on, are a desirable minimum. A broken axle a hundred miles from anywhere may otherwise result in a pretty dilemma, and though there is normally little danger of dying of thirst in the Palmyrene desert, stories of such deaths continue to be told, at any rate in the towns.

Though the lost traveller would find it impossible to cross a hundred desert miles in the heat of summer without water, he would in all probability never be called upon to do so, for, as one soon discovers, Palmyrena, though desertic, is not unpeopled. It has its own slow traffic, its own curious ambulant life and society: the stranded traveller in this country of wide horizons will almost certainly find Bedouin, or more probably be found by them. It is extraordinary how often he will stop and set up his bed for the night in a solitude apparently absolute, thinking his presence unseen and unsuspected, only to find Bedouin shepherds watching, from any convenient hummock, the stirring of his camp at dawn. Palmyrena offers such good grazing and is so constricted by comparison with the greater deserts southward, that the traveller continually sights Bedouin encampments or finds himself among their great loose flocks of pasturing camels. As he drives past, the testy beasts make a tremendous pretence of stampeding, charge off with great jolting strides, and then as suddenly forget his intrusion and fall again to browsing.

A European rarely remains indifferent to these Bedouin and even more rarely is the judgement that he passes on them a balanced one. They seem to evoke either an exaggerated distaste or an equally exaggerated romanticism. Both attitudes are not without excuse. On the one hand the Syrian Bedouin are quarrelsome, suspicious, litigious and limited in interest; yet equally they are hospitable, brave, independent and skilled in their own techniques. Reflection reveals their faults and virtues to be complementary. Both are conditioned by their background and their history.

Hospitality in the desert is the recognition of want; it has grown into a social grace. The stranger who comes to a tent comes, or at least in the old days came, because there was nowhere else to go. To turn a man away was equivalent to murder. Such a society for its own sake could not afford to be anything but hospitable. All ran the same risk and trusted to find the same asylum. Bedouin hospitality is part of a routine imposed by the desert, and as such has existed from the earliest times. Though Muhammad, with his characteristically practical sense, might wish to enforce the routine ('Whoever believes in God and the day of resurrection must respect his guest'), its sanction is essentially social and not religious. In a similar way environment has made bravery a Bedouin necessity. Where differences of opinion, or the right to scanty pasturage, are always, and have always been, settled by cunning and force of arms, only the wily and intrepid can hope to survive. The Bedouin is both of these almost by definition. His liberty and independence of spirit are also due to the life he leads, and are a direct by-product of his migratory habits. Had he been settled he would have been subjugated long ago; his mobility has ensured his freedom and the spirit that freedom brings. Only the methodic Roman really dominated these deserts, enrolling the Bedouin in his Camel Corps. Later the great sheiks shook themselves free, and for centuries managed to maintain a practical if not a theoretic independence of Cairo and Baghdad. Even the insistent Turk could not gather taxes from these people. With the coming of the aeroplane the situation has, of course, changed. The bomber and the Vickers gun can make light work of a task which baffled Abbasids, Fatimids and Ottomans. When the twin pipe-lines crossed the desert in 1935, they symbolized the end of a very long era of freedom – though the loss of virtual independence has not yet modified that bearing which travellers have always admired. Finally, the uncompromising desert environment, leaving the smallest margin between success and starvation, between life and death, has imposed on the Bedouin a complete command of his own limited techniques. Within a specific range he is, and has had to be, a virtuoso. He has thus acquired the particular self-confidence and *cachet* that come to the man who can do one thing superlatively well. Camels and camel gear, the vagaries of sand and wind, the spoor of wild animals, the management of tents – in the knowledge of such and similar things he excels. But it is well to remember that the mysteries of any profession, even stock-broking or the law, appear impressive in direct ratio to one's own ignorance of the subject.

But all this happened, as it were, a very long time ago. For centuries the challenge in response to which these virtues were evolved has in no way altered: the desert that created Bedouin society also immutably fixed it. They pitch their tents exactly as Abraham pitched his, and the range of their interests goes hardly further. Their costume has not changed in a thousand years, and the Bedouin today dress in every

* E

particular as the traveller Maqdisi described in the tenth century. It is all understandable enough: the desert is a self-contained unit into which new influences can only penetrate with difficulty. It is a defined and strictly limited area and the interests of those who live there reflect this fact. What happens beyond the borders of the deserts is so little their preoccupation that throughout history the Bedouin themselves have never apparently initiated or maintained a caravan traffic. They have taken a toll on such traffic, and they have provided transport; but they have never organized it, the termini of such traffic lying outside the deserts and thus outside their possible range of interest. Their vision is limited by the deserts.

Other Bedouin failings, as seen through the eyes of the West, are also attributable to their peculiar environment. Time nowhere hangs heavier than in the desert; sometimes for days the Bedouin is steeped in profound and corrosive inactivity: it is then that the endless litigations are set on foot, and in the shadow of the tent those quarrels hatched, or remembered and brooded on afresh, which end in blood vendettas. Bedouin suspicion, the strange concomitant of Bedouin hospitality, is also a desert product: in those spaces unexpected contacts are rare; you know pretty well in which direction tribes and families may be wandering and their reasons for doing so. Surprise visits from unknown callers too often take the form of raids. For centuries it has proved wiser not to divorce wariness from good manners; the habit persists. Lastly those quarrels on a larger scale, the chronic tribal feuds of the Bedouin, though probably grounded in the material fact that in bad years there is barely enough pasturage to go round, only recur with their traditional frequency and violence because these ill neighbours do not live upon each others' doorsteps. When the *razzia*, the looting raid, is over, the desert parts the combatants and, until the next encounter, migration gives them a respite. The environment prevents disunity becoming intolerable, but has also prevented the discovery of any cure.

The Bedouin are thus an odd mixture of qualities and limitations which the desert goes far to explain. Those Bedouin whom the traveller finds today in Palmyrena and southward are, for the larger part, of the 'Aneza tribe. The 'Aneza are not indigenous to Syria but, as tribes have done time and again, came up from Arabia in search of better pasture. Their passage was not easy, and only after a century and a half of migration and intertribal warfare, did they establish their supremacy in the Syrian deserts about a hundred years ago, forcing Shammar tribes, their predecessors, into Mesopotamia. The Rualla tribe is by far the most important of the many subdivisions into which the 'Aneza are divided, and constitute their real strength and backbone. The size of a tribe is computed by the number of its tents, its wealth by the number of its camels: the Rualla have seven thousand tents, and their camels are over a quarter of a million. In cohesion and warlike spirit the Rualla are outstanding. Outstanding also among Bedouin is their enterprise: in 1929 when Europeans were just beginning to realize that the Ford would replace the camel as the ship of the desert, the Rualla had already supplemented their racing camels and Arab horses – the military transport for their raids – by some twenty first-class American cars. This gave them a tremendous advantage over their neighbours until the latter began to develop mechanized transport.

Most of the true Syrian Bedouin lead more or less the same life and are subject to more or less the same social organization. They must be clearly distinguished both in these respects, and in respect of moral worth, from the Bedouin in process of becoming sedentary, along the fringes of the desert and in the Euphrates valley. Such semi-settled Bedouin are the rejects of the desert; nomads for whom the nomad life has been too much. With dwindling flocks, squeezed out first from one pasture and then another, they have at last come to scrape a living on the edge of the cultivation. They are in a state of transition. Peasants, who have not yet acquired a peasant morality, they have lost the desert code of honour and the desert virtues. The contempt which they know the true Bedouin feel for them on the one hand, and the distrust which the peasants feel on the other, does not bring out the best in them. They are, in fact, reputed to be thievish, treacherous and untrustworthy; whereas there is practically no known instance of travellers receiving anything but good treatment from the Syrian nomads, these riverain and settled Arabs have a less honourable record.

The true nomads enjoy a semi-democratic social organization. All affairs of importance are settled by the sheiks in council. These, the important men of the tribe, who have established their right to sit in the tribal council either by the weight of personal character or as representing powerful family units, administer justice, direct policy and make tribal peace or war. The Saiyid, or paramount sheik, presides over the council, but the weight that his word carries in its deliberations depends as much upon his character as his office. By virtue of the latter which is not even hereditary in principle, though practice tends to make it so, he is no more than first among equals. In matters of religion the Syrian Bedouin are often Muslim in name and little more. That fanaticism and respect for the minutiae of dogma which cramps the life of towns on the desert edge is almost unknown among these nomads. Their vagrant life has made conformity with dogma impossible: migrating tribes cannot, and do not, keep the Great Fast. Their Islamic faith is worn easily; it still overlays, and barely hides, a number of pagan beliefs.

The Syrian Bedouin are of two sorts, those who rear camels and those who rear sheep. The former, who look down on the shepherds, are richer and more powerful. In range and territory they also differ; the shepherds frequenting more northerly pastures and tending to keep closer to the cultivation, while the camelherds with their mobile, thirst-resisting flocks, are the men of the great spaces, crossing the arid wastes and straying far south of Syrian territory. Both, however, live by their flocks, and their flocks only, and this accounts for the cycle of their lives.

They are a wandering people because their beasts, which constitute their whole wealth, must in these thin-grassed lands move continually in search of fresh pasture. The camel-breeding tribes, migrating with the regularity of birds, move south into the Great Desert after the winter rains when pasture is easily come by; later as the summer heats draw on they edge slowly north, and at the moment when pastures are most sere and dry are to be found at the extreme northerly limit of their range where a more copious winter rainfall provides a meagre grazing right through the droughts. This is the essence of their lives, a leisurely shifting from pasture to pasture, following the green film on the desert that means food for their flocks and preservation – rather than prosperity – for themselves. Prosperity only the great sheiks can hope for. The average Bedouin lives and dies not far from poverty. His beasts, his brown tent and blankets, and a few cooking utensils, are nearly all that he possesses except the right to wander the deserts and rule himself. The life is perhaps not unpleasant. The Bedouin knows nothing of the sanitary problems and accumulated dirt of the peasant and settled Arab; always on the move his tent is pitched on clean ground and he leaves his refuse behind him. His progress from day to day and pasture to pasture may not be stimulating, but, since many of the true Bedouin do not work, it is at leastly lordly and idle. Every family of consequence has its slave or slaves who tend the beasts and do the menial chores. These slaves are usually of African origin and darker than their masters. They cannot intermarry with the Bedouin, but they have their own wives and, if fidelity is any criterion, seem contented enough with their existence.

In Syria the life of the Bedouin, picturesque though it is, remains an
echo, a reflection. The grandeur that once came to these nomads still
sets off their meagre lives and the memory of the Umayyads lends
splendour to their ragged tents. The shadow of these great caliphs and
the ruins of their summer palaces are still the most real thing in the
Syrian deserts. Thirteen hundred years ago, and only some forty years
after the Hegira, the Umayyads, Meccans in origin but with strong
Bedouin affiliations, profited by dissensions among the prophet's
successors and seized the caliphate. Syria, the basis of their power, thus
became the centre of Islam and of a huge empire. Forsaking its ever-
repeated role of province and satellite, the country for a brilliant and
dramatic century came into its own. Syria was a world power. It is to
this historical realization that romantic sentiment in Syria still looks
back. The Umayyad period, thanks to the flattering distortion which all
peoples practise, looms preternaturally large over the disappointments
of succeeding centuries.

This distortion is perhaps more forgivable than most of the tricks
which feeling plays with historical perspective, since the empire of the
house of Umayya was surely one of the strangest and most poetic
'sports' of history, and its desert-loving princes among the most
attractive and sympathetic of rulers. When Mu'awia, the first Umayyad
caliph and brother-in-law to the Prophet, secured supreme power in 661
on the murder of the Caliph 'Ali, he chose to be invested in Jerusalem
and not in the holy cities of Arabia, for the Umayyad power represented
the reaction of Syria and the desert men against the townsmen of Mecca
and Medina on the one hand, and of Iraq on the other. It represented
also, since most of the desert people wore the new faith simply and
naturally, a reaction against the tight-lacing of Islam. Love of the
desert and a liberal scepticism in matters of dogma, together with
imagination and good sense, were to characterize most of Mu'awia's
successors.

In order to picture Syria during this hundred years of Umayyad rule,
it is important to bear in mind that the complex and efficient Greek
bureaucracy, which had made possible the cultivated and pleasant life
of those hill towns of which we have spoken, still continued to function.
The Arabs overran, but did not at first destroy. The Umayyads therefore found a going concern and an administration composed of government officials whose religious differences with Byzantium inclined them
to be friendly. The Umayyads had the good sense to accept the administration as it stood. Upon this Byzantine administration they simply

imposed a ruling Arab caste. The latter was a *Herrenvolk*, but a *Herren-volk* of peculiar attainments and vision. While enjoying the military superiority essential to such a caste, they omitted to persecute their inferiors, set about acquiring the knowledge and attainments of which the latter were possessed, and in their new environment cultivated, with the happiest results, the nomad sense of poetry and style.

The tolerant policy of the Umayyads and their co-operation with the native Christian population enabled the latter to play a role of the first importance by handing on to the conquerors much of their Graeco-Aramaic culture and civilization. What Greece had been to Rome, Syria was to the Arabs, saving and transmitting a great culture. The transition from Emperor to Caliph was there effected with a minimum of loss. The five military areas into which the Umayyads divided the country corresponded closely to the earlier Byzantine districts, and the general survival of pre-Arab machinery is reflected in the names for coins, weights and measures, which the Arabs adopted. Thus the *dinar* and the *dirhem* – though the former became a gold coin – prolonged the memory of the *denarius* and the *drachma*, and the *oke* and *rotl* (measures still in use today) reflected respectively the Greek word for an ounce and, by the inversion of 'l' and 'r', the Greek *litra*. The non-Muslims, enjoying autonomy under their own religious heads and their own legal system, showed their gratitude in whole-hearted co-operation with the government, supplying the administrative technique which the desert Arabs still lacked. As late as the tenth century Maqdisi could write, 'verily the scribes here in Syria are all Christians', adding in explanation that the Muslims 'do not hold letters a profitable study'. In Umayyad times the same thing applied to doctors and the liberal professions generally. The relations of that remarkable man St John the Damascene, an Aramaic-speaking Syrian, with the new princes was characteristic. Son and grandson of men who had administered the finances of Damascus, and had also connived at the surrender of the city, he was brought up as the close companion of the second Umayyad caliph, and in due course succeeded to the office which his family had held for two generations. The fact that he was the last of the great Fathers of the Church, and a devotional poet, was no disadvantage to him in the execution of duties which he carried out with distinction until his retirement to a monastery in the reign of the Caliph Hisham. Indeed throughout the Umayyad period (and for a hundred years afterwards), the majority of the population, with the exception of Damascus, remained Christian, while at the same time the relations of conquerors and conquered continued in most districts, until the caliphate of Umar II, to be satisfactory. The Homs district was even for a time under a Christian governor, and it is stated by Maqdisi that an edifice there did service both as church and mosque. In Damascus, where at first mosque and church existed side by side within the great temenos, Christians and Muslims apparently entered the holy area amicably through a common doorway. The truth is that the rulers did not wish to see the privileges of their caste extended to the people of the country, and after a time did their best to discourage conversion to Islam. The Syrians, it was decreed, could only become Muslims by attachment as clients to an Arab tribe, and even then the converts were not exempted from the tax imposed on non-Muslims, and continued to be regarded as inferiors. It was not the Islamic faith, but Arab blood, which conferred distinction. As regards administration, it was only with the reign of Abd el-Malik, fifty years after the first Arab occupation, that important steps towards the arabization of Syria were taken, such as the substitution of Arabic for Greek in the state registers and the minting of an Arabic coinage.

This strange dual control was, moreover, not merely responsible for a wealthy province (the Damascus revenue alone amounted at the end of the Umayyad period to 420,000 dinars [1]), but directed one of the largest and most spectacular empires that history has known. The Umayyad territories stretched from the sea of Aral to the Sudan and from the Atlantic Ocean to the Indus, and it is not without irony that Islam should have achieved its maximum territorial expansion (an area greater than that covered by the Roman Empire) under these sceptical caliphs. Their military initiative, their dash, and perhaps their good fortune, were phenomenal. While their generals in the west were sweeping up through Spain to meet Charles Martel at Tours, two caliphs successively reached the walls of Constantinople. Indeed, summer incursions into the heart of Byzantine territory became a regular Umayyad tradition, and the story of the thirty Arabs who penetrated into Asia Minor, burnt a quantity of Byzantine shipping, and got away without the loss of a single man, typifies the initiative and confidence of these Bedouin warriors. They were remarkable people, and their conquests had an inevitable effect on the tone and scale of life in Syria. Foreign slaves poured in – the great princes might well own as many as a thousand apiece – and it was in Damascus that Suleiman marked the apogee of

[1] Worth in gold today, quite apart from the decline in purchasing value, nearly three-quarters of a million.

Umayyad magnificence when he received the conquerors of Spain, bringing among their countless prisoners members of the fair-haired Gothic royalty.

This mushroom empire was, as we have said, in the hands of a series of exceptionally endowed princes. It was a dynasty of individuals and one Umayyad caliph after another stands out by virtue of his personality. Not only did they signally possess the desert virtues of courage, endurance, hospitality and respect for true speaking, but they combined them with a lively aesthetic sense, a liberal humanity and invaluable humour. In a cruel age the Umayyads were extraordinarily clement. The position of women, too, was relatively free, the harem system being introduced only at the end of the period. As for their humanity and humour, it could hardly be better illustrated than by the story of the caliph who, on discovering that a plebeian poet was addressing love poems to his daughter, instead of cutting out his tongue, took the practical step of providing him with a wife. The relations between the caliphs and their subjects is well summed up by the tribute paid to one of them by a local Syrian who said *communis cum omnibus civiliter vixit*. But it was their aesthetic sense which perhaps gave the court its most characteristic stamp. Lovers of music and poetry, they fostered the old Arab tradition and brought lute, song and wine into Islam. The caliphs themselves were glad to be known as poets or gain a name for their expressive handling of the lute or the wailing one-stringed *rebaba* of the deserts. A love of poetry played an important part even in the life of the ordinary soldier. Verse was discussed round the camp-fire and the winners of poetic contests acquired enormous prestige. Naturally poetry itself flourished in such an atmosphere and notable poets appeared, among whom Akhtal, a Christian, and Jarir were outstanding.

Few dynasties can have produced so many idiosyncratic and agreeable people, who were at the same time effective. Mu'awia, who established the line and showed his beaten opponents a fine clemency, ruled with a wise mixture of tact and strength, pliant when it was possible and strong when it was necessary; it was characteristically Umayyad that he should have passed a third of his nights in listening to the history of the Arabs. His son, known as Yazid of Wines since he abandoned rose sherbet for the grape, an amiable and democratic prince, a sportsman, musician and poet, was for hundreds of years perhaps the most black-guarded ruler of history. It was his misfortune to have to sack rebellious Medina and bear the responsibility for the battle of Kerbela where Husain, grandson of the Prophet and pretender to the caliphate, together with his followers, was defeated and killed. It is difficult to see how Yazid could have acted differently: in Arabia the rebellion was dangerous, and at Kerbela Husain and his pathetic band of followers were given every chance to surrender and avoid inevitable massacre. In spite of the opposition both of the Shi'ites and of Muslim Orthodoxy, the Umayyads continued to prosper. Under the rule of Abd el-Malik (685–705) and, subsequently, of his four sons the Empire reached its greatest extent and power. Of these sons, Walid I, an indefatigable builder, Suleiman, among other things a famous gourmet, and the youngest, Hisham, were exceptional men. The foremost historian of the caliphate has called Walid 'the greatest and in every respect the most powerful ruler amongst the so-called Commanders of the Faithful'. The wise and conscientious Hisham who guided the empire for nineteen years, though less spectacular than his elder brother, was hardly less effective. Hisham was, however, the last of the Umayyads with administrative ability, and when the son, whom he had educated to succeed him, was killed hunting, the dynasty passed into inefficient hands. When he heard of his son's death, Hisham, retaining even in his bitterness something of the Umayyad humour, briefly remarked: 'I brought him up for the caliphate, and he pursues a fox!' The Umayyad house only lasted seven years after Hisham's death, and of the four caliphs who succeeded him only one was in any way remarkable, and then hardly for qualities desirable in a ruler. This was Walid II in whom the aesthetic and pleasure-loving element in the Umayyad character ran riot. Whereas Yazid had enjoyed his wines and Abd el-Malik got drunk but once a month, Walid II bathed in a swimming-pool of wine. The court indeed lived with brimming cups, but the drinking always went with poetry, music and the dance. The caliph himself was an accomplished musician and poet and one of his verses which has survived runs as follows:

> There's no true joy but lending ear to music,
>   Or wine that leaves one sunk in stupor dense.
> Houris in Paradise I do not look for:
>   Does any man of sense?

The scepticism is characteristically Umayyad, but it must have been a little too much even for the desert Arabs when Walid used the Koran as a practice target for his arrows and allowed his mistresses to take the caliph's place at public prayers. Only outside the towns could he satisfactorily escape from the irksome pressure of state papers, and so it was that the last remarkable Umayyad wandered from one desert palace to

another with his Bacchic train, staining the sand with wine and making
music, until in the desert he met his end.

Given the wealth and power which policy and history suddenly
showered upon them it is curious enough that the Umayyads should not
have failed sooner than they did. Their vitality must be ascribed
primarily to the instinct which prompted them constantly to renew
their vigour in the deserts. There they found the toughness and stamina
to offset the delights of empire. When Mu'awia, the first caliph, sent the
heir apparent off into the deserts, in charge of his Christian-Bedouin
mother, to acquire an education in desert endurance and desert virtues,
and incidentally a pure Arabic free from Syrian Aramaicisms, he set a
fashion which subsequent caliphs followed. The young Umayyads were
bred in the strict and stimulating desert air. Their tutors were instructed
to make them tough and, as the Caliph Abd el-Malik phrased it, to
'accustom them to little sleep'. Further, the caliphs themselves,
prompted by a desire to avoid the summer heats in the dry and relatively
cool atmosphere of the steppe, and also wishing to avoid the plague
which visited the cities in the hot season, often assumed a semi-nomad
life for certain months in the year. The court at first moved out in tents,
though in due course on the most favoured camping grounds appeared
those desert castles and palaces which are so remarkable. Abd el-Malek
died in one of his country residences, and not only Walid II but the wise
Hisham, for very different reasons, elected to spend most of their reigns
in the desert.

The desert entailed not only a simple life, but also the trial and education of the chase. The Umayyads one and all were huntsmen. Game
was plentiful: lions existed in the Euphrates valley until the middle of
the nineteenth century, and the large herds of gazelle which still range
the steppe must in the days before cars and rifles have been even larger.
The Umayyads pursued their game with hawks, seluki dogs, and the
tame cheetah. Yazid of Wines, particularly distinguished as a huntsman,
was the first person to train cheetahs to ride on the croup of his horse,
and his pack of selukis, adorned with gold anklets and each one attended
by a special slave, must have been a splendid sight. These princes were
also inevitably good horsemen and breeders of horses, and racing was a
common alternative to the chase. It was organized under royal patronage, and apparently there were as many as four thousand entries, an
all-time record, for a great race arranged by the Caliph Hisham. It is
this aspect of Umayyad life, the hunting and the horsemanship, that
provides the most effective link between the Rualla in Palmyrena today

and the eighth-century grandeur of the desert nomads. The great sheiks still hunt much as the House of Umayya did, and like them still recite the poetry of the chase in the tents at the day's end. The cheetah has disappeared but the selukis and the obedient hawks remain, and when the great sheiks with slaves and servants set out to hawk for gazelle, swaying high on their camels (their finest Arab horses are led unridden in reserve for the contest), the desert men come into their own again. Their hawking for gazelle is a very skilled and complex affair and perhaps the most curious thing to be seen in the deserts. Since the gazelle will outrun even the seluki, its death is only to be compassed by the elaborate co-operation of hawk, hound and huntsman. This co-operation is effected in the following way: the hounds start a gazelle at which the huntsman in full pursuit loosens the falcon from his wrist. The bird, climbing quickly, soon overtakes the game and stoops at the gazelle. Each time the falcon stoops the gazelle must break its stride and try, with a flourish of its horns, to stop the bird burying her talons in its shoulder. In this way, unless the falcon becomes exhausted, the selukis close in on the game and the kill is effected. Why, it may well be asked, should a falcon stoop at so large and unnatural a target as a full-grown gazelle? This indeed is the most interesting feature of the Bedouin technique and is the result of a long and ingenious training. The young falcon is first of all given its meat on the shoulder of a straw-stuffed dummy over which a gazelle skin is sewn. After some days an incision is made in the skin and the meat half hidden so that the bird must pull it out. Finally, the meat is tucked out of sight and the skin sewn up, so that the falcon to get its meal must tear open the dummy shoulder with its talons. In this way a conditioned reflex is achieved: to the falcon mind gazelles come to mean food, and a good falcon can thus be relied on to stoop even at a moving gazelle.

That the Umayyad princes with their desert sojourns should have been skilled huntsmen was natural enough, but that they should at the same time have encouraged good building is perhaps surprising. Not content with introducing the minaret into Islam (derived from the Christian churches of Syria) and evolving the *mihrab*, perhaps from the Christian apse, the Umayyads were responsible for a series of magnificent monuments. The first of their caliphs, Mu'awia, built a palace at Damascus known as Qubbat al-Khadra, the Green Dome, where the royal audiences were held. Though it disappeared long ago, other even more famous Umayyad monuments have in part remained. At Jerusalem Abd el-Malik raised the Dome of the Rock to divert pilgrims from

Mecca, a town with which Umayyad liberalism made it impossible to be
on good terms, and Walid I built the Great Mosque at Damascus,
demolishing the cathedral for the purpose and getting large numbers of
skilled workmen from Byzantium.[1] The original Great Mosque at
Aleppo, built by Walid's successor, was unfortunately destroyed by the
Byzantines in the tenth century and has thus disappeared, like the
Qubbat al-Khadra. Not content with such achievements, and with
building activity in provinces farther afield, the Umayyads left their
mark in their own deserts. At Qusayr 'Amra, Mshatta, Kasr at-Tuba
and not least at Kasr el-Heir, they raised palaces or castles in the
solitudes of the steppe for their summer retreat. It is in these, the ruins
of their favourite residences, that the spirit of the Umayyads is least
overlaid with history. When the Umayyads departed, no builders
succeeded them and the palaces, though ruined, remain eloquent in the
deserts where they were first set up. Qusayr 'Amra with its murals
(where the last Visigothic king of Spain shares the wall space with nude
dancers, musicians, and the Muses of Philosophy, History and Poetry);
and Mshatta, the unfinished residence of Walid II, whose magnificently
carved façade is now in the Berlin Museum, both lie south of the present
Syrian border.

But Syria itself contains perhaps the most important and impressive
of these desert buildings, Kasr el-Heir.

The best approach to Kasr el-Heir is from Palmyra, whence it lies
some hundred and fifteen kilometres in a north-easterly direction.
The track leads across a great wide plain with mountains to the north.
A nap of spare feathery grasses is variegated by the deeper green of
depressions and faint wadis where a more generous share of winter rain
has left a legacy of small succulent shrubs. Presently the scene changes,
and the country grows more broken and more arid; the grasses and the
shrubs disappear, and the track winds its way through stones and a
grey, friable, intensely dusty earth. A white scarf of dust, like smoke,
hangs out behind the car for miles, and the going is slow and bad.
Through a universal drabness the traveller jolts at last, past a few poor
fig-trees and meagre plots of green, into the Arab village of Sukna, the
only habitation between Palmyra and Heir. Ragged and grey, it has a
grim absence of charm which is impressive. History explains its desolation, which is not purely a result of dust and the inhospitable landscape.
Sukna is an example of one of those caravan posts which have died with
the caravan traffic. It lay on the route from Damascus over Palmyra

[1] See pages 16–18.

to the Euphrates at Deir-ez-Zor, and, with its hot springs, constituted
a convenient stage for the camel trains that for centuries came and went.
Then the traffic failed. Today the untiring American car, that carries its
own fodder and water, traces a more direct southerly route, making
Deir-ez-Zor in one flight from Palmyra. So Sukna is abandoned. In the
mid-fourteenth century, Ibn Batuta found it still chiefly Christian, a
state of affairs which is not surprising since the desert dwellers, with the
immunity of isolation, were particularly tenacious of their old faith.
Today the Orthodox Muslim inhabitants, in a desolation which progress
has made so much more profound, sustain a precarious life on an acre or
two of green, and scrape yearly a little barley from the hard wrinkled
slopes. Choking in the dust, under a sun that pulses over the ragged
stones that stretch in all directions, the village is plainly expiring.

Without a good sense of direction, or familiarity with a sun-compass,
it is wise to pick up a guide at Sukna, for the track to Kasr el-Heir, some
thirty kilometres on, is almost non-existent though marked on the maps.
As Sukna drops behind, the character of the country again changes. To
the north-west a line of hills, the Jebel Bishri, rises dramatically in
precipices from the desert plateau, but eastward towards Kasr el-Heir
the landscape becomes more steppe-like. The dust and stones disappear
and are succeeded by a considerable amount of vegetation. The traveller
moves into sparse rolling grassland, dotted with shrubs and bushes, a
foot or two high. As he approaches Kasr el-Heir, the going becomes
excellent, and – the track long since faded out – his car cruises at
random across the extended width of green, leaving the pattern of tyre
tracks on the crushed herbs and grasses.

Here, if anywhere, the desert smiles. The vegetation attracts gazelle
which scamper off in compact terrified parties as the car approaches,
taking the little bushes in their stride like hurdlers. Here too one sees
the bird life of the desert in greater profusion than in most places: the
cream-coloured coursers mincing away from the car on their stilt-like
legs; the whirring pin-tailed sandgrouse that make poor eating; the
common bustard with its ridiculously affronted look; the black-and-
white desert chat and others of the same family; the Isabelline wheat-
ear with its exclamatory rump; and a whole gamut of larks, from the
sandy desert varieties to the horned lark with its black cheeks and the
bi-fasciated lark that reveals unexpected colour as it opens its wings.
In the migration periods there are numberless other birds in the deserts.
They are to be seen in the best possible circumstances, for they have
usually alighted for food and rest and the vegetation offers little cover.

In these expanses you may often meet hundreds of voyaging storks standing about in studious deliberation, for once quite removed from the haunts of men, or a party of glossy ibis, hunch-backed and solemn, regarding each other with characteristic gravity.

In this green country of bird and gazelle, the traveller first catches sight of Kasr el-Heir. It stands in a wide shallow saucer whose sides slope so imperceptibly that the faintly 'cupped' nature of the landscape is at first hardly realized. These walls, that shine out white in the middle distance, have had – since their desertion at some uncertain date centuries ago – a romantic history. Situated close to an old route from Aleppo to Baghdad they were seen by various European travellers who made the desert crossing between the early seventeenth and early nineteenth centuries. Pietro della Valle, that indefatigable person, saw them in 1616, as did Niebuhr some century and a half later. Two or three less eminent English travellers also noted them, one of whom in 1778 stated with an engaging provinciality that the quality and colour of the masonry reminded him of Bath stone. Soon after 1800, however, there is no further word of Kasr el-Heir and the ruins, unvisited by travellers and for all practical purposes lost, pass into a century of oblivion. Though Alois Musil, the distinguished archaeologist-traveller, made his way there in 1908, it was not until 1925 that the ruins were systematically visited and described. They are thus, in a sense, a discovery. The reason for their curious withdrawal from history is bound up with a chain of events which made the central Syrian desert more 'deserted' in the nineteenth century than perhaps at any other time in its history. When the Cape route was opened to India, Indian goods largely ceased to flow across the overland route to the Mediterranean. They could be shipped far more cheaply by sea, and indeed Indian goods reaching London via the Cape could often be re-exported and sold in the Levant cheaper than those arriving directly overland. Yet for the individual traveller, the merchant, the diplomatic agent on his way to Persia and the express messengers of the East India Company – for whom speed was of greater account than cost – the land route still had its advantages. Though abandoned by goods, it continued to be used by personnel until the early part of the nineteenth century. At that time the declining power of the Porte enabled the Red Sea – formerly closed to Unbelievers – to be opened to British ships. Almost at once fast traffic was diverted to the new route and by 1840 an important travel agency, The Transit Company, took charge of passengers arriving at Alexandria from European ports, shepherded them across Egypt, and re-embarked them at Suez. The time saved on the Red Sea journey was enormous, and from this date travellers abandoned the desert route, as goods had done over three hundred years earlier. With the change Kasr el-Heir was forgotten.

Today in its isolation, with the gazelle grazing right up to the walls of 'Bath' stone (which have acquired with time that remarkable apricot tinge to be found also at Palmyra), Kasr el-Heir is most impressive. The ruins consist essentially of two roughly square 'castles' standing side by side, of which the western is a good four times greater than its neighbour. In the vast scale of the desert their size is not at first apparent, but the larger of the two actually measures over a hundred and sixty metres square. They stand a stone's throw apart, and in the corridor of desert which separates them rises an isolated tower, which must once have served as watch-tower or minaret. The walls of the lesser castle, flanked by round towers, are relatively well preserved, and were once topped with brickwork which in places remains. It is possible to reach the rampart walk by clambering up on the inside at the south-west corner. The interior of the castle consisted, as may still be seen, of a central courtyard, around which were arranged vaulted chambers backing on the fortified wall. The most satisfying thing about the building is its single gate, on the west side, with two flanking towers. The gate is topped with a straight lintel above which is a round relieving arch. Directly above the arch is a fine early double machicoulis. The treatment of the towers on each side, however, is the feature which makes the castle entrance so impressive. On either tower the masonry some way up gives place to courses of brick, used for purely decorative effect; these in turn are succeeded by a further course of stone-work, on which rests a remarkable series of blind arcades set with stucco panels. Above these again is more decorative brickwork terminating in a small cornice. Each tower is crowned with a small brick dome.

The larger castle to the west repeats the lesser castle in its general scheme, though the work as a whole appears to be less careful. It is in a poor state of preservation. There are the same fortified walls, two metres thick, built of the same stone, and round flanking towers. The gates, however – there are four – though similarly provided with machicoulis and surmounted by a straight lintel, are relieved with slightly pointed arches. In each case the tympanum (the area between the lintel and the relieving arch) is pitted with holes set at regular intervals, the supposition being that some sort of decoration was applied, either ceramics or more probably stucco. A ruined mosque stands in the south-east corner of the enclosure, but it is otherwise impossible to reconstruct the interior layout of the castle. Time and treasure-hunting Arabs have almost completely destroyed whatever buildings once stood there.

The architecture of the twin castles of Kasr el-Heir is of great interest and importance. The local prototype of such square fortifications is undoubtedly to be found in the square garrison fortresses built by the Romans from Akaba on the Red Sea to the Euphrates, and serving to protect their lines of communication. The *strata Diocletiana*, one of their great Syrian roads, passed quite close by Kasr el-Heir on its way from Palmyra to Resafa and thence to Sura on the Euphrates. The present buildings are, however, of later date. The discovery, over a century ago, of an inscription on one of the pillars of the mosque in the larger castle dates this building exactly. The inscription, which was removed and has unfortunately disappeared, stated that it was built in A.D. 728–9 by the Umayyad Caliph Hisham, whose favourite residence, Resafa, was only some eighty kilometres northward across the steppe. This means that the castle has the distinction of being the oldest certain example of a fortified Muslim enclosure.

As to the date of the smaller castle, expert opinion varies. There are features – such as the use of the acanthus and other ornamental motifs essentially hellenistic – which seem to link it with the Byzantine period, and more particularly with Resafa and the Christian churches of Northern Syria. The way the moulding of the relieving arch over the gate is continued in each direction to meet the flanking towers, achieving the effect of a flowing ribbon of decoration, is directly reminiscent, for instance, of Kalat Seman. It has therefore been dated as early as the sixth century. On the other hand, Professor Creswell, the foremost authority on early Muslim architecture, for various reasons ascribes it, like the larger castle, to the Umayyad period. The strong Mesopotamian influences, both in the stucco work and in the treatment of the bricks, which are set in characteristically thin mortar, are said to bear out his supposition, since the Umayyads habitually recruited workmen of talent from all corners of the empire. Further, the hellenistic features in the decoration are not necessarily a sign of Byzantine origin, since we have seen that the Umayyads compromised with the established culture at every point. If Professor Creswell is correct, the lesser castle must dispute with the larger the honour of being the earliest fortified Muslim enclosure, and will claim to preserve in its gate towers the earliest known example of Muslim stucco work, foreshadowing those magnificent stucco designs which were later to adorn the mosques in Cairo and elsewhere

Perhaps for the traveller the most significant thing about it all is that the Umayyad assimilation of classical influences in Syria should have been so complete that a division of opinion as to Byzantine or Muslim origin should still be possible among experts.

As one looks out from the *chemin de ronde*, or better from the summit of the isolated tower, at the deserts stretching unbroken in all directions, the question inevitably arises as to what these large buildings were doing there at all. Their extent and nature make it quite evident that they were not simply another of those summer palaces which the Umayyads put up in the desert. They must have sheltered a far larger community. The clue to their nature is provided by certain walls, in places destroyed and in others only faintly indicated, which stretch southward from Kasr el-Heir for a full five kilometres, enclosing an immense area. A closer inspection reveals that these walls served no defensive purpose, since they are buttressed both within and without, an arrangement contrary to all accepted rules of fortification. Further, at the south end of the vast rectangle enclosed, the walls are provided with openings which quite evidently served as sluice gates. The whole area was, in fact, a huge garden, irrigated by water brought through channels several kilometres long, vestiges of which still remain. The sluice gates served the same purpose as they do in gardens at Palmyra today, namely to draw off an excess of water after the sudden and violent storms which sometimes occur in the desert. (The supposition that the whole area was an artificial lake is untenable, since it has recently been discovered that there were gates in the walls and that the top courses of the walls were of mud-brick.) The implication of this great irrigated and cultivable area is that Kasr el-Heir housed a colony of people working on the land, and at the same time provided the security of which they were certainly in need in the open desert. Kasr el-Heir, like Resafa, was an artificial desert oasis whose existence demanded a highly organized administration. Its florescence in the Umayyad period indicates the way in which these Arabs knew how to utilize and incorporate the Byzantine administrative genius, introducing into their own deserts talent which centuries of acclimatization had made less Greek than Syrian.

In spite of their organization, their palaces, their poetry, their enlightenment and the democratic touch of the desert, the Umayyads were doomed. They were an Arab minority in a world where the bourgeois townsmen outside Syria (the Syrian townsmen were fanatically pro-Umayyad) were becoming progressively more hostile and more important. Only the unity of the Bedouin tribes, those chronically

centrifugal units, could have maintained their power, and this unity
they could not preserve. The succession of weak caliphs after Hisham
provided that opportunity for which orthodoxy had long been waiting.
Respectable opinion, entrenched in the Persian cities and the sanctuaries of Arabia, and with astute Abbasid direction, was able to engineer
an effective revolt. Propaganda was easy. Of all the Umayyad caliphs,
only Umar II had been an orthodox believer, a belief which he demon-
strated primarily in the humiliating measures which he imposed on
religious minorities.[1] Umayyad scepticism was a convenient target
which everywhere enabled religious feeling to be marshalled against
them. As opposition grew, the religious issue obscured the more funda-
mental struggle – the contest for empire between the paramount Arabs
basing their strength and organization on hellenized Syria, and the
Persianized civilization farther east. A contemporary poet went to the
heart of the matter when he said, writing of the Abbasids, "'Death to
the *Arabs*", that is all their creed.' After the defeat of the Umayyads in
the field, death was indeed meted out to them with systematic thoroughness. No member of the House of Umayya, on whom the Abbasids
could lay their hands, was spared. The treatment they received offered
an ironic contrast to the clemency which they themselves had shown to
their conquered opponents a hundred years earlier. The last caliph,
Marwan II, was captured and beheaded in Egypt, and over seventy
members of the royal house, who could not be disposed of in any other
way, were treacherously murdered by the appointed representatives of
Abbasid orthodoxy after having surrendered on an oath of indem-
nity. At Resafa the corpse of Hisham was exhumed and the dead
bones flogged. Almost alone of the members of the great house his
grandson escaped, to found in Spain the kingdom and dynasty of
Cordova.

The new Abbasid power was based on Iraq and Persia, and the capital
of Islam was thus transferred to Baghdad. This shift of power eastward
had incalculable effects. It involved the Persianization of Islam, and
was to colour the whole future of the Faith. Muslim dogma came to be
interpreted in the light of Persian ideas, and the possibilities of a fruitful
union with classic thought gradually disappeared. The free, priestless,
essentially practical faith of Arabia grew in the Tigris valley tortuous
and restricting, and the oriental Abbasid court, with its luxury and its

---

[1] These measures were later widely adopted in Islam. Umar decreed that
Christians might not testify in the law courts, wear a turban or use a saddle, and
must wear distinctive clothing.

deaf-mutes, its veiled women, its ceremony and its Median absolutism, modified the Islamic outlook to its grave injury. In addition, the rise of the Abbasids meant the eclipse of Syria. The new rulers, jealous of the role that Syria had played and continually fearful that Umayyad sympathies might lead to revolt, did everything in their power to weaken and impoverish the country. No doubt was to remain in Syrian minds that they were again provincials. Syrians accepted the position grudgingly. Time and again the white banner of the Umayyads was raised, and time and again the Abbasids stamped out the revolts. As the chances of effective insurrection grew less, the white banner became more and more the symbol, the almost mystical symbol, of Syrian independence. Around it, and around the person of the *sufyani*, the messianic representative of the House of Umayya who was to return and restore the country to its imperial glory, the hopes of Syria were centred. Such hopes were a necessary tonic through the lean centuries that followed, when one foreign governor after another – Abbasid, Fatimid, Ayyubid, or Ottoman – ruled or misruled from the old Umayyad capital.

The Abbasid neglect of Syria could not for strategic reasons be as absolute as the rulers might have wished. The caliph Al-Mamun built a great fortified town at Raqqa on the Euphrates some two hundred kilometres from Aleppo, and it was oddly enough the most magnificent and satrapic of the Abbasids, Haroun-al-Raschid of the *Thousand and One Nights*, who for a time took up his residence there and moved his court into Syrian territory. The ruins of the town still show the scale on which these Abbasids built. Al-Mamun's town was not the earliest foundation nor Raqqa the first name given to the site. The way in which it has often been rechristened neatly illustrates how Syrian history has accumulated in regular stratifications. Such changes of name are the rule rather than the exception. The town was founded by Alexander the Great and baptized Nicephorion. Later it became a border town in Parthian hands, and reappears in the third century A.D. as Callinicon, so named after a sophist executed there in the reign of Gallienus. Finally in the fifth century it became known as Leontopolis after the short-lived Emperor Leo II. Plundered by the Persians and refortified by Justinian, the classic city, already ageing, became known at the time of the Muslim conquest as Raqqa (= morass) owing to the presence of a swamp in the neighbourhood. It was near the Raqqa of this period that the battle of Siffin was fought, where in 656 the Umayyads with shrewd cynicism secured the caliphate by raising the Koran upon their spears and appealing to arbitration. A century later Al-Mamun's new town was built beside the old; it took the name of Rafiqa (= companion), possibly because a 'companion' town to the older foundation. Changes in nominal identity were not yet over. Before the mid-fourteenth century, when the town went into complete eclipse, the older name of Raqqa had again become current, replacing Rafiqa. It still does duty for the excessively ugly little town which has sprung up in the last sixty years.

It is not for the modern town that one visits Raqqa, but for the unpeopled Abbasid city. Its immense walls enclose an empty world where sheep crop a sward that in the dry friable East seems graciously green and smooth. The grassy undulations cover and confound the plans of streets and palaces. A glance at the surviving work and the curious horseshoe shape of the walls is enough to indicate that here is something very different from the other great monuments – Palmyra, Halebiyah, Resafa and the rest – that are to be visited in the Syrian desert. At Raqqa one passes the frontiers of the classic world. The place is representative of another outlook and civilization, for the Abbasids when they came brought Iraq and Persia with them up the Euphrates. Al-Mamun's city (A.D. 772) was indeed in many respects a reflection of the great circular city which Al-Mansur had built at Baghdad ten years earlier. Like the latter its walls were of brick, though it was horseshoe shaped rather than round, the open end of the horseshoe, facing the river, being closed with a great wall. The walls, with their round flanking towers, are still the most impressive thing at Raqqa and in the Middle Ages two horsemen could ride comfortably abreast upon the rampart walk. Indeed, at that period the main wall – still in existence – was preceded by a lower and less formidable outer wall and this in turn was protected by a deep ditch. Within the walls there stand a brick tower-minaret, said to be of the twelfth century, and the remains of a mosque contemporary with Al-Mamun, which shows eastern influences more particularly in its square ground plan, its bastioned walls, and the way in which mud brick and burnt brick are used respectively for walls and arcades. The most important of the town gates, and today the only one preserved, was that facing down the river to Baghdad. Its importance was symbolic of the direction in which Abbasid allegiance lay.

Raqqa impresses the traveller more than any mere enumeration of its remaining architectural features would lead one to expect. The immensity and quiet of the area that was once a town, whose carpet of green covers the indecencies of time and dilapidation, is satisfying.[1] To the south the hurrying Euphrates; northward a desert country; and, within the ramparts, an extraordinary *absence* of things: the walls insist on the presence of a town which is quite obviously not there. The resulting effect is curious, for the imagination supplies what the site appears to demand: Raqqa is one of those places which are popularly said to be 'haunted'. In the perspective of history, Raqqa has a melancholy flavour, which perhaps adds to the atmosphere of loss the place inspires. It stands at the beginning of a long period of Syrian provincialism. Outside Aleppo and Damascus there was to be nothing of importance built for centuries. The next people to conceive anything on the scale of Raqqa, Kasr el-Heir or the buildings of earlier periods, were the Crusaders over three hundred years later.

[1] In places the ground is pitted and pocked under its film of green where the Arabs have for centuries been desultorily digging for treasure. They hope to find pieces of that Raqqa pottery for which the town in the Middle Ages was so rightly famous and which still turn up occasionally.

CHAPTER VII

CRUSADER CASTLES

———————————— ·❦· ————————————

THOUGH it is six and a half centuries since the last Crusaders embarked for Cyprus, the architectural imprint of the crusading enterprise lies heavy on the Syrian littoral. Immense, and immensely solid, their castles couch on the mountain spurs, clawing the rock and the spare soil. They dominate the passes that lead from the Muslim hinterland to what was for so long the Frankish seaboard. It is symbolic of the liberality with which the Latins built these fortress works that some can no longer be identified; no name mentioned in the crusading chronicles will fit and we ignore who built them, what sieges, if any, they sustained, and when they fell at last into Saracen hands. Such anonymity is inevitable when castles seem to have sprung up fully armed, like the soldiers of the Jason legend, on almost every promontory and *tell*, and beside every ravine, from Edessa to the Gulf of Akaba on the Red Sea. From this multiplicity stand out in due and impressive prominence the greater castles, the best of the Crusader endeavour. As a group they constitute the cream of medieval military architecture and are known by their names and deeds. No anonymity here. Banias under Hermon, Beaufort, Safita, Markab, Sahyoun, Krak of the Knights: these and others are famous and embody half the history of the Latin kingdom.

Not only the architectural achievement of the Crusaders, but their drive and determination are brought home in sheer weight of stone; the repeated triumph of setting up these land leviathans, often in the most inaccessible places, still astounds. Yet it is not a matter of bulk alone; the castles impress equally in the skill of their masonry, the strategic cunning of their layout, and unexpectedly (in buildings of such severe purpose) by sudden beauty of detail. The lovely capitals and columns of the chapel doors at Markab, the Warden's Chamber at Krak with its ribbed vaulting and roses carved in stone, are an essential expression of the building sense which produced in the same castles the huge cisterns that held water for a five years' siege, and the towering south

146

wall of the inner ward. Great strength and great delicacy: in fact, the architectural genius of twelfth- and thirteenth-century France, but doubly impressive in these hills and in such alien surroundings.

To visit all the major castles takes more time and energy than the average traveller has at his disposal, yet – to get a proper impression of the literal *weight* of Frankish achievement – it is important to see more than just one or two of these monuments. On grounds both of geographical position and function, the castles are separable into two main types. There are on the one hand the mountain castles, set to control the passes that lead through from the Muslim hinterland to the sea across the Lebanon or the Jebel Alawi, and on the other the coastal castles whose duty was to watch the coast road and the ports, and to protect the littoral if necessary against the Muslim fleet centred on Egypt. Dotted up the coast from Tyre to Latakia, these maritime castles are not on the whole so large, so well-preserved, or so impressively placed, as the mountain fortresses. None the less they have the advantage of lying on the main road and a normal progress up the coast brings one automatically to the castles at Sidon, Byblos and Tripoli. Of such coastal Crusader sites, two – Nephin and Tortosa – are perhaps particularly worth mention. The first for the intrinsic charm of its position and because it is so easily overlooked; and the second both for its architectural beauty and for the insight which it gives into ecclesiastical and civil life in the Latin kingdom.

The site of Nephin, some ten miles south of Tripoli, is hidden from the road by the houses of Enfeh village. It is a narrow peninsula of rock running out at right angles from the coast into deep water. Two great trenches carved in the solid rock to water level isolate it from the mainland. The largest of these trenches is a good hundred feet across, and it is characteristic of the thoroughness of the Franks that they should have expended so much labour to create so tiny an island fortress. Though almost nothing remains of the castle itself, the place has charm. The island-peninsula rises from blue-green water and the grass among the boulders is dotted with salty marine flowers. The local fishermen paint their boats brown and white and moor them in the lee of the island, and they themselves come there to dry their nets. Otherwise the site is deserted and the castle, of whose history almost nothing is known, has disappeared. It was presumably taken, as time passed, by the ancestors of these same fishermen, to supply stone for Enfeh village.

Northward from Tripoli, the road to Tortosa runs through country surprisingly un-Phoenician. The strip of cultivation that is elsewhere wedged between the mountains and the coast gives way, as the Lebanese heights recede, to a dun unfruitful plain. The sandy soil looks devitalized and carries expanses of yellowish nodding grass. Sluggish streams curl and twist their way out through saltings to the sea and gulls stray far inland. The dead character of the landscape is somehow accentuated by infrequent flocks and their shepherds, giving, as they sometimes do, an impression of aimlessness and loss. Even the barrel-roofed huts of the pasture people, constructed of reeds, fail to break the monotone and are as colourless and unobtrusive as the plain itself. It is where this country ends and the mountains – the Jebel Alawi – again approach the sea that the fishing town of Tartus stands. There, at Tortosa as the Crusaders called it, the Order of the Templars established their principal fortress. In the great banqueting hall, nearly fifty yards long, hung their standards and trophies, and there the Order met for counsel and deliberation. The castle is now sadly mutilated; modern houses and hovels have intruded upon it without ceremony, and it is difficult to form any adequate idea of its original importance. Little even remains of the great keep from which in 1188 the Master of the Order and the Knights successfully repulsed the attacks of Saladin when the town and outer precincts of the castle had fallen. One is still shown, however, the small postern giving directly on the sea, whence after the fall of the town the last Crusaders left the soil of Tripoli and sailed to Cyprus.

Separated from the Templars' castle and standing within its own wall there existed also in Crusader times the episcopal town, centring round the cathedral shrine of our Lady of Tortosa. Of the town wall on the north and east a considerable stretch, including the North Gate, still stands; but it is the cathedral itself, preserved through a series of misadventures as storehouse, mosque and garrison, that creates the special interest of Tortosa. Tortosa was from early times an important Christian sanctuary. Its altar claimed the honour of being the first dedicated to the Virgin, and St Peter was vaguely reputed to have there celebrated mass. The earthquake which at an early date destroyed the church, but by miraculous good fortune preserved the altar intact, only served to increase the prestige of the shrine. It was thus upon a site already revered that the Franks in the twelfth and thirteenth centuries erected the present cathedral. It soon acquired reputation as a place of pilgrimage, and people from all over Europe – including Joinville the historian – came to pay homage to the Virgin of Tortosa. The exterior of the cathedral gives no impression of what is to come. It is a little heavy, almost squat in appearance, and was indeed reinforced in the thirteenth

17   Stonecarving at Kalat Seman

18 The so-called baptistery at Kalat Seman

19 The *Méharistes*, the Syrian camel corps

20   Bedouin woman

21 Nomad family

22   Aerial view of Raqqa, showing the 'horseshoe' fortifications

23   Interior of the Cathedral at Tortosa

24   Krak of the Knights (aerial view)

25   Krak, showing the concentric fortifications

26   The Castle at Masiaf

27   The water-wheels of the Orontes

28 Lebanese weaver

29   The 'Mountain', looking towards the summits of the Lebanon

30   Goatherd in the High Lebanon

31   Lebanese cedars

32   An Alawi bride

century for purposes of defence. The west front also, before which Raymond of Antioch was stabbed by two of the Assassins, though said to be remarkable, is certainly unsatisfactory, and the arrangement of the windows and their relationship to the west door cannot have been altogether pleasing even before disfigurement by the Muslims. The effect of the interior is very different. One discovers with surprise and admiration what is in essentials a fine French church of the transition period, reminiscent of buildings to be found both in Burgundy and Provence. To specify a nave carried on four arches, with side-aisles, three apses at the east end and a fine barrel roof, is to say nothing. It is the proportions that count, the way in which the weight and solidity of this fortress church are translated into symmetry and grace. The effect is undoubtedly increased by the magnificent colours – a range of ambers marbled with verdigris – which the stone has acquired through time and a happy neglect. Yet there is more to it than this. One realizes after a moment that here is one of the few churches, not in a ruined state, that one has really been able to *see*. Custom dictates that architectural bodies must wear clothes. This one is utterly bare, pure masonry: not a lamp, not a pulpit, not a piece of plaster, not even – creeping discreetly along the bottoms and angles of the walls – the inevitable electric wiring. Here is a church naked, largely as the inspired masons left it, and the beauty of fine construction in stone, essentially an architectural beauty, comes home to one with great effect.

Castles are necessary for defence, but works such as the cathedral of Tortosa suggest a settled civilization, and imply that their builders envisaged the permanency of that civilization. One glimpses at Tortosa the laborious effort to establish a permanent Frankish culture and society that must have continued in the many quiet intervals between the alarms and excursions of two hundred years. The cathedral at Tortosa, though the greatest, is merely one of a number of ecclesiastical monuments which speak with greater intensity and pathos of the failure of this endeavour than do the sombre castles. At Tyre more than eighteen churches were built, excluding the cathedral of which the historian William of Tyre was at one time the illustrious archbishop. All these have disappeared, but elsewhere many such monuments still exist: among them one might mention the cathedral of St John at Beyrouth, now sadly mutilated and beplastered; or the church looking out to sea at Byblos with its elegant baptistery; or, not least, the modest little church at Kouabba, just off the main road before one reaches Ras Chaqqa. It stands alone on a hillock among vines and olives, unassuming and

F

deserted. The chameleons which haunt its walls stare down at the
intruder like gargoyles, and even under a hot Levant sun it is incongruously but unmistakably occidental. Few modern travellers visit it, yet
in its simplicity and silence it evokes better than many more imposing
remains the strange nature of the Latin effort.

Of the great mountain fortresses that guard the approaches to the
coast from the hinterland, the most splendid and the most impressive
is undoubtedly Krak of the Knights, and for this reason it should be
reserved to the last. Any castle after Krak is an anti-climax. One may
properly lead up to Krak by visiting Beaufort, Markab and Sahyoun, all
giant Crusader castles of the first order which have the advantage of
being tolerably accessible from the coast. The best view of Beaufort is
from the east. There the sprawling ruin hangs nearly a thousand feet
above the Litani River, the Leontes of the Ancients, and you look
straight across to it from the Merdjayoun road on the other side of the
gorge. It is an impressive vantage-point. The abyss acts like a sounding-
box, and in the stillness every note from the castle precipices comes
faithfully across. You hear the noise of goats clambering across the scree
below the castle walls before you have spotted them, and you recognize
the goat-boy's whistle, that limpid but somehow inhuman note common
to all the hillsides of the Mediterranean.

The castle belonged first to the lordship of Sayette and later to the
Templars, but, in spite of that forbidding gorge, fell to the arms of both
Saladin and Beibars. It is said that during the first siege the Lord of
Sayette, in spite of having received a safe-conduct from the Saracens,
was tortured in view of the castle walls in order to break the defenders'
morale. Whether such an episode occurred or not, it is typical of many
others which go to prove, if proof were necessary, that chivalrous
relations were rarely the rule between Crusader and Saracen. It is true
that Saladin sometimes exercised a clemency, both humane and politic,
which created a legend in Christendom (and was explained with
delightful *naïvete* by the supposition that he must have had an English
mother); but he was an exception. After the fall of Safad, Beibars, in
spite of his oath, massacred two thousand of the defenders. The same
thing had happened earlier at Edessa, and was to recur later after the
fall of Acre and of Beyrouth. The Franks were no better. Raymond
of Chatillon's perfidy was a byword, and when as a prisoner he was
cut down with his own sword, it was an appropriate end. The massacre
of the tenacious Muslim garrison on the fall of Tripoli, and the dis-
graceful and tragically ironic sack of Jerusalem, after hymns had

been sung in procession about the city walls, were among the exploits of Christian chivalry.

Markab lies north of Tortosa. Here, though the mountains come down close to the sea in the usual way, they are less rocky than elsewhere. There is chalk in the soil. The skin of earth is more ample, and only here and there does the underlying skeleton of rock split through. Precipitous, the hills are yet smooth and carry turf. It is in such country that one suddenly sees against the sky the great mass of Markab, its black basalt walls and towers standing out in contrast to the white chalk ridges they dominate. Standing on a spur two or three miles inland, Markab combined the tactical position of the mountain fortress, guarding as it did the route through to Kadmus and Masiaf, with the duty and possibility of watching the port of Banias and the coast road. Its strength was such that Saladin, even after his victory at Hattin, dared not attack it, and for a hundred and fifty years it remained in Frankish hands. Only in 1285, when the game was up and the end of the Crusader occupation was in sight, did the fortress capitulate and the defenders depart with safe-conduct to Acre.

From the coast at Banias a bad, and finally precipitous, road crawls up to the castle. It was one of the great strong points of the Hospitallers, and the finer parts of the fortifications were erected by them in the thirteenth century. The water cisterns which lie under the great paved court, the chapel with its north and west doors, and finally the round keep, are particularly impressive. The last, second in size only to that at Coucy, built in Northern France a century later and destroyed by the Germans in the First World War, must be climbed both for the clear map-like impression of the fortifications to be gained from the summit, and for the tremendous view over coast, sea and mountains. From this vantage-point the size of the area girdled by the double castle wall becomes at once apparent. Upon those walls four knights and twenty-eight men-at-arms kept watch night and day, year in and year out. Within them whole villages with their livestock retired for shelter, and a five years' supply of provisions was comfortably housed. By nature fortified perhaps more strongly than any of the great Crusader castles, one sees how Markab is posed on the summit of a triangular spur which is joined to the main mountain ridge by a narrow isthmus at its apex. One sees clearly, too, how the great works of the castle are piled up to face this single danger-point, and the isthmus itself severed from the mountain by a deep moat.

Sahyoun is within a couple of hours' drive of Markab. The road inland to the castle from Latakia follows the gracious valley of the Nahr el-Kebir. The landscape is no longer like the coast country. The river winds and sweeps in a wide gravel bed; watering cattle come down to the shingle and stand knee-deep in the current. There are solid-looking clumps of blackberry bushes, and here and there a few plane-trees. On either side of the valley, coombs, whose streams are fringed with dwarf poplars, run up into the foot-hills. Up one of these coombs the road turns, and climbs at last to the village of Haffeh. There a track – it is hardly more – branches off to Sahyoun and one emerges into mountain country: boulders, evergreen shrubs and tenacious dwarf oak. Sahyoun does not stand out, like most of these mountain fortresses, but grasps a rocky ridge, one among many such ridges. After a precipitous descent into a ravine – just practicable by car – the track climbs out again and up to within a stone's throw of the castle walls. The traveller is there immediately confronted by the most remarkable feature of Sahyoun – a tremendous channel, cut in solid rock, separating the ridge on which the castle stands from the hillside behind. This extraordinary divide, whose towering sides are haunted by that decorative bird the black-and-scarlet wall-creeper, was spanned by a drawbridge carried on an isolated pinnacle of rock whose hundred and ten feet still rise sheer from the bed of the hewn channel.[1] There could be no more astonishing testimony to the energy and determination of the Franks. The tragedy, their tragedy, was that in spite of such labour the castle fell to Saladin in 1188 after a bare seventy years' occupation and was, unlike many other castles, never recaptured. Their loss was in a sense our gain, for almost alone among the great castles Sahyoun did not pass later into the hands of the military orders, those indefatigable building corporations who in the thirteenth century remodelled all they touched, and so it remains a unique example of the earlier twelfth-century Crusader work and of the modifications which the Franks first introduced into the fortresses which they occupied. The long ridge on which the castle stands lies between two precipitous ravines and appears deceptively narrow. Actually Sahyoun from the two-floored keep with its vaulted roofs, rising above the rock-channel, to the extreme end of the lower fortress, covers a greater area than any of the other castles in Syria. So large is it that two hundred years after the Franks had left, a considerable town, the capital of the district, stood comfortably within the walls.

---

[1] Sahyoun is a Frank remodelling of earlier Byzantine work; it is therefore probable that the great rock divide was an enlargement of the artificial ditch which the Byzantines habitually set to guard the approach to their fortresses.

The approach to Krak seems to announce something special. North of the Tripoli–Homs road the country grows steadily wilder, and it is in almost moorland landscape that the great pile of Krak is first revealed on a spur of the foot-hills, jutting out over a marshy snipe-frequented plain, the Boquée of the Crusaders. Fine at any time, the scene is perhaps most impressive in winter when clouds are hanging on the hills and the castle looms dark against the sky, and the marsh below is desolate.

T. E. Lawrence thought Krak 'perhaps the best preserved and most wholly admirable castle in the world'. It is difficult not to agree. The solidity and the art which appear to be the salient features of Crusader architecture are at Krak combined in supreme fashion. To stand on the top of the south-west tower gives one the impression of being on a ship's bridge, and the kestrels, that wheel in the air above these Syrian castles, scream as bitterly as gulls. The fortress buffets the wind and rides above the extended landscape with the confidence and mastery of a ship. There is the same strength, together with the same beauty of design. As on a fine vessel, the precision of the scheme transcends the utilitarian and creates a work of art. The plan of the concentric walls, the disposition of the flanking towers, and the whole layout of the inner castle, are infinitely pleasing, and at the same time are contrived with the exactitude and economy of a naval architect's blueprint. But the comparison ultimately fails. In its immense solidity and weight the castle is pure mountain. And indeed the great slant wall that slopes outward beneath the south-west tower, a wall eighty feet thick, was known to the astonished Muslims as 'the Mountain'.

This creation stands, owing to the skill of its builders, time's leniency, and the faithful restoration of the French, much as it did when the Crusaders left it over six hundred and fifty years ago. It is thus one of the few medieval castles that the amateur can not only 'feel', but, owing to its full preservation, understand. Indeed the perfection of this preservation makes Krak seem incongruously empty, and its silence out of place. These halls and passages, essentially functional architecture of the best sort, ought to be filled with the knights and sergeants for whom they were designed; the babble of medieval French ought to reach one from the guard-room and the chanted Latin Mass from the twelfth-century chapel. For a hundred and fifty years without a break the Crusaders *were* within these walls – as many as two thousand men when the place was fully garrisoned. The Hospitallers received the castle from Raymond of Tripoli in 1142, and it was they who were responsible for remodelling it and creating the present fortress. Not long after the Order had taken over, Nur-ed-Din attempted the place and was roundly beaten under the walls. Saladin, twenty-five years later, marched on the castle, saw its strength and marched away again.

Inside the walls life continued from generation to generation, and with it continued the daily business and routine, the policy and administration, that the maintenance of an important feudal fief involved. Meetings and banquets took place in the thirteenth-century hall; great figures came and went. The King of Hungary was a visitor and left behind him, as a gift in perpetuity, the rents of many Hungarian acres. Geoffrey de Joinville died in the castle, who seemed to his brother knights the type of the true Crusader, and to Richard Cœur-de-Lion worthy, for his bravery, to quarter the arms of England with his own. He was perhaps buried in the chapel near the six Crusaders whose bodies were found not long ago. From their airy vaulted chamber in the south-west tower, the Wardens of the Castle looked down on it all and in due course succeeded one another. Their names, such as Hughes Revel, Armant de Montbrun, typify the fundamentally French nature and composition of this curious monastic enterprise.

Elsewhere the Crusader tide began to ebb, at first slowly – the fall of Edessa as early as 1144 had been the initial sign – and then after the middle of the thirteenth century with catastrophic speed. One after another towns and castles fell: Jerusalem, the capital of the kingdom, had already gone in 1244 and Antioch fell in 1268. Soon only the coastal belt and a few strong points remained. All the hinterland of Homs and Hama over which Krak had once exercised suzerainty became hostile territory, and the bastion castle, guarding the vital rift between the Lebanese and Alawi Mountains, became more and more isolated. True the garrison could signal to the great keep-tower at Safita, whence a message might be flashed on to the castle at Arima, and so to the coast; [1] yet yearly the Saracens ventured with greater impunity beneath the castle walls and communications grew more hazardous. No longer a bastion, Krak became a vast and lonely outpost. A letter written by the Grand Master of the Hospitallers in 1268 speaks of his financial difficulties now that most of the Kingdom of Jerusalem was in enemy hands, and, even more serious, of his reduced numbers. Whereas Krak alone had maintained a garrison of two thousand at the beginning of the century, Krak and Markab at this date, he says, could muster only some three hundred knights between them. Three years after this letter, in

[1] The Crusaders had also learnt from the Muslims how to use carrier pigeons.

1271, the Sultan Beibars, that competent general who had started life as a slave in Damascus, brought up an army against the castle. Until Krak was taken there was no safe access to the sea. It was, as a Saracen chronicler maintained, 'a bone stuck in the very throat of the Muslims'. The castle, however, was still marvellously strong and the fighting monks who defended it, in spite of their depleted numbers, experienced and determined. Though the Saracens pierced both *enceintes*, they could not win the mountain-like wall and the south-west stronghold. The siege, moreover, was costly and, among many others, the Sultan's own squire fell in the assaults. It was at this point that Beibars devised an expedient which Christian contemporaries called treachery, but which indeed was only one of those ruses that the morality of war approves. A letter, which the defenders took to be genuine, was conveyed into the castle. It purported to come from the Count of Tripoli and instructed the garrison to surrender. Thus after a century and a half Krak capitulated; and the knights, granted a safe-conduct provided they returned to Christendom, rode away to the coast, leaving behind them this architectural monument to their long occupation.

Before passing on to discuss various aspects of these castles, mention must be made of two fortresses of the Crusader period, not, however, primarily connected with the Crusaders – Sheizar and Masiaf. Both are accessible from Hama and, though they do not compare in size with the great castles that have been mentioned, their associations and their dramatic situation render them remarkable. Sheizar lies in the rolling plain that stretches far southward from Aleppo, having on one side the blue line of the Alawi Mountains and on the other the emptiness of the desert. It is a plain of mud villages, with conical bee-hive huts, where the men wear magnificent saffron robes, and the women dresses of red and blue. It is the plain where they rear the best horses in Syria, descended perhaps from the stock of the Seleucid cavalry whose stud farm was situated there, at Apamea. No vista but seems to have a man cantering on a horse, showing off his mount and trappings. No vista either is without a bald trodden threshing floor for corn and barley crops, the sole wealth of the district. It is in this treeless rolling country that Sheizar stands, on a bend of the Orontes River. There, as often in its course, the river is sunk well below the level of the surrounding plain and the traveller looks down from steep escarpments to a winding cleft of green, where huge wooden water-wheels lift and parcel out the water to shady orchards and gardens. The castle stands above the river on a long thin spur of rock whose shape acquired for it the name of the 'Cock's

Comb'. Its importance lay not only in the strength of the position but in the fact that it controlled one of the major fords of the Orontes.

The ancients realized the value of the site and it is mentioned in the inscriptions of the Pharaoh Totmes III. Though fortified in very early times, the present castle dates mainly from the twelfth century when it was rebuilt after a disastrous earthquake. It is of Saracen workmanship and was in fact one of the chief Arab fortresses. Its interest is thus that it gives one a glimpse of what the people on the 'other side' were doing. The stronghold belonged to the princes of the Banou Munqid family, and it is closely associated with Usamah Ibn-Munqid, perhaps the most readable and entertaining of the chroniclers of the early crusading period. His memoirs not only reveal the picture of an exceptionally cultivated Muslim gentleman, but describe the chase, life in the castle, the expeditions against the nearest Frankish stronghold at Apamea and the successful resistance which Sheizar itself put up on more than one occasion against the crusading armies. Today, though the entrance with its Arabic inscription and the keep to the south are still impressive, 'La Grand Césare', as the Franks called it, is in a sorry state. A stinking village squats among the ruins and emphasizes the disappearance of the arts of war and peace which were so successfully cultivated at Sheizar in Usamah's lifetime. It is the old story, so often repeated in Syria, of six hundred years of haphazard neglect and destruction under Mameluke and Turkish rule. Only poverty remains.

The castle of Masiaf introduces the traveller to another factor of considerable importance in the history of the Crusades, the Assassins. They were members of a heretical Muslim sect, the Ismailis, followers of the Prophet's son-in-law Ali. Their beliefs at the time of the Crusades were also held by the Fatimid dynasty in Egypt, but fortunately for the Franks they quarrelled with their fellow heretics and adopted on the whole a policy of co-operation with the invaders. The name of Assassin they acquired from the inveterate habit, first contracted in Persia, of taking the drug *hashish*. The perfection to which they brought the use of assassination as a political weapon accounts for the sense given to the word 'assassin' in the West. The chief of the Ismailis in Syria in the middle of the twelfth century was Rashid el Din Sinan, known to the Franks as the 'Old Man of the Mountain', a title which they conferred without distinction upon his successors. Joinville describes with great picturesqueness the embassy and the gifts – including a giraffe in rock crystal and a set of chessmen – which the Old Man of the Mountain sent to St Louis. The value to the Franks of the Ismaili alliance lay largely

in the fact that the latter were established in the Alawi Mountains and
thus protected a sector of the Latin flank. To bulwark their mountain
stronghold the Assassins built a series of castles, often on earlier Byzantine sites, of which Masiaf was, and remains, the most impressive. The
castle itself is nothing – the Assassins at their best were mediocre
military architects – but the position is admirable and the ruins stand
on a bold rock that detaches itself, with a sense of the dramatic, from
the eastern flanks of the Alawi Mountains. The village and the surrounding country are also attractive. The road from Hama winds up a
small valley, whose stream, tributary to the Orontes, is overhung with
azaleas; and the descendants of the Assassins, the Ismaili inhabitants of
Masiaf, now turned industrious peasants, plant their lanes with pomegranate hedges. Castle and village were once a compact unit, enclosed
in an encircling outer wall. Though much of the latter remains, the
village pays little attention to its stone boundary and spills pleasantly
into orchards and gardens. The general air of cleanliness and well-being,
of stone-built houses and mountain activity, provide a striking contrast
to the rags of Sheizar, the dust and abjection of the villages of the plain.

To return to the great Crusader castles. It is impossible for the
stranger to visit them without wishing to discover the answers to
various teasing questions. Why, first of all, were they built in such
numbers and on such a scale? What architectural influences were
predominant in their construction? How were such vast defensive works
ever captured? And lastly, what was the society of which they were so
often focal points? The answer to these problems involves consideration
of certain aspects of the crusading enterprise.

The twelfth and thirteenth centuries in Western Europe inaugurated
the golden age of military architecture, but that in itself is not sufficient
to account for the fever of Crusader building, and for the great number
and the vast size of their castles. The latter were brought into being by
a serious problem non-existent in the West – lack of manpower. The
huge Crusader army that crossed the Bosphorus had dwindled, it has
been estimated, to 100,000 when it sat down before Antioch. On the
subsequent march south each fief and feudal principality, as it was
created, drained off its complement of men, leaving an ever smaller
force available for quick concentration against the enemy. Of the
original army perhaps not more than one in twenty reached Jerusalem.
When that city fell and yet others sailed home, it is said that only five
hundred knights remained in the southern province of the Latin kingdom. For every armed knight one must count ten, or perhaps more,

* F

foot soldiers; even this, however, only makes a total force of somewhere over five thousand men. Anyway, only the knights really counted. They were the decisive element in the battles of the time, and it was essentially the net superiority of the mounted Crusader over the Muslim horseman that made possible the capture of the Holy Land. Time and again the charge of the Crusader knights, with their heavier armour and larger breed of charger, achieved victory against forces of overwhelming superiority. Though the disparity in numbers was exceptional, that defeat which Raymond of Toulouse, with three hundred French gentlemen, inflicted outside Tripoli on a Saracen army of many thousands was symbolic of the military superiority of the armed and mounted nobility who constituted the striking weapon of the Crusader force. During the twelfth and thirteenth centuries no new developments in tactics arose to challenge this superiority. Though the Muslim horse-bowmen with their skirmishing methods, light armour and small fast Arabs could work havoc on a disorganized force, they never learnt to meet the weight of a Crusader charge.

However, when knights were numbered by scores every casualty counted. The reinforcements that trickled in, younger sons, adventurers, pilgrim-knights, were barely enough to make up losses. Thus when the first properly organized reinforcement – the Second Crusade – came to hopeless grief in Asia Minor in the middle of the twelfth century, it was evident that the inadequate forces available in the Latin Kingdom could not hold it without intensive fortification. Lack of manpower necessitated the Crusader castles. Even with a sizable army the country would, for two reasons, have been difficult to hold without strong points: first it was elongated in shape, a maritime belt stretching from the last spurs of the Taurus range to Akaba on the Red Sea; and second the Crusaders did not control the route running north and south on the desert fringe to the east of Palestine and the Lebanon. Along this the Saracens could bring in reinforcements from Egypt, or from Baghdad via Aleppo, and thence they could continually harass the Latins. It has been said, and probably with truth, that it was the tactical error of not seizing Damascus, and with it this inner route, at the time of the First Crusade that, in the end, cost the Crusaders their kingdom. Had this hinterland been taken at once, when there was a force adequate for the enterprise, the Latin Kingdom would have had its back to three hundred miles of almost waterless desert, not easily traversed by any large armed force. In addition Egypt would have been isolated from Baghdad and the Islamic world effectively cut in two. The hinterland, however, was not taken. Later, when manpower failed, the great inland castles were built to watch it and to hold, as best they might, the long Crusader flank.

The major castles soon created problems of their own. Their upkeep was so costly, and the charge of garrisoning so great, that the ordinary feudal lords found them difficult to run. Such men had other obligations whereas the supervision of these mammoth fortresses was a whole-time occupation. Further, life in the frontier castles was inevitably of a semi-monastic sort and over long periods could have little attraction for the secular knight and his retainers, who knew and appreciated the pleasures of the coast. Again, continual vigilance was necessary, and continuity of command; on the death of a feudal owner, who might even leave a minor as heir, continuity was inevitably broken. The solution to these problems was supplied by the creation of the military orders, the Hospitallers and Templars. The former had been established in Palestine in a civil capacity since before the Crusades, and had supervised the pilgrim traffic, supplying accommodation and, as their name suggests, creating hospitals for the sick. With the foundation of the Latin kingdom they acquired immensely increased importance. Forming themselves into a highly organized military-monastic order, responsible directly to the papacy, they soon acquired lands, wealth and power. The Knights Templar, an offshoot of the Hospitallers created in 1118, were a parallel organization taking their name from the Temple enclosure at Jerusalem, where their first quarters were situated. These orders of armed monks, wearing on the surcoat that covered their mail respectively the white cross or the red, familiar from the illustrated history books of one's childhood, came to provide the backbone of resistance to the Saracens, and in due course acquired the charge of the great castles. This was a task for which they were eminently fitted. Their monastic vows suited them to the dour life, their direct responsibility to the papacy placed them beyond local feudal quarrels, and their character as undying corporations ensured continuity. Finally they possessed both the necessary wealth, acquired through vast endowments, and the necessary organization. The latter was strict and impressive. Each order was composed of three classes of men – knights; sergeants recruited from the bourgeoisie; and chaplain-clerks. Each order, moreover, levied its own taxes, possessed its own diplomatic service and ran its own marine. Such were the states within the state on which devolved the defence of the great castles. To the Hospitallers fell the monster fortresses of Krak, Markab and Banias; to the Templars,

Tortosa, Safita, Chastel Rouge, Arima and finally Beaufort. By 1166 there were only three castles in the Kingdom of Jerusalem which the military orders did not control.

The next question that arises is an architectural one: what conception of military architecture do these Crusader castles express, and what was the predominant architectural influence in their construction? The whole problem is a specialized one, and angels tread the ground with considerable circumspection. One theory, in its extreme form, is that the Latins were initially pretty naïve in these matters, but that after seeing the Bzyantine castles in Asia Minor, and as a result of prolonged contact with the Byzantines, they adopted the methods of fortification with which the Eastern Empire had been familiar since the time of Justinian; that they had in fact everything to learn and that the inspiration for their architecture came directly from Byzantium. Another theory, again expressed in its extreme form, is that the inspiration of crusading architecture came directly from France and Italy. Certainly neither of these extremes represents the truth, which probably lies somewhere between the two. Arab influence further complicates the problem, for Arab fortresses of Byzantine inspiration, such as Kasr el-Heir (see Chapter VI), had gone up in Syria centuries prior to the Crusades, and Arabo-Byzantine contacts had resulted in the evolution of indigenous Arab fortification.

One thing is certain: if the Franks came in ignorance, they proved remarkable pupils and, whether exploiting their own knowledge or that of Byzance, they rapidly evolved a military architecture more formidable than anything that had been seen before. This is not the place to go fully into the subject, but a tentative review of the main features of crusading architecture in relation to their Latin or Arabo-Byzantine origins cannot be avoided.

The Sites. The Crusaders raised most of their major castles on natural defensive sites, which thus in some degree determined their shape (cf. Markab), and which had also sometimes been used by the Byzantines and Arabs before them. In the latter instance existing fortifications were often incorporated (Sahyoun is a good example).

Masonry and Walls. Massive walls and the use of large building stones were in the ancient tradition of Syrian and Phoenician construction. (Baalbeck in this context at once springs to mind.) The Frankish architects seem to have revived this tradition. Their masonry is excellent and their massive walls are so well put together that the mortar is often hardly visible and the work at first sight resembles freestone building. However, unlike the freestone workers of the Byzantine period who built Kalat Seman and the dead cities round Aleppo, they often filled the centre of their walls with rubble and mortar in conformity with the practice of medieval castle building. The face of their walls is also characterized by what is known as *bossage*, an effect produced by only levelling the fitting surfaces of stones and leaving a rough 'boss' in the centre of each stone. This treatment, which both adds thickness to the wall and economizes labour, was not used either in medieval Syria, or in France before the thirteenth century. It had, however, been common in Syria in classical times, and the Franks, who adopted it soon after their arrival, may well have copied it from classical models. The Arabs did not begin to use it until about a century later.

The masonry of the earlier Byzantine fortresses was on the whole relatively light. Eastern siege tactics in the Middle Ages prior to the crusading period were extremely imperfect, and thin walls were thus adequate. Sometimes, indeed, they were so thin that the *chemin de ronde* had to be carried on corbelling or on interior arcades (cf. the town walls of Resafa). The Byzantines calculated also on supplementing the fragility of their stone-work by ample garrisons, which – as we have seen – the Crusaders could not usually afford to do, and by deep protective ditches.

1. Rectangular curtain-tower.   2. Round half-tower of same diameter.
Arrows indicate lines of fire from given points on the curtain wall.[1]

Towers and Flanking Fire. At the time of the First Crusade towers in Europe were not built along curtain walls to provide flanking fire, and the Franks in Syria probably took over the idea from the Byzantines. The latter had for centuries strengthened their walls in this way, but had usually been content to employ towers that were square in shape and projected a relatively small distance from the castle walls. In Syria, Halebiyah is a nice example of such fortification (see Chapter V). The Byzantines also tended to place their flanking towers wide apart. In

[1] T. E. Lawrence, *Crusader Castles*, Vol. I, plate 12.

these matters, in the centuries immediately preceding the Crusades, the Arabs followed the Byzantine practice. It would give the wrong impression, however, to pretend that the Byzantines and Arabs had never used anything but shallow square towers. There are, for instance, four round corner-towers at Resafa. The walls of Kasr el-Heir are wholly furnished with round towers, and at Ukhaidir, south-east of Syrian territory, the walls are flanked with round towers only some ten yards apart.

The Franks with their flair for military architecture at once realized the importance of the Byzantine flanking towers. But they also grasped that the fire provided along the walls was more effective if the towers had considerable depth, and that the round tower was definitely better than the square. Not only was the round tower more solid, but it was more defensible, as the diagram on the previous page illustrates.

In Syria round flanking towers of considerable salient providing carefully schemed covering fire are characteristically Latin. It was the Hospitallers who best exploited their possibilities, and in the great castles of that Order the transformation which the Franks effected in the old Byzantine conception of the flanking tower is clear. Indeed lines of fire came to be so admirably devised by the end of the twelfth century that Richard Cœur-de-Lion boasted of his castle at Les Andelys, which incorporated all the Crusader innovations, that it 'might be held even if its walls were made of butter'. The influence of the military architecture of the Holy Land reached England as early as the middle of the twelfth century, and at Alnwick Castle (1140–50) the importance of flanking towers is already recognized.

The Keep. Though the Byzantines had erected keep-like citadels in their fortified towns, the square keep was essentially a Norman creation and came into fashion with the Tower of London, built by William the Conqueror just before the First Crusade. Almost more solid than anything except the concrete fortifications of the twentieth century, the keep was admirably suited to the conditions of early feudal warfare when forces were small and siege tactics not fully developed. On the other hand, the keep suffered from the weakness inherent in purely passive defence. It provided no flanking fire, and could accommodate for obvious reasons only a very small force and that force could be hopelessly blockaded, since, with the one small entrance that defensive prudence dictated, sorties were almost impossible. It has been said that a keep could be defended by one man; it has also been rightly pointed out that 'it could certainly be besieged by two, standing one each side of the doorway to prevent egress'. The weakness of the keep had not, however, been made clear at the time of the First Crusade. It was in its heyday, and the Crusaders on their arrival built keeps in what was then the latest style of European architecture. The massive square keeps of Sahyoun, Safita, Chastel Rouge, Byblos and Banias are examples of this importation. Local conditions, however, necessitated an important modification. In Europe keeps were not normally vaulted, but in Syria owing to the lack of timber each storey had to be carried on stone vaults. This meant that though tremendously massive – the walls of the keep at Sayhoun are over twenty feet thick at ground level – the Syrian keeps did not attain the height of their European prototypes.

The early keeps in Europe had been placed at the strongest point in the castle. This was soon discovered to be an error, since it was the point of weakness which called for the greatest strength of fortification. Thus the keeps, or fortress-keeps, at Sahyoun, Krak and Markab, are situated at the point where the natural defences are weakest. By the thirteenth century this disposition had become universal. The keep simultaneously underwent a change in shape and the round keep displaced the square. The angles of the latter were too susceptible to mining, and it offered the same disadvantages from the point of view of flanking fire as the square curtain tower. As we should expect, the early twelfth-century keep at Sahyoun is square, while the later fortifications of the Hospitallers have round keeps, or at any rate round towers to their fortress-keeps.

Portcullis, Bent-Gateway, Machicoulis. The portcullis, though known to the Romans as early as the end of the third century B.C., was apparently in Syria a Frankish importation and was not used in the Byzantine and Arab castles of the Middle Ages. The device of employing a bent entrance at castle gates to avoid the danger of the gate being 'rushed', especially when the defenders were withdrawing into the castle after a sortie, was of even older origin, since two isolated examples have been found in Egypt dating back to the second millennium B.C. However, in spite of an eighth-century example at Baghdad, the bent entrance did not come into general use until the time of the Crusades. The Arabs were then the first to exploit the device, and the finest remaining example is their magnificent five-angled entrance to the castle at Aleppo, built in the thirteenth century.

Though, in twelfth- and thirteenth-century France, castle walls and towers were finished with wooden hoardings to provide cover for the defenders, the timber shortage in Syria made this impracticable. It has been suggested that this difficulty was directly responsible for the development of machicoulis. This device is apparently purely Syrian in origin and is first found, though not always employed for military purposes, in the ruined Byzantine towns near Aleppo, and later in the eighth-century fort at Kasr el-Heir. After this date it seems to have been forgotten, only to be revived in the crusading period. However, though there are examples at Krak and Banias, the Crusaders did not so much make local use of the machicoulis as introduce it into Europe from the East. As a result of this importation, continuous machicolation appears in Europe from the fourteenth century.

The Concentric Castle. The origin of the concentric castle (i.e. a castle having a double or even triple girdle of walls), of which Krak is a perfect example, is much debated. Byzantium and other imperial towns had double walls, and the fortifications of the Caliph Al-Mansur's circular city at Baghdad also foreshadow the concentric castle. It has thus been supposed that the Latin kingdom adopted such a scheme of fortification from the Byzantine east, whence it in due course passed to Europe and revolutionized western castle-building. Richard Cœur-de-Lion's château at Les Andelys (1196) has been pointed out as the most important and immediate example of the transference of this Byzantine conception to the West.

It seems equally plausible to suppose that the concentric castle may have been a natural development of the keep-castles of Europe. There, as the disadvantages of the simple keep became evident, architects began to replace it by the shell-keep, essentially a keep-fortress built round an open courtyard. These shell-keeps were supplemented by outer defences. The latter usually consisted in a curtain wall springing from the keep itself, and encircling a considerable outer area known as the 'bailey'. From this to the further enlargement of the shell-keep (until it virtually resembled an inner ward) and to its complete isolation from the surrounding 'bailey' wall, was a natural step. Once this step had been taken the concentric castle was in existence. It is maintained that so simple and organic a development was inevitable as siege tactics improved and the prestige of the traditional keep declined, and that it was thus hardly necessary for architects to travel to the Holy Land to evolve the type. Further, if models were really needed, western builders had them at hand in the concentric earthworks of the Roman and Saxon castles. In view of such opposing claims as to the origin of the concentric castle it seems difficult for the amateur to arrive at a conclusion. Perhaps the problem at present does not admit of a definite solution one way or the other.

The architectural genius of the Crusaders found its highest expression in the buildings of the Military Orders. The Templars did not choose to exploit the new conception of the concentric castle as did the Hospitallers and the architects of Western Europe. Unfortunately many of their major castles, such as Arima, Chastel Rouge, Safita and Tortòsa, are today sadly ruined. Time has been kinder to the work of the Hospitallers and the exact character of their building remains clearly visible at Krak and Markab. Particularly in the former the typical Latin solidity and mass are evident, together with the provision of careful flanking fire, ensured by round curtain towers of adequate depth spaced at reasonably close intervals, and – here the revolution appears – the fullest possible acceptance of the principle of concentric fortification. Krak consists essentially of two castles, the outer and the inner, and the latter remains a self-contained unit, workable for offence and defence, even when the outer ward is lost. In the vast strongwork above the 'mountain' wall survives the last echo of the old Norman keep. Perhaps nothing shows more clearly than this great bastion with its linked towers how far the Crusaders had taken military architecture in little over a century.

It is not difficult to see that such castles were immensely strong, and looking at Krak the further question arises as to how the great Crusader castles came to be taken. Built on natural sites where attack was only possible from one side, and usually on rock to prevent mining, provided with narrow elbow-entrances easily defensible, and with a careful system of towers providing fire along every yard of the curtain walls, it seems inconceivable that such strongholds should have fallen before the introduction of gunpowder. Yet they did. The old weapon of famine of course existed and was sometimes effective. Thus Saladin managed to starve out the defenders of Beaufort, and of the impregnable Kerak in Transjordan. Yet capitulation on this ground was rare and, when one recalls that Markab was planned to hold provisions for a five-year siege, it was evidently not easy to bring about. The besieger had, however, at his disposal a variety of other weapons, and as is usually the case, the steady progress in fortification stimulated a corresponding improvement in siege methods.

Two plain alternatives lay open to the besieger – to get over the walls or to get through them, to scale or to effect a breach.

Of the direct methods of assault, scaling-ladders were the simplest but also the most easily repulsed. It should be remembered that the task of the defenders in meeting direct assault was complicated by the fact that the numbers available at any given point were strictly limited by the width of the wall and the wooden planking which might supplement it. Overcrowding could only provoke confusion. Loopholes in the body of towers and buildings, though useful enough in providing light, offered a very ineffective arc of fire. The essential defence of a castle had to be made by men manning a narrow wall-top. In direct assault numbers were, of course, of the first importance to the besieger. If attacks were made at various points and the attacker prepared to sustain heavy losses, results might be obtained. In the matter of numbers the Saracens had an overwhelming superiority. Where the Latins could bring a hundred knights and their retainers to man the walls, thousands were available for the assault.

If scaling-ladders failed, there was always the alternative of piling up earth in primitive fashion against the wall and thus making a ramp up which the besiegers could deliver their attack. Such a procedure, besides being lengthy and laborious, involved – especially where there was strong flanking fire – a high percentage of casualties, since those engaged in the work were continually exposed to the fire of the garrison. For protection under such conditions, the besiegers worked under mantlets, light shields made of twisted hurdles covered with hides and held above their heads.

More effective than either of these methods of assault were movable wooden towers of which frequent use was made in the crusading sieges. These towers, built somewhat higher than the wall against which they were to be advanced, fulfilled a double function: while acting as posts from which a fire could be directed down on the enemy with a view to clearing a portion of the wall, they possessed drawbridges, which could be lowered at an opportune moment. Across these the besiegers could advance on to the wall. They offered, on the other hand, an easy mark for the defenders and, a more serious handicap, could only operate on even ground.

What might be called the siege artillery of the time was of three main sorts, and, of course, available to defenders and besiegers alike. The mangon, essentially a huge sling, was worked by *torsion*, and could project bodies of vast size. It had, however, a high trajectory which made accurate aim difficult, and was therefore used to best advantage in hurling missiles indiscriminately into some wide objective, such as a camp or beleaguered castle, rather than in aiming at a specific target. (It was some form of mangon that Saladin probably used for hurling missiles into Sahyoun across the ravine from the south. An Arab chronicler tells how the Crusaders when besieging Sheizar hurled a

millstone from one of their mangons which razed a whole building.)
With the second type of artillery, the *ballista*, markmanship was
possible. This machine worked by *tension*, and was in essence a gigantic
long-range crossbow. It hurled javelins, or more often iron bolts,
'feathered' with wood, four times the thickness of the ordinary arrow
and half its usual length. These missiles could easily pierce mail, and the
point to which the *ballista* had been developed before the Crusades began
may be gauged by the fact that at the siege of Paris a lucky shaft went
right through several besieging Danes who happened to be in the way.
The third type of siege artillery – the trebuchet – only came into use
after the First Crusade. It was worked not by torsion or tension, but by
counterpoise. A long pole was fixed across a strong upright, in see-saw
fashion, but with its butt-end considerably closer to the pivotal point.
The longer end of the pole, to which the missile was attached, was fixed
to the ground, while the butt-end was loaded with heavy weights. To
set off the mechanism, the longer end of the pole was released and the
counterpoise of the weights discharged the missile. The trajectory of the
trebuchet was not unlike that of the mangon, but it developed greater
power, and owing to the use of a counterpoise that could be moved up or
down the pole, rather as the little weight is slid along a weighing-
machine, greater accuracy could be obtained. These machines, and to
a lesser degree the *ballista*, could be used for throwing Greek fire. The
Saracens had learnt the secret of this incendiary weapon – so deadly
against the wooden siege engines of the period – from the Byzantines,
and by the end of the twelfth century were employing it with great
effect against the Crusaders.

Only when direct assault had failed was an attempt usually made to
force a breach in the walls. This could be achieved by any one of three
weapons – the ram, the bore or the mine. The first of these was the
most formidable, but also the most difficult to work. A giant tree, the
largest available in the district, was slung from two great uprights and
the whole affair trundled on wheels up to the castle wall. To swing the
great beam might call for anything up to sixty men, and these in their
turn would need a mobile pent-house with a strong roof to protect them.
If allowed to batter away at will, loosening the mortar and piling up
hour by hour one shuddering blow upon another, a large ram could
effect a breach in almost any wall. But no ram was allowed to work
unmolested. If the pent-house was not crushed or set on fire and the ram
put out of action, great mattresses or beams would be lowered over the
castle walls to take up the shock, or, perhaps most effective of all, the

defenders by means of a heavy forked beam would catch and pin the ram just after it had delivered its blow.

The object of the bore was to create a breach; not by shattering the wall, but by slowly gnawing its way through. For this reason the Romans had, centuries earlier, aptly nicknamed it *musculus*, the mouse. While less effective than the ram, the bore had the advantage of being less unwieldy and of needing fewer men to work it.

Lastly there was the mine, though this could not be used effectively against castles, built as was Krak, on solid rock. Mining in the days before gunpowder was a primitive business, but necessitated considerable skill. It was laborious, but, as technique improved in the thirteenth century, often surprisingly successful. Richard Cœur-de-Lion employed Aleppine sappers who were apparently particularly cunning. The method used was the following: earth was removed from under the castle wall to a considerable depth, and the cavity so created was temporarily shored up with beams; when a sufficiently long stretch of wall had been thus undermined, this artificial 'cellar' was piled with brushwood which was set alight. In due course the beams which supported the masonry were consumed, and the length of wall came crashing to the ground. How effective mines could be is exemplified in the story of the fall of Markab. The Sultan Kalaoun having taken the outer defences, the Hospitallers retired behind the walls of the massive inner ward, whence they repulsed a Saracen attack with heavy losses to the enemy. The Sultan, considering the chances of direct assault to be slight, set to work to drive a mine right under the main keep. The sappers were so successful that the whole structure was in due course resting on wooden props alone. The Sultan, who wished to preserve the castle intact for his own purposes, thereupon sent an embassy to the defenders, inviting them to delegate experts to examine his mine under safe-conduct. This they did, and their report bearing out the claims of the Saracens, the defenders had no alternative but to surrender.

To all these methods of breach and assault, the defender naturally had his replies, and the more one considers the weapons available the more one begins to suspect that something else must have contributed to the fall of the great castles. Before the use of gunpowder the siege weapons hardly seem in themselves adequate to the reduction of places like Sahyoun and Markab. The answer probably is that the defenders, mewed up for months and years in these great piles, developed a peculiar mentality. Immobility killed initiative and defence grew more and more passive. The interminable business of waiting for the other man to do something affected the garrison. Inevitably they were always one move behind; they were always countering, never attacking. The mentality of the old garrison hand who had spent half a lifetime in these prisons must have been a special one. As a siege dragged on, nerves must have become more and more frayed, and false alarms, especially at night, more frequent – someone had heard the sound of sapping under the great tower; men were already scaling the west wall; the postern had been betrayed. The great castle in fact imposed an immense psychological strain on the defender, and as the strain month by month increased, capitulation must have seemed an ever more desirable release. 'Castle-mentality' therefore must be classed among the most important weapons of the besieger, and was perhaps often decisive.

The fall of these castles presents, as we have seen, something of a problem. Conversely a problem is posed by the fact that, though often isolated, they should have remained so long – in more than one case for a hundred and fifty years – in Frankish hands. Had these frontier castles been set in hostile country so long a resistance would hardly have been possible; in hostile country a castle might maintain itself for five, ten, fifteen years, but not for five or six generations. In truth each fortress formed the centre of a not unfriendly community. This brings us to a final question: what was indeed the society of which these castles were often focal points, and what were the relations between the Franks stationed there and the local population?

The First Crusade occurred when the prestige of feudalism was at its height. Thus, though the Military Orders were extra-feudal and the maritime powers on the coast – Venice, Genoa and others – secured for their merchants a special autonomy and privilege which placed them outside the feudal structure, a rigid feudalism prevailed in the countryside. The Syrian population formed the basis of a feudal society of which the castles dotted all over the country were among the administrative centres. Further, it is important to realize that the majority of the population accepted this society. Had they not done so, it would have been impossible to hold the country with the forces available. They accepted it for a variety of reasons.

After the initial seizure of the kingdom, made possible primarily by the military superiority of the Crusader knight and by the political divisions of his opponents, a military expedition turned into a colonial venture. The ensuing organization of the country offered, in many ways, improved conditions for the native population. The feudal organizers started with two advantages; they possessed the support of the local Christians – the Maronites turned out to be valuable archers – and of the Old Man of the Mountain and his followers. On the other hand, they had to contend in the Muslim population with a very natural religious and racial antagonism. It was to offset this that a policy of orientalism was adopted with considerable success. At Jerusalem, Baldwin, the first of the Crusaders, sat cross-legged to receive audience, decked in a gold-embroidered burnous, and Tancred at Antioch assumed a turban, though decency demanded he should pin a cross upon it. The Venetians, with their ever-watchful eye on opportunity, sped their trade inland by striking coins – *Byzantini Saracenati* – bearing an Arab inscription, a Koranic text and a date calculated from the Hegira. Well might Fulcher of Chartres, King Baldwin's chaplain, exclaim, 'We are all becoming Orientals'. Antagonism, however, in the long run was appeased by more practical considerations. Stimulated by the energy of the maritime powers, trade revived. Caravan traffic with the interior flourished; on the coast Tyre enjoyed a prosperity it had hardly known since Phoenician days, and Acre bustled into new and brilliant importance. At the same time feudalism provided a better internal administration than had been seen since the time of the Umay-yads. Even the Muslims admired the equity with which the taxes were collected and justice administered. Cases involving the local population were tried in special native courts, where a Frank magistrate presided with the help of a jury of six, four of whom were native Syrians. It was the principle of the Mixed Courts of Egypt, but devised by Crusaders eight hundred years earlier. Finally social welfare, in the hands of the Hospitallers, was not overlooked; orphanages and hospitals were created, and in Jerusalem alone two thousand poor were fed daily. It was the old story: precision and organization, seeking their own ends, yet bringing order and prosperity as a by-product.

At this time the Saracens had no alternative to offer. Islam in the East had passed its zenith. It was symbolic that the Caliph in 1150 should have burnt the philosophical library at Baghdad, consigning to the flames the works of Ibn-Sina, and that in Syria medicine should have been almost the monopoly of the Jacobite clergy. The old idea that vandal Latins burst in upon an advanced and flourishing Arab civiliza-tion can no longer be accepted. The Latins had indeed a lot to learn from the Byzantines, and a good deal from the Saracens, but essentially the West at this time was vigorous and effective, the East aged and corrupt.

Syrian merchants and peasants saw where their material advantage lay. They accepted the methods and the rule of the feudal kingdom. Ibn Gubayr, a Muslim traveller visiting the country not long before the military disaster of Hattin, gives, in spite of his strongly anti-Frankish sentiments, a striking picture of the treatment accorded to the Syrians and of their favourable reaction to that treatment. 'We passed', he says, 'through a series of villages and cultivated lands all inhabited by Muslims, who live in great well-being under the Franks. Allah preserve us from such a temptation! The Franks allow them to keep half of the harvest and limit themselves to the imposition of a poll-tax of one dinar and five kirats.[1] Apart from this they only levy a small tax on timber. The Muslims are proprietors of their own houses and run them as they wish. Similar conditions apply along the littoral and in all the districts, towns, and villages, inhabited by the Muslims. The majority of them cannot resist the temptation of comparing their lot with that of their brothers in regions under Muslim rule – a lot which is the reverse of agreeable or prosperous. One of the chief tragedies of the Muslims is that they have to complain of the injustices of their own rulers, whereas they cannot but praise the behaviour of the Franks, their natural enemies. May Allah soon put an end to this state of affairs!' In such circumstances it was not surprising that Muslims often emigrated into Frankish territory. Such immigrants, whom Ibn Gubayr severely censures on religious grounds, found in the shadow of the frontier castles not only security, but a highly developed agricultural, social and financial policy. It was indeed the purely civil functions of the great castles, that by securing the co-operation of the populace, enabled them to exist for so long in their military capacity.

[1] Considerably less than the similar tax imposed on Christians in Muslim territory.

CHAPTER VIII

TURKS, TRAVELLERS AND THE MOUNTAIN

———————————— ❦ ————————————

I N men like Nur-ed-Din, Saladin, Beibars and Kalaoun, the Latins were confronted by soldiers and administrators of outstanding ability. Their successors in the two centuries that intervened between the departure of the Crusaders and the arrival of the Turks were, unfortunately for Syria, of lesser calibre. The country, as a dependence of the unstable Mameluke sultans of Egypt, was ruled from Damascus by a series of governors whose tenure of office was usually brief and whose exercise of power was commonly inefficient and oppressive. The transference of power from Cairo to Constantinople in 1516 brought no improvement in internal administration and the Turkish pasha merely replaced the Mameluke governor. The ruling power never had confidence in its own delegates; suspicion and intrigue thus forestalled any possibility of firm planned rule. Governors were appointed and removed with nervous haste. In a hundred and eighty-four years (1516–1697) there were a hundred and thirty-three pashas at Damascus, and in the Mameluke period a governor was removed, as a contemporary writer tells, for no better reason than that 'he had long held power and his prestige had increased'. In such circumstances governors came to Damascus only to acquire wealth quickly and left, often enough, only to be executed. Exactions were the rule and chronic disorders their natural consequence.

In the Mameluke period internal difficulties were further aggravated by the Mongol menace and Crusader raids from the Kingdom of Cyprus. The Mongols twice took Damascus. On the second occasion, in 1400, Tamerlane, after sacking the city, deported all the best artisans to Samarkand and permanently crippled the local crafts. The Mongol invasions though catastrophic were brief; the western menace on the other hand was semi-permanent. Numbers of Crusaders after their

172

expulsion from the mainland had retired to Cyprus, which became a base for raids on the Syrian coast. Owing to the superiority of the western marine these raids were extremely effective and there were few ports which did not suffer from the Crusaders' lightning descents. They occupied Tortosa in 1302, 1367, 1369 and as late as 1518 the knights seized and held the fortified island of Ruad opposite the town. A year later they held Beyrouth, then the foremost port on the coast, for three days. The Mamelukes in desperation adopted a 'scorched earth' policy, undertaking the systematic destruction of the coastal ports. Tripoli, Tyre, Acre and Jaffa were among the places dismantled and evacuated. Though such negative measures made descents on the littoral less tempting for the Crusader pirates, they can hardly have contributed to the comfort or well-being of the population. It was not until the growth of Turkish naval power in the sixteenth century that life became more normal and secure along the Lebanese coast.

The conjunction of foreign invasion and administrative ineptitude was not favourable to the arts. Outside of Aleppo and Damascus there are few buildings of architectural importance. None the less, the Turkish period in Syria has a particular interest for the European since it saw the arrival of the Marseilles merchants and the Levant Company, followed in due course by the learned travellers of the Age of Reason, and ultimately by Lady Hester Stanhope and the Romantics. As a result of these contacts the western conception of Syria during this period gradually changed: from being the evocation of Hattin, Acre and the hostile Saracen, it became successively the country of Baalbeck and Berytus, and the home of the glamorous Arab. In spite of subsequent political developments, the romantic conception, as standardized somewhere about 1830, is still current today. The Turkish period is that which remains the most 'alive', in the sense of being the least changed. It is directly accessible to the traveller. In Hama, and one or two places like it, the Syria which the *savants*, the romantics and the merchants knew has survived almost intact. Further, it is the period which saw the clear emergence of the Lebanon as a separate entity and is thus bound up more closely than any other with the romantic history of the Mountain.

At the beginning of the Turkish period there were over three thousand taxable villages in the pashalik of Aleppo; about three hundred years later there remained only four hundred. Syria was thus entering a period of profound economic decadence when the French and English merchants began to arrive, a decadence which their activity counteracted only at specific places. The European trade which brought them to Syria had first arisen to satisfy a taste for eastern luxuries developed during the Crusades; it only later came to be regarded as an indispensable channel for the outlet of western goods. The traffic initially had been in the hands of the Italian maritime powers (Venetian merchants in the fourteenth century penetrated even to Hama); with the memory of the Crusades still fresh, it was only their perseverance and skill which achieved a compromise between hostility and interest. It was with the seventeenth century that the greater share of the trade fell to the French and the English. Jacques Cœur, that enterprising merchant prince and ambassador, came out to survey the ground for the French as early as the fifteenth century, and the French later established a monopoly of trade at Sidon, where the shrewd Emir Fakr-ed-Din lodged them in the magnificent *khan* which exists today. So important was their business there that a French traveller could write in 1658: 'Si les François abandonnoient Saida, la ville deviendrait deserte, les habitants iroient loger ailleurs.' The English did not put in an appearance until after the foundation of the Levant Company by Queen Elizabeth in 1581, and then they opened their main trade counter at Aleppo. As the terminus of the annual eastern caravan from Basra and the depot for Persian silks, Aleppo was the most important European market in Syria, and the English found the Venetians and French already entrenched there. In due course they outstripped their rivals, and the English 'factory' as it was called became in the seventeenth century the most important in the place. It numbered in 1662 about fifty merchants. They were represented by a consul whose salary at about that time amounted to three thousand thalers exclusive of special allowances, and they enjoyed the services of a chaplain. The trade driven was considerable, and the value of the goods which these merchants sent home to England via the port of Alexandretta brought them a comfortable profit. One merchant, John Verney, returned to England a rich man after twelve years' trading, and Sir Paul Pindar, who was consul in Aleppo from 1606–10, built up in the Levant the basis of that fortune which enabled him to donate £19,000 towards the repair of St Paul's Cathedral.

Though the Aleppo trade was less profitable in the eighteenth century (there were eighty European firms represented there in 1775), it must still have been remunerative, for only a solid return could have reconciled the merchants to the life they led. Sojourners in a strange and hostile land, the European merchants passed a hermetic existence in the Frankish quarter. There each of the European powers had its own *khan* or hostelry, allocated by the Sultan, where the merchants were compelled to lodge and where they lived a semi-collegiate life. Each *khan* was built round a courtyard; on the ground floor the merchants had independent lock-ups for their wares, while the sleeping apartments were situated above. Many of these *khans* still exist, and it is thus possible in Aleppo to envisage the communal life of the Frankish merchants. Long since abandoned by their original owners (the English factory was closed in 1791), and lapsing now into desuetude with the final decay of the caravan traffic, the courtyards of the *khans* are empty; but the simple functional architecture remains most pleasing, and the imagination easily enough recreates in them the life of the exiled trading colonies. The old Venetian *khan* has belonged for generations to the Pokhe family, who are kind enough to show strangers their house and furniture. The *khan* that once belonged to the East India Company, who were represented in Aleppo, lies just across the way, and a little farther on is the French *khan*. Huddled together for company and protection, the Franks could communicate with each other by ladders across the roofs without having to venture down into the streets. Such means of communication was also useful at night, for the gates of the *khans* had to be closed at sunset, after which the merchants were not permitted abroad. Such a regulation was made as much for the merchants' safety as anything else, for the contempt with which the true Muslim regarded these commercial Unbelievers was apt to translate itself into violence on the slightest pretext. With violence went economic exactions. These exactions, known as *avanias*, were a constant menace, and hardly a year went by without some individual merchant, or the colony collectively, being bled by the authorities on a trumped-up charge. This in spite of the privileges and exemptions, in the form of Capitulations, granted by the Porte to the foreign merchants of each nation.

These were not the only disadvantages of expatriate life. While the merchants were hopelessly cut off from home – an exchange of letters took four to five months – it was almost impossible owing to religious prejudice to develop social relations with the Turks or Syrians. Though for their safety the Franks wore native costume, their local contacts were usually limited to business interviews or visits of courtesy to officials. Women who play so useful a part in breaking down national and religious barriers could effect nothing, since every Christian who went with a respectable Muslim woman risked the death penalty. The majority of the European colony of necessity remained bachelors. In these circumstances they were thrown wholly upon each other's company: 'Our delights are among ourselves', wrote an Englishman from Aleppo in 1699. The nature of these delights, at any rate among the members of the English factory, was largely dictated by the fact that in the wild country around Aleppo they could escape from the crowded and hostile town. There, twice a week, the whole factory went out hunting, coursed their greyhounds, enjoyed the duck-shooting in winter, and even played cricket. On their return there was, for some, the quiet of the factory library, which at the end of the seventeenth century boasted two hundred and twenty-eight volumes, and for others a convivial drinking society which went by the name of the Knights of Malhue.

Such diversions can hardly have mitigated the boredom and apprehension of the life, a life led in Aleppo and elsewhere by scores of Frenchmen, Dutchmen, Venetians and Englishmen over a period of centuries. One must not, however, be over-sentimental about these people. If they were martyrs, they were martyrs to their purses. Their own interest brought them there, and the interest of the authorities saw to it that the indignities and violences they had to support rarely became intolerable. The romance of difficulty and adventure attach far more to the travellers who from the end of the seventeenth century came in ever-increasing number to explore the Syrian countryside; archaeologists, scientists or simply inquisitive minds, they were a striking advertisement to the alert interest of their age, and included men such as Wood, who first mapped Palmyra, the conscientious Bishop Pococke, Niebuhr, Volney and not least the great Burkhardt. Accused of digging for treasure when they were mapping ancient sites, robbed of their scientific instruments which were thought to be magical apparatus, these travellers rediscovered Syria and the Levant in difficult circumstances.

Their rediscovery helped to awake in Europe 'the glamour of the East', and on their heels followed romantic travellers such as Lady Hester Stanhope. With the handicap of being both a woman and a Christian, Lady Hester achieved a position in Muslim Syria which would appear incredible had it not been attested by numbers of her contemporaries. Granddaughter to the great Chatham, and hostess to the younger Pitt, she had already passed her first youth when, disillusioned with European society, she arrived at Sidon in 1812. Of the stories that followed her, the majority were untrue. Though completely unconventional, she was nothing of a libertine. She was indeed rather the reverse, and it is characteristic that her love for Sir John Moore, which she came to regard as the great sentiment of her life, should have remained platonic.[1] Her vitality and force of character rather than her feminine charm enabled her for a generation to play the part she did in Syrian political affairs and in the affections of the Syrian people. Neither beautiful nor pretty, she was both noble and imposing; her manly qualities of courage, generosity, enterprise and boundless self-confidence won her the respect of the Arabs. 'She thinks no more of money than of dirt,' one of them said, 'and as for fear she does not know what it is.' The woman who as a child had planned to launch a boat and row alone to France was perhaps the only woman in Europe who could have established herself in this hostile anti-feminist country.

That she exercised her talents in Syria rather than in Europe may be explained on two grounds. Incorrigibly romantic, she was caught, like so many others after her, by the glamour of the Arab world. Further, and perhaps even more important, she was something of a megalomaniac. Difficult and self-obsessed, she could bear neither contradiction nor rivalry. Chatham's granddaughter would divide the honours with no one; she needed a stage to herself, and in Syria she found one.

From the moment of her arrival she set out to impress the authorities, and did so with astonishing success. Soon, as no other woman had been, she was talking on terms of equality with pashas, and making her entry on horseback and unveiled – an unbelievable audacity – into the sacred city of Damascus. It was in the flush of her first triumph that she devised and executed the expedition to Palmyra which won for her the freedom of the Bedouin tribes and with it a position which remained hardly shaken until her death. The authorities regarded the scheme as fantastic and impossible. Friends and pashas alike tried to dissuade her; no white woman had ever been to Palmyra, and no pass could take her there, for the Bedouin tribes that ruled the inner deserts did not acknowledge the authority of the central government. Lady Hester Stanhope with characteristic directness went straight to the Bedouin themselves. In March 1813 the thing was accomplished, and this extraordinary woman rode into Zenobia's ruined capital. The determination with which she had surmounted the considerable difficulties of the journey, her air of imperturbable authority, and not least her horsemanship, had profoundly impressed the Bedouin. With a fine sense of the dramatic they prepared a worthy reception. Arab dancers and Arabic music greeted the cavalcade at whose head she rode clad in Bedouin dress, and

---

[1] Moore paid her the tribute of his dying words at Corunna: 'Stanhope, remember me to your sister.'

among the ruined columns she was solemnly crowned Queen of the East and given the freedom of the desert. It was her great moment, perfectly appealing to her sense of power and sense of the romantic. She had stepped into the middle of the stage; she was to monopolize it until the day of her death.

After the limelight of Palmyra the idea of return to Europe grew distasteful to her, and she finally decided to settle near Djoun, a village in the hills behind Sidon. The half-ruined convent that she had taken soon became the most important place in the district. From its walls her secret agents were dispatched all over Syria. There was indeed nothing in which the Queen of the East with her restless energy did not presume to interfere, often to the embarrassment of the authorities. It was said that no one came to her in vain for help or protection, and at times of political disturbance Djoun assumed almost the appearance of a refugee camp. Even the Porte respected such a sanctuary, while on different occasions she openly defied both the Emir Bechir of the Lebanon and the great Mahomet Ali of Egypt. The latter, when in control of Syria, said that Lady Hester gave him more trouble than all the insurgents put together. The author of *Eothen*, who stayed at Djoun for a couple of days, describes how this strange woman preserved a free enclave in a world of tyranny: 'In truth this half-ruined convent, guarded by the proud heart of an English gentlewoman, was the only spot throughout Syria and Palestine in which the will of Mehemet Ali and his fierce lieutenant was not law . . . and so long as Chatham's granddaughter breathed a breath of life, there was always one hillock, and that too in the midst of a most populous district, which stood out and kept its freedom.'

Lady Hester's renown brought a stream of visitors to Djoun, until in the later years of her life she closed her doors to Europeans. These visitors brought back strange stories. Less kind than the Arabs, who regarded her as a holy woman, a being apart, they plainly said that she was mad. Eccentric she undoubtedly was, and as time went on she became more and more wrapped in occultism and subject to curious fancies. A sacred horse lived in her stables and a mad soothsayer – an old general of Napoleon's – enjoyed the hospitality of her house. At the same time her prejudices were on a comprehensive scale, and she developed a morbid dislike of women, missionaries and the English nation. In her later years she rose only in the afternoon and received her visitors in the twilight. They were not to see how the almost fabulous face was ageing. A European who first met her in the house of one of the

great Druze sheiks thus described her: 'Reclining . . . with crossed legs
à l'orientale, smoking a long and elegantly mounted nargileh, was a tall
and splendid figure dressed in a long saffron-coloured robe with red
stripes, an embroidered sadrieh, fastened at the throat by an aigrette
of gold, whose appearance, though somewhat wan, was dignified and
majestic. . . . Her right hand grasped the stem of her pipe . . . and in
her left she held a long rosary of amber, the beads of which she let fall
one by one in slow succession.' [1] In spite of her position it was really a
lonely life that she led. Her qualities commanded obedience and admiration rather than affection. Her visitors were many, but her friends were
few. As the years went by, financial difficulties were added to her
loneliness. She had lived a legend on a very expensive scale.

Djoun is situated in the hills inland from Sidon, and the journey is
worth making. Lady Hester's convent is some twenty minutes away
from the village. The little hill on which it stands falls sharply away on
three sides, affording tremendous views seaward and northward. The
only tenants now are a peasant family who live in two or three of the
rooms. Chickens wander across the courtyard, and there is a single cow
in the stables that once housed her blood mares. The crickets are vocal
in the sun, and a barley field grows up to the sills of the windows. The
atmosphere is melancholy, and the desertion cries for the bold eccentric
figure that once gave a meaning to the rambling buildings. Her tomb – a
simple and satisfactory affair – lies amid olive-trees, in front of the house
where the views are widest. One would like to think that it marks the
spot where her arbour stood, and where, on a bearskin rug, embowered
with jasmine and rose laurel, she received with royal dignity Kinglake,
Lamartine, and so many more who made the pilgrimage to see her.

The treatment accorded to Lady Hester Stanhope in Syria was, as
we have indicated, very different from that experienced by the Franks
in general. It is to Hama, not to Djoun, that one must go to recapture
the 'feel' of the Turkish period as the average Frank knew it. To Hama
the West has penetrated less than to any of the other large towns in
Syria, and there, in a very lovely setting, the world of the Levant
Company merchants has survived. Islam colours and conditions its
temper, and there can be few places outside the Holy Cities of Arabia
where the Faith has remained so aggressive and fanatic. As in the
eighteenth century, the Muslim is ipso facto the master and the Christian
dog exists on sufferance. As for Jews, not one is allowed in the town.
Faith prohibits the sale of alcoholic drinks in hotels and public places

[1] Quoted in Joan Haslip's Lady Hester Stanhope, London, 1934.

(though beer fortunately is not regarded as alcoholic). The women are
veiled with the greatest strictness, a practice in part responsible for the
effective survival of the vice which the West calls 'unnatural', but which
came easily enough to the Turks. Even the Syrian Christians adopt a
protective mimicry, veiling their women and assuming a Muslim pose
whenever they can, while the sisters of the *Sacré Cœur* are obliged to
tuck their crucifixes out of sight when they go abroad. The mosques are
always crowded at prayer time and the movement of the *suks* seems to
overflow into them spontaneously. Faith intrudes even on merchan-
dising, and it is with something like envy that the European observes a
pressure of conviction that admits no teasing query. There are times
when the intensity of the town's belief seems to excuse all that it
involves of intolerance and prejudice.

The Great Mosque with its wide sunlit court and columned treasury,
the latter not unlike that in the Great Mosque at Damascus, is the focus
of Hama's life. It is built upon the site of an earlier Byzantine basilica.
The carved lintel and capitals of what was once presumably the west
door of the church are particularly fine, but it is inappropriate here to
regret the classical and Christian past. That even such stones should
remain is recognizably fortuitous in a place where the tide of Islam runs
so strongly and so deep. At Hama the stranger understands better than
elsewhere in the country what must have been the initial force of that
religion which overspread half the Byzantine Empire and submerged
all ancient Syria. The terrifying power of belief, and the absolute
demands its makes upon passions and energies, good or bad, remain
evident in this lovely and aggressive pocket in the plains. It is the spirit
of the Islamic past that moves in the narrow streets, and the European
will wish to pay it due respect.

The economic organization of the town and district dates with equal
completeness from the past. Most of the wealth is in the hands of four
families who rule the town and its dependent 'slave' villages with a
power almost absolute. Even the great wheels which furnish the town's
water supply are privately owned. In such a setting of faith and
feudalism it is not surprising that the population should be notoriously
farouche, hostile not only to the European, but even to the neighbouring
inhabitants of Homs, and indeed to all ideas and persons unfamiliar.
Their mood is expressed in sudden violences and rash riots, such as the
Frankish merchants once feared. Prior to 1932 disturbances closed the
Hama *suks* twenty-one times in three years, and the same sporadic
unpredictable outbreaks still occur. It is a place of fanatical certainties

and uncertain passions which it is difficult for the western mind to comprehend.

Even the position of the town symbolizes its enclosure in Islam and the past. The Orontes eats its way – no other phrase describes it – through the dry plain, and the windings of the river are overshadowed by cliffs and high escarpments. Hama, lying on the river, is thus in a sunken world. Above are the plains and winds; below there is no view outward and the escarpment encircles the town. The lower air is motionless, hot, damp and rich, bringing passions and plants to equally sudden fruition. The stranger, descending into this sealed town where, from the world above, no thought or sound can penetrate, breathes the atmosphere and is drugged. He is also delighted, for the winding Orontes is beautiful. The endless gardens that the river waters and creates, with their bewildering variety of fruit, are famous. The Hama houses cling to the river, press upon it, are built over it, and the activity of the people follows the water. They drink it, use it for their mosques and gardens, and the boys bathe in the deep pool in the middle of the town. It is impossible to lose consciousness of the river; not only is it always reappearing in its serpentine course where the stranger least expects to find it, but the drone of the water-wheels, not unlike the sound of a distant aeroplane, is never for a moment absent. These gigantic wooden water-wheels, *norias* as they call them, are the things most characteristic of Hama. Built, many of them, centuries ago, they continue to supply the town and orchards with water to the accompaniment of their droning and oddly nostalgic music. They function with a minimum of efficiency, slopping in long cascades half the water they raise, and creaking and groaning in every wooden joint. Into this setting of water-wheels, and houses that overhang the water, modern building barely intrudes, and there are only a handful of shops. To buy anything the purchaser must go to the *suks*. These remain extraordinarily unspoilt and, with their local costume and colour, have preserved a fine tradition of cotton and linen printing, perhaps the most attractive of the remaining Syrian handicrafts. Printing by hand on natural stuffs, the craftsmen employ designs, mainly in black, cobalt blue, or red, which have been handed down for generations. The result is a product of great simplicity and charm.

Hama, besides taking one back to the Turkish past, provides a clue to a most important aspect of that past. By eleven o'clock on a summer morning the café-terrace by the river, shaded with vines and mulberry-trees, is already filling up; with the air of having more than all the day to

G

spend, the clients drink their coffee or sherbet and pull ruminatively at their long pipes. Already, throughout the town, courtyards, fountains and wells of shade are playing their part in the elaborate cult of idleness. This cult, the despair of the administrator, makes for half the charm and preserves half the charming things in the towns of Syria. The traveller, who has no reason to demand immediate activity from the lounging hierophants, can only be grateful for a tradition which contributes so much to the grace of his surroundings. The Turkish pashas and the rich men of the country, in their time, brought this cult to a fine perfection and in so doing made a contribution to civilization whose value the West is inclined to ignore. Over-critical of the Turkish period rather than the reverse, the European ironically enough condemns the Turk as much for his virtues as his vices. Suffering himself from chronic activity, he finds it difficult to appreciate the ability to be gracefully still. Whatever his failings, the Turk organized his leisure with studied good taste. Even the nagging, persistent heat of the East was, in his private life, turned to good account, since the elaborate search for secluded cool and quiet produced the most successful and salient features of the houses of the Turkish period. The qualities of these houses are nowhere better revealed than in the Azem Palace at Hama.

Built in the first half of the eighteenth century by the governor of Hama, Azad Pasha el Azem (who was responsible for the more famous but no more charming palace of the same name at Damascus), the Hama palace exhibits many of the best features of Ottoman architecture in Syria. The general characteristics of such buildings are fairly uniform: the masonry for decorative effect is often laid in courses of different coloured stone, black and white or buff and white, and the rooms give directly on an open courtyard in whose centre is a fountain. (At Hama the view across the Orontes was a cool and natural attraction, and the architect who built the Azem Palace made the most of it by placing a second courtyard on the first floor overlooking the river.) An important feature in the arrangement of these buildings is the main courtyard. In a country where for months at a time it never rains, the courtyard is regarded as an essential part of the house, and there exists no rigid distinction between indoors and out. The courtyard is treated with almost the same care as the interior. One or two trees are carefully grown for shape and shade, and every inch of the floor is tiled and spotlessly clean, while, at one end, house and courtyard actually mingle in the *liwan*. This is a high-roofed room open to the court, with divans arranged around three sides, where in the hot weather the inmates can

sit and enjoy the air. In the interior of the house proper, the tiles and
the fountains are repeated, for the Turk in a hot country wisely saw no
reason why water should not be as appropriate in a room as in a courtyard. Marble floors and fountains, faience tiles, carved and painted
ceilings and walls of painted panelling (where fruits and birds and
cypress-trees look cool and fresh) characterize the enclosed privacy of
the women's *haremlik* and the *qaa*, the room of stately reception. Much
thought and labour are expended on a triple objective: coolness, dignity
and quiet. In such settings the Turkish governors and the great men
reclined in their Damascene silks and upon their Damascene brocades,
and in such a favourable atmosphere, with their amber-lipped pipes
at hand, they cultivated the elaborate Turkish courtesies and the ritual
of doing nothing with elegance. It is possible for the West to disapprove
of such static activity, but quite impossible not to admire the excellence
of the technique.

Of the more ambitious houses of the Ottoman period that remain,
only the Emir Bechir's eyrie at Beit-ed-Din rivals (in splendour if not in
taste) the Azem Palaces at Damascus and Hama. More modest houses
are, however, to be found all over Syria and one such, of particular
charm, lies just across the river from the Azem Palace at Hama. It is a
long, low, rambling building whose feet are in the water and whose
balconies overhang it; the rooms echo the sound of the river. Dating
from various periods, it has for centuries ministered to the eastern love
of cool retirement. No windows give on the street, and beyond the low
doorway the dust and heat of the East are excluded with calculated care.
As in all these houses, the sudden transition from noise and dirt to
stillness and scrubbed stone creates much of the effect. Belonging to the
Keylani family, one of the four powers of Hama, it remains in use as a
private house and thus serves to give the stranger an insight, juster
perhaps than that derived from more imposing buildings, into the
graces of a traditional way of life that survives among many well-to-do
Syrians. In such houses the ritual of courtesy and quiet unostentatious
leisure continues, hardly modified by the bustle of the West.

Such things alone do not, alas, make a civilization. Though private
life might survive the slow rot of maladministration and the inertia,
which beginning in the Mameluke period was accelerated under the
Turks, the country as a whole was tragically affected. Only the Lebanon
in some degree escaped.

This resistant capacity of the Lebanon was due to the special history
of the area which, in its turn, was largely the outcome of Lebanese

geography. The Lebanon is a mountain, or more properly a brief but emphatic mountain range. The very word Lebanon means the White One, and it is not unnatural that in the dry desertic Middle East the Mountain should have derived its name from its snows. The range is narrow and only some eighty or ninety miles long. Running due north and south, it rises on one side with determined splendour straight from the lapping Mediterranean. In some places the climb, which takes its summits to just short of ten thousand feet, seems to have begun far under water and the cliffs rise dripping, as it were, from the sea with no natural pause for beach or coastal road. Rarely is there more than a mile's momentary hesitation between sea edge and the first mountain rampart. To the east, facing the deserts, the mountains fall away with a similar dramatic abruptness, dropping in great jolting steps, a thousand feet at a time, down to the alluvial plain of the Bk'aa. Facing sea and desert, the range is a natural retreat and fortress, and such history has for centuries proved it, associating its name indissolubly with that of the Maronite Church.

It is not easy to approach the Maronites objectively since their history is coloured with the glamour that attaches to the struggle of a determined minority. In the East religious minorities usually pay for their continued existence in deformation of character. Cunning and servility are their only weapons. The mountain Maronites, through the preservation of a precarious independence, have escaped this fate. They have not only survived, but have survived uncowed. The remarkable nature of their history is paralleled by the strange birth of the sect some thirteen hundred years ago. At that date the Emperor Heraclius, energetic and well-meaning, fresh from his conquests over the Persians and keen to achieve unity within his empire, was casting about for some compromise, some religious platform, which would enable him to reconcile the schismatics of Syria and Egypt, who maintained the existence of a single nature in Christ (hence their name *Monophysites*), with the orthodox Byzantine Church. On his way back to Byzantium from the east, perhaps in A.D. 629, it is said that he happened to stop at the Monastery of St Maron which lay on the Orontes between Homs and Hama. There he found current among the monks, side by side with an orthodox belief in the dual personality of Christ, an original insistence on the single nature of His *will*. This appeared to offer just the loophole for which the Emperor was looking.[1] The new doctrine received imperial

[1] Actually the Emperor had probably been conversant with Monothelite ideas several years before the time of his supposed visit to the monastery of St Maron.

support and the Christian world was asked, indeed ordered, to settle its differences upon the basis of this compromise. At first it looked as though the Emperor might be successful. Fate, however, was against him. Though the four great patriarchal sees – Rome, Constantinople, Alexandria and Antioch – appeared initially favourable to the new belief, the Bishop of Jerusalem, in his zeal for orthodoxy, sounded the alarm. Rome soon took up the note, and the belief in a single will was finally and officially anathematized by the Sixth General Council of the Church in 680. Thus the Emperor in the end succeeded only in creating one more obscure heresy, the Monothelite.

However, in the region where the new belief had first been formulated, the heresy became orthodoxy and the imperial intervention launched the Maronite Church. Macarius, patriarch of Antioch, at the Council of 680 set the tone that the Maronites were for many centuries to adopt when he cried that he would rather be hewn piecemeal and thrown into the sea than acknowledge the existence of two wills in the person of Christ. Of the early fortunes of the sect little precise is known. Justinian II, invading Muslim Syria in about 685, did all that he could to cripple the Monothelites whom he probably regarded both as Christian heretics and political traitors. Twelve thousand were transported to Thrace. The famous monastery on the Orontes (which his predecessor Justinian I had fortified) was destroyed and five hundred of the schismatic monks were executed. It was at about this time that the Maronites in despair deserted the plains and took to the fastnesses of the northern Lebanon which were to be their permanent stronghold. In so doing they limited the sphere of their influence but ensured its continuity. The name of Maronite, first used by John the Damascene in the eighth century, is of uncertain origin. It may have derived from St Maron, the fifth-century hermit whose retreat on the Orontes provided the site for the great Monothelite monastery (the name being thus, as Gibbon says, 'insensibly transferred from a hermit to a monastery, and from a monastery to a nation'), or again the eponymic may have been derived from John Maron, reputed to have been the first Maronite patriarch, and the moving spirit in the exodus to the mountains and in the subsequent organization of the mountain church. Not long after this exodus, the Mardaites appeared in the northern Lebanon, a Christian group with whom the Maronites have often been confused. The arrival of the newcomers was a result of Byzantine policy. Semi-independent auxiliaries of the Empire, they came down from the Taurus under the leadership of Byzantine officers who established them in the mountains to act as a thorn in the side of the Muslims. As such they were outstandingly successful until the Umayyad administration managed to buy off imperial support. The ensuing discomfiture of the Mardaites proved pure gain to the Maronites; their routed units were in part absorbed by the mountain sect. Henceforth they were to be indistinguishable.

Abbasid rule which brought humiliation to Umayyad Syria did not fail to bring persecution and exactions to the Syrian Christians. In the northern Lebanon revolt followed. The Maronites at first were successful, doubtless owing to the military experience of the Mardaite elements which they had incorporated. Initial victory, however, tempted them from the Mountain and in attacking Baalbeck they met with disaster. Severe repression followed, and little more is heard of the Maronites for over three hundred years. However, they were still established in the Mountain when the Crusaders arrived. With the latter, apparently after some hesitation, they decided to throw in their lot and, in due course, became so committed to their new allies that some of them thought it wiser to leave for Cyprus with the eventual failure of the crusading enterprise. Alliance with the Crusaders meant closer ties with Rome, and thus had far-reaching results, which have modified the nature of the Maronite Church through subsequent centuries. Though the union then achieved, by which the Pope recognized the right of the head of the Maronite Church to his picturesque title of 'Patriarch of Antioch and All the East', did not outlast Frankish rule, it marked a change in religious policy. The advantages of alliance with the powerful Latin organization were thenceforth evident, and in future Maronite theologians preferred to stress their orthodoxy rather than their separatism. A century and a half after the Crusaders left, the Maronites began again to tighten those bonds which ever since have linked them closely to the papacy. In 1441 a Maronite and Druze delegation left for Italy, and in 1584 Gregory XIII founded the Maronite College at Rome, which not only played a decisive part in the organization of the Lebanese Church throughout the Turkish period, but produced a series of scholars of the first order, whose learning, infiltrating the local Church, enabled the Maronites to maintain a decided intellectual superiority over their neighbours. The material was there – a Maronite had translated Homer into Syriac, and for centuries the Maronites had provided scribes and financial secretaries up and down the coast – and the college at Rome gave it shape. Joseph Assemani, an eighteenth-century scholar of international repute, to whom the Vatican library owes many of its finest manuscripts, was typical of what the college could produce at its best.

In 1596 a papal legate appeared at the synod of the Maronite Church to smooth out differences of ritual and dogma. He was to be followed by many others. Of these the most prominent was the same Joseph Assemani, the moving figure in the important council which in 1736 virtually achieved a union of the Churches. This union has been interpreted in a sensible and tolerant way. Though the Maronites recognize the Pope and have adopted various Roman usages and symbols, such as the bishop's mitre and crozier, they continue to permit the marriage of priests, take the rite of confirmation immediately after baptism, and retain their own fasts and saints and not least their own Syriac liturgy.

When the Crusaders retired they did not leave the Maronites to face the displeasure of the Saracens alone. Between the seventh and eleventh centuries two important minorities, the Druzes and the Metwalis, had made their way into the southern Lebanon. Heretical offshoots from Islam, they were united in their opposition to Muslim orthodoxy, and like the Maronites had been gravely compromised during the Crusades. Their relations with the Maronites in the early centuries of their proximity are obscure; it is certain that when, with the co-operation of the Nosairis or Alawis (another religious minority who had reached the extreme north of the Lebanon from the Latakia district), they rose against the Muslim government of Syria a few years after the departure of the last Crusaders, the Maronites did not throw in their lot with the revolt. The rebellion was crushed and the rebels dispersed and decimated. Maronite neutrality proved extremely advantageous, as they indirectly profited from their neighbours' discomfiture, extending their own control over villages which the Druzes had deserted, and acquiring a numerical preponderance in the Lebanon. So successfully indeed did they consolidate their power that the more mountainous parts of Maronite territory had grown virtually independent in the second half of the fifteenth century. It was the effort to maintain this semi-independence which dominated Maronite policy throughout the subsequent four hundred years of Turkish rule and which led to the development of a long and satisfactory understanding with the Druzes, with whom in effect they shared the territory of the Mountain. United the Mountain could stand; divided, as the Turks realized, it must fall. Lebanese history from the sixteenth century until 1840 thus largely records the efforts of the Turk to divide the country, and of one local emir after another to unite it against Ottoman rule. On the whole the emirs were surprisingly successful.

Two among them, the Emirs Fakr-ed-Din and Bechir, were

outstanding, and are the national heroes of the Lebanon. The first was
an exceptional man and has, with reason, become the chief focus of local·
romantic sentiment. For fifty years (1585–1635) he planned, intrigued
and fought for Lebanese independence, and in so doing created the
Greater Lebanon for the first time. His achievement cost him a five
years' exile, and finally his life. In 1613 he was forced to fly the country,
and escaping on a French vessel found a welcome at the court of the
Medicis. Eighteen years after his return to the Lebanon, he left the
country again, a prisoner, going to his death at Constantinople. To
regard him as a Lebanese patriot would be to interpret the early seventeenth century in terms of the twentieth. He was a capable, imaginative
and ambitious man, who had the wisdom to realize that his own future
and fortunes were bound up with those of the Mountain. They prospered
together. Fakr-ed-Din's administration laid the foundations of that
security which made the Lebanon in the seventeenth and eighteenth
centuries as safe as any district in the Turkish Empire. A wise agricultural policy allowed no land to lie fallow, increased the mulberry and
olive plantations, and created new villages. A brilliant commercial
policy had even more striking results. Fakr-ed-Din realized that the
position of the Lebanon made it the natural channel of trade with
Europe. The devastated and idle ports were accordingly repaired and
everything done to attract European merchants. Their capitulations
were honoured and the humiliating disabilities from which they suffered
elsewhere in the Ottoman Empire were swept away. As the Emir had
expected, the Franks came in force and the ports of Sidon and Beyrouth
knew a period of thriving activity. Finally, the Emir's breadth of
character and policy enabled him to disregard local sects and jealousies
and to give the Lebanon a new unity. Carefully non-committal himself
in matters of religion – his subjects hardly knew if he were Muslim,
Druze or Christian – he enlisted support from all quarters and from
all sects, and insensibly drew the Mountain together. The resulting co-
operation of Druze and Christian was, for nearly two hundred and fifty
years, an embarrassment to the Turks. Fakr-ed-Din's contacts with the
Florentine Renaissance were as useful to him in the pursuit and elabora-
tion of his policies, as were his Florentine engineers in the execution of
his harbour works. A remarkable prince, and in some senses an enlight-
ened one, his reputation was outstanding in his lifetime, and history has
done him more than justice. His political methods were dubious. He
stabbed his closest adviser with his own hand. On other occasions
proxies were no doubt available.

Apart from the *khan* which the Emir established for the French merchants at Sidon (*see page 50*), little of his building survives. It is possible that in his lost palaces the Italian Renaissance style may have made a brief and early appearance on the Syrian littoral.

Time has been kinder to the buildings of the Emir Bechir, though not to his reputation. If he is a national hero, it is chiefly because throughout a life of over eighty years (1767–1850) he dominated the fortunes of the Lebanon, disputing its control with all comers, and extending its territories and autonomy almost to the limits achieved by Fakr-ed-Din. Like his predecessor he realized that his own strength was bound up with that of the Mountain, and accordingly gave in prosperity and justice as much as he took in taxes. But if his public justice was inflexible, so was his private revenge. His magnificent head with its piercing eyes, and his huge black beard, told of amazing physical and mental vitality; they were responsible for much of his personal magnetism, but they successfully concealed, as many found to their cost, an unscrupulous cunning that did not spare even his own family.

The success and character of the Emir are exemplified in the romantic and curious palace that he built. He was a mountain man, and the site he chose was therefore his mountain stronghold of Beit-ed-Din; but he was also an oriental potentate and into his mountain palace he accordingly introduced every refinement that a sense of luxury and the ingenuity of the time could contrive. Warburton, writing of the palace soon after it was built, described it as an 'Isola Bella, with all its gardens, terraces and pavilions, upheaved from the Lago Maggiore, and placed like a crown on a majestic mountain'. The setting still remains wonderfully impressive, as do the terraces and gardens whose fountains are fed with the waters brought by the Emir's nine-mile aqueduct. The buildings seem to float above the valley and their wealth and scale are unexpected in a setting of mountain peasants and spare mountain earth. On the other hand it is impossible to be as whole-heartedly enthusiastic about the details of the palace as were the early nineteenth-century travellers. Even the architectural and decorative fantasy which has gained so wide a repute is neither very original nor very daring when compared to many contemporary Turkish rococo buildings, such as the palaces on the Bosphorus or the *papier mâché* splendour of Shubra in Egypt. The severity of the Mountain appears to have exercised a certain restraint on architect and craftsmen; thus the outstanding feature of the place today is the simple excellence of the stone-work, everywhere so characteristic of the Lebanese builders. This excellence

* G

is best appreciated in the main courtyard, where the masonry has taken
on a pleasant patina and the delicacy of the arches creates an impression
of unusual lightness. Inside the palace, though the stone carving is
good, there is too much dull geometric-arabesque, in mosaic or inlay,
and too little is preserved of the painted walls and painted stucco which
must have constituted the main charm of the interior when first completed. This charm is best recaptured in what was apparently the Emir's
private study where an amusing oriel, some delightful flower-panels
and vestiges of plaster decoration remain. On this room and on the
palace *hammam*, or Turkish bath, the Emir evidently expended much
care. The latter was unfortunately badly damaged during the allied
advance in 1941, but has since been well restored. Its size and the care
lavished on the decoration of each of its chambers illustrate well enough
how important a part the *hammam* played in that cult of leisure which,
as we have seen, gave grace to the Turkish period. Warburton, who was
privileged to enjoy the baths as a guest of the Emir's, tells of the
impression that they made upon him with their pale marble walls, their
crystal streams falling into alabaster basins, their muted subaqueous
light. Wooden pattens inlaid with mother-of-pearl, silver ewers, exquisite linens, iced sherbets, drowsy heat, all provided an appropriate
contrast to the dry burning sun and craggy roads which had led the
traveller to Beit-ed-Din. The sequel to the bath, when the traveller
reclined on silken cushions by an arched window, through which cool
breezes filled with orange perfumes reached him from the gardens, was
equally delectable. 'The bubbling of fountains, the singing of birds, the
whispering of trees, were the only sounds that reached the ear. The
slaves glided about silently and somnambulistically; or stood with
folded arms watching for a sign. If the languid eye was lifted to the
window, it found a prospect of unequalled splendour over the mountains
to the sea; and nearer were rich gardens, and basins full of goldfishes,
swimming about with such luxurious motion that it rested the eyesight
to follow them. There were amber-mouthed pipes of delicious Latakia,
and fragrant coffee, and sherbet cooled in the fountain, and black slaves
to wipe our hands with gold-embroidered napkins.'

It is curious to think of the muscular Emir, come direct from some
deep-laid ruse or sudden catastrophic vengeance, in the passive relaxation of the marble hot room with the perspiration pearling that vast
spade beard. Later, cooled and freshened, in the magnificent Turkish
robes which his pictures reveal, it was from the baths that he must often
have gone to receive and charm the curious Westerners who were

granted an audience in the throne room. Lamartine has described romantically enough his introduction into the Emir's presence.

Nous fûmes introduits [he says] dans une très-belle salle dont le pavé était de marbre, et les plafonds et les murs peints de couleurs vives et d'arabesques élégantes par des peintres de Constantinople. Des jets d'eau murmuraient dans les angles de l'appartement, et dans le fond, derrière une colonnade dont les entre-colonnements étaient grillés et vitrés, on apercevait un tigre énorme, dormant la tête appuyée sur ses pattes croisées. – La moitié de la chambre était rempli de secrétaires; . . . d'Arabes riche-ment vêtus et armés; de nègres et de mulâtres attendant les ordres de leur maître, et de quelques officiers égyptiens . . . – L'autre partie de l'apparte-ment était plus élevée d'environ un pied, et un large divan de velours rouge, régnait tout autour. L'émir était accroupi à l'angle de ce divan. – C'était un beau viellard à l'œil vif et pénétrant, au teint frais et animé; . . . une robe blanche, serrée par une ceinture de cachemire, le couvrait tout entier, et le manche éclatant d'un long et large poignard sortait des plis de sa robe . . . et portait une gerbe de diamans de la grosseur d'une orange.

Bechir's extraordinary career, with its no less extraordinary vicissi-tudes (he had to escape from the country on four occasions), coincided with a period in which Lebanese affairs were taking a new turn and growing yet more complicated. In the first place foreigners, from the time of Napoleon's expedition onward, had played an important part in Turko-Lebanese politics, and even the Emir, scheming in his mountain palace, found it at times impossible to play off all the interests involved. In the second place there was a serious deterioration in Maronite-Druze relations and their fruitful co-operation was drawing to an end. This was primarily due to the growing influence of France in the Lebanon, used exclusively to bolster the Maronites, and because the Druze jealousies and apprehensions so created were exploited and encouraged by the Turks and apparently also by the English. Further the Maronite and Druze communities were themselves undergoing structural altera-tion and their old feudal organization was breaking down. As long as the Emir Bechir, who could command the obedience of both parties, remained on the scene there was no serious open rupture. Not until his final exile in 1840 did the trouble begin which was to culminate in the Druze massacre of the Maronites in 1860. This event, by precipitating the intervention of the European powers, marked a new era in the history of the Mountain. In 1864, owing to European pressure and the French military expedition, the Porte was prevailed upon to provide for the peculiar position of the Mountain and officially to recognize the semi-autonomy for which the Maronites had so long been struggling. A Lebanese enclave was created, much smaller than the Greater Lebanon of the Emirs, but containing the majority of the Maronites. It was

given a Christian governor and depended directly from the Porte rather
than from the local Turkish pasha. This arrangement persisted until the
collapse of the Turkish Empire after the First World War.

The centuries during which the Maronites schemed, and intrigued, to
maintain a semi-independence against the Turks are those in which we
know most of the organization of the Mountain and of the life they lived
there, for it was the age of the travellers. The traveller Sandys in 1611
saw the Emir Fakr-ed-Din, and others before and after him penetrated
into the Lebanon. The picture they have drawn is an attractive one.
The Christian Mountain was in spirit a theocracy, comparable almost to
Mount Athos, but with one essential and salutary difference; owing to
the hostile forces that permanently surrounded it, this theocracy dared
not antagonize its own members and was thus forced to avoid a despotic
absolutism. The Patriarch of Antioch and All the East, the first man in
the Mountain, resided at Kanoubin; under him the same liberal supply
of bishops as had characterized the early Church presided over a number
of minute sees. Convents and monasteries were perched, as they are
today, on every crag and mountain spur. There were some two hundred
of them in the eighteenth century, observing the rule of St Anthony
and on the whole successfully escaping the accusations of immorality
which laymen level at such institutions. To say that ecclesiastic intrigue
did not trouble the Mountain would be untrue, but the framework in
which these churchmen lived usually served to keep holy plots and
tongues within bounds. The civil administration, representing the
Mountain in its relations with the Porte, was closely linked to the
Church. Officially the Mountain depended from the Pashalik of Tripoli,
but it was not garrisoned by Turkish troops and the administration in
each area was in practice left to local Maronite officials with the title of
mokaddam. These were usually chosen from among the sheiks of the
Mountain, and their dealings with the Turks were apt to be limited to
the dispatch of the annual tribute which the Mountain was expected to
furnish. Even this tribute, usually raised from the profits on their vines
and silk-worms, was at times withheld, as happened during Fakr-ed-Din's
lifetime. The tendency to independence of action was most marked in
the heart and height of the Mountain, and though the Turk might
encroach along the seaboard, at Becharré, perched above the precipitous
Kadischa Valley, the *mokaddam* for considerable periods maintained a
token autonomy for the whole Maronite nation.

If the internal organization of the Mountain had differed, the role of
oppressor, in the absence of the Turk, might well have been filled by the

local chiefs and those prominent families from among whose members the various *mokaddams* were chosen. At it was, the Maronite feudal system incorporated strong democratic elements, and each village community elected its chief in much the same way and spirit as do the Bedouin their paramount sheiks. Government was by usage and custom and the governors on the whole found it necessary to regard the wishes and interests of the mountaineers. Further, the nature of the country, which enabled each village to be turned into a strong post capable of self-defence, made the extension of power from any one centre and by any one man extremely difficult. Finally, the even distribution of wealth, or perhaps more truly its general absence, tended to produce an egalitarian way of life. All lived by their labours and their orchards, the sheik as well as the peasant, and even the priest, six days a week, turned out to work the land. They were in the main, as a European noted in the sixteenth century, an active and intelligent people. A nation of hard-working peasant communities, with a love of independence, they exhibited the characteristic peasant conservatism and respect for order. This respect unfortunately ceased where blood-feuds were concerned. Though vendettas troubled the Mountain, it was none the less possible in the eighteenth century for the stranger to travel in the Christian Lebanon by day or by night with a security almost unknown elsewhere in the Levant. In a country where the only military force was a local militia, spontaneously created when external danger threatened, no soldiery infested the roads, and in the mountains where only habitual hard work could squeeze a living there was nothing to attract a vagabond population. It was the peasant traditionalism of the Maronites that made them cling to the Syriac tongue, a last sign and legacy of their Aramaic origin, which in the Mountain fortress held out for centuries against all-invading Arabic. As late as the fifteenth century it was the tongue that Latin missionaries among the Maronites had to learn if they were to win over the population and, though from the eighteenth century it disappeared as a spoken idiom, it still persists in their church services. Today in the Lebanese villages, though the gospel readings are in Arabic, the peasants respond to the liturgy in a language they do not understand, but whose survival symbolizes their own. Both have come through a thousand years of storm.

Established originally in the high mountains at the northern end of the Lebanon, the Maronites have changed their boundaries, withdrawing or extending as population pressures increased or diminished. In the fourteenth and fifteenth centuries they pushed into Kasrawan and began infiltrating down the coast southward from Byblos. In the sixteenth century, though Becharré remained the Maronite stronghold, their whole centre of gravity shifted south, due to the pressure of the Alawis who were coming into the Lebanon from the north. It was at this period that they crossed the Adonis River and established themselves in the mountains and foot-hills near Beyrouth where they have remained ever since. Though their territory varied, their population seems until the late nineteenth century to have remained remarkably stable. William of Tyre, the Crusader chronicler, speaks of forty thousand men capable of bearing arms, and a late eighteenth-century estimate puts the figure at only five thousand less. The nation over this long period probably amounted to something like a hundred thousand or a hundred and twenty thousand. It was only after the constitution of 1864 brought added security that the Maronites began to increase seriously in numbers.[1] Since the population that the Mountain can support is strictly limited, this increase brought with it that tide of emigration which has carried so many of the Lebanese southward to the easy wealth of Egypt or westward to America. Wherever they have gone, the industry and initiative which squeezed a living from rocks and snow have brought them wealth on more fruitful soils. The Maronite Church in America today has tens of thousands of members, *émigrés* that with proper filial gratitude send back a huge sum yearly to enrich the Mountain.

The Mountain is not a place for ruins and antiquities. In Roman times an imperial forest, it later became as we have seen an asylum for struggling minorities, who had not the wealth to build great churches or palaces, and who discouraged the presence of those Mameluke and Turkish governors whose only virtue was often the stone memorial which survived their own removal. Mention has been made of Byblos, and of the monuments to the cult of Adonis situated in the gorge of the river named after him. Of the other historical remains in the Lebanon the famous inscriptions, fifteen kilometres north of Beyrouth, are the most interesting. Their existence, characteristically enough in the Mountain, derives from the way in which geography interferes with human activities. Where the Nahr-el-Kelb River issues into the Mediterranean, the mountains come down to the shore. At certain periods in history they left no room even for a track between the mountainside and the sea. Past this natural obstacle conquerors, moving up or down the coast, have had to squeeze their armies from the beginning of time. The place is striking and – the rock faces offering a good field for the

[1] There are now rather over 300,000.

graver and sculptor – these same conquerors from the second millennium before Christ paused to record on the rocks either their passage or their triumphs. Their inscriptions, in hieroglyphics, cuneiform, Greek, Latin and Arabic, evoke in the most striking way the long, magnificent and depressing pageant of history. Rameses II returning from his campaign against the Hittites, Assarhaddon returning from his victories against Egypt, Nebuchadnezzar having subdued Phoenicia, Caracalla's Third Gaulish Legion on duty far from home, these, and many others, carved history and their names upon a few square yards of rock. Here have always passed men of war, 'captains and rulers clothed most gorgeously, horsemen riding upon horses, all of them desirable young men . . . with chariots, wagons and wheels, and with an assembly of people'. The iron language that soldiers talk and the rattle of arms are almost audible above the noise of the river. In the nineteen-forties the pass was heavily guarded: there were tank traps across the road, and a modern centurion examined your papers. The traveller will also notice, not without a smile, that the nineteenth and twentieth centuries have recorded their exploits on the rock space still available. The Emperor Napoleon III, with customary bad taste, commemorated the French Expedition of 1860 by obliterating one of Rameses II's inscriptions with his own stucco memorial. Other vainglorious graffiti have followed. Allenby's campaign, Gouraud's expedition to Damascus in 1920 and the Anglo-French capture of Syria in 1941, are all momentously recorded, though in none of these operations did the forces concerned come anywhere near the place.

The first conquerors who left their names at the mouth of the Nahr-el-Kelb probably did so not only because they were impressed with it as a strategic obstacle, but because the river from early days appears to have had religious importance. Its course is extraordinary and exhibits those elements of the mysterious and the spectacular likely to appeal to the primitive imagination. Rising from springs under the snows of Mount Sannine, the river passes under a fantastic natural bridge, a massive stone arch some fifty yards across, and carves its way down towards the sea among picturesque but giddy ravines. It is in this setting that the river abruptly disappears into a system of caverns which in size appear to rival the finest in Europe. Though they have been partly explored by boat, their full extent is even today unknown.[1] The river reappears above ground only a few miles from the sea.

[1] There is an interesting account of these caves and their exploration in Edward Thompson's *Crusaders' Coast*. London, 1929.

Flowing parallel to the Adonis River, some eighteen kilometres away, the Nahr-el-Kelb was inevitably connected with the cult of Byblos and Adonis, and a temple to the latter apparently existed near its source. Its more particular association was, however, with the god Anubis. A native of Egypt, this deity was represented as a jackal or as a human being with a jackal's head, and his particular function was to open the way to the land of the dead. He presumably came to the Lebanon with the Osiris legend, for it is related that Isis when searching for her dead husband (*page 60 above*) was aided by the dog Anubis, who became her guide and champion. A connection with the underworld was particularly appropriate for the deity of this underground river, and in the popular mind the caves and the disappearing waters may well have been linked with the land of the dead. The river today retains its association with Anubis: Nahr-el-Kelb means in Arabic the River of the Dog, and is a rough translation of the Roman name, *Lycus Flumen*. At some early period a colossal statue to the dog-god was raised at the mouth of the river, which is reported to have howled whenever enemies approached and to have been audible miles away. Possibly the dog, like the statues in *Erewhon*, became vocal when the wind lay in the right quarter. As late as the eighteenth century, travellers were shown not far off under the sea a mossy rock which they believed to be the fallen god, and today one may still view above the road the emplacement on which the statue is said to have rested.

Down the course of the Nahr-el-Kelb the emphasis is on geography, on landscape, on the visual scene; and this is typical of the Mountain. The emphasis and the interest fall on the country and the people. As nowhere else in Syria the present attracts as conclusively as the past.[1] One's glance is not always directed backward. From a blue sea to a blue sky the Mountain climbs in gigantic terraces. In the foreground are the warm easy foot-hills, Italianate, swathed in olives; plane-trees and acacias overhang the roads, and azaleas the watercourses; there are tidy, red-roofed monasteries each with its clump of umbrella pines and unpretentious views across vineyards and villages to the sea. A stage higher the air tightens and is no longer moist and Mediterranean; the soil is thinner and rock peers through. The world climbs; a long laborious

[1] It might have been expected that the Crusaders, with their love of formidable sites, would have left a strong impress on the Mountain. For strategic reasons, however, they concentrated on the foot-hills north and south of the main Lebanon mass. Monestir, above the source of the Adonis River, guarding the route over the Mountain to Baalbeck, and the large castle of Akkar, appear to have been their only fortresses in the High Lebanon.

heave upward through wild myrtle and laurustinus, with wiry scrub oak gripping the slopes. Where the ravines wind up into the heart of the Mountain the villages assail the rock face like mountaineers. Every patch of cultivation is precious and man-made; the orchard is shored up over the abyss. A voice that floats across to you, and seems a mere stone's throw away, will be three hours by mule track. Only the birds communicate easily. The rock strata here are twisted and torn, and the rock faces betray the action of ice. Your way climbs where the glaciers once came down.

At five or six thousand feet comes the next stage, that graceful pause which every mountain range seems to make between the first long ascent and the bare peaks above. This is the region of cow-bells and yellow broom, of huts that the shepherds inhabit only in summer, of small unexpected valleys crooked in the Mountain's arm. Here in the hollows you meet the first patches of unmelted snow and tread on sward, most green and un-Levantine. It is the region of the large white-bellied Alpine swift, and of small Alpine flowers (unlike the rest of Syria, these mountains have a Mediterranean flora).[1] It is the region where you sit and measure the long way you have come against the peaks that are still three thousand feet above. Along the coast the towns and villages are like toys, and the roads run as they do on maps. The sea appears flat and glassy, and sails scattered across it look like scraps of white paper. On the horizon an isolated pile of cloud hangs over Cyprus. Sometimes at sunset you can even see the island, over seventy miles off. This is a region where you would like to stay.

The last stage is bareness, beyond the last fir and the last juniper. White clouds pull across the mountain summits like birds and you know it means wind above. Their shadows, creating a play of light and shade, give pinnacles and walls of rock the appearance of fluidity and move-ment: palpable deception, for this is essential solidity, *the* solid thing, even grim in its immobility and fixity, in the frightening absence of mov-able gadgets, of handles and appurtenances. The bare slopes lengthen below you as you climb, and the rock faces in the sun shine like steel. This is the region of eagles, of shale, of giddiness, of cutting wind; it is the region of six months' snow. When there is at last nothing more above, and you are yourself the skyline, the urge that drew you up from the café on the coast, from the orange groves and the sound of the waves, is finally and logically satisfied. You have looked over the other side; and there was nothing between you and Persia.

[1] Mount Hermon and the Gebel Druze are also exceptional in this respect.

It is a wonderful range, and the villages and people of the Mountain are worthy of their setting. Only on the narrow beaten track of the tourist, or where the people have been spoilt by contact with the West, does the harmonious compatibility of man and country fail. In most places the people remain much as the earlier travellers found them, and have not lost the virtues that these same travellers admired. Their long political struggle and the effort to squeeze a livelihood from rocks and precipices have made them independent, courageous and provident; the Church has ensured their piety. As Warburton noted a century ago, 'the change from the lowland vassal to the mountain freeman is very striking', the people still retain 'their fearless look, their bold bearing and that respectfulness which so generally accompanies self-respect'. The openness and confidence of the mountain men makes them pleasant to meet or journey amongst, and enables Maronites and Shi'ites, mountain neighbours, to get on well and generously together. To qualities of character is added the picturesque: they are good-looking, and like most mountaineers have an 'air', to which their costume contributes. They favour gay waistcoats, round tight-fitting caps of fur or sheepskin, sheepskin jackets and the characteristic baggy trousers that are associated with old Turkey. These trousers have at the back a curious, non-functional fullness which has been accounted for in various ways. The most ingenious explanation relates to a legend that the Messiah at his second coming is to be born of man, and maintains that the trousers were first adopted in the hope, cherished by every pious wearer, of finding himself the chosen vessel.

The people have remained wholly agricultural, and the ingenuity and perseverance with which they tame the hillsides is remarkable. Whereas in Syria proper they strive for water, here they strive for soil, capturing it from the rocks laboriously, foot by foot. Their terraced vines, piled vertically one above the other, climb to the snows. Their minute orchards are often wedged literally in the faults and crannies of precipices. Such industry has its reward. The very rocks have grown fertile; the Mountain yields oil and wine, figs, peaches, apples, chestnuts, cherries; and its mulberry-trees feed the silk-worm. The forced inactivity of winter, when the ground is under snow, has helped to maintain the local crafts which flourish in the more isolated villages. The charm of these crafts is that they persist without affectation and are usually practised coincidentally with some other occupation. Thus the village barber, when no clients appear, will retire to his loom at the back of the shop, or the grocer to his wood-carving. Though contact with western models has debased the taste of these craftsmen, their technique remains excellent. Happily, where building is concerned, both taste and technique still prevail, and the local tradition produces houses as satisfactory as may be found anywhere around the Mediterranean. The Lebanese are master-builders, with a genius for using stone sensibly and decoratively. As a result the poorest mountain village has a certain architectural dignity. Only near Beyrouth and one or two other places do pretentious and inappropriate villas creep up into the foot-hills, or even, as at Bhamdoun on the Damascus road, find their horrid way four thousand feet up. The salient features of the older local tradition are its beautifully cut stone, which takes with time a fine warm patina; its vaulted ground floors which frequently present an open loggia to the street; and the tall triple ogive window which in houses of any consequence sets off the heavier arches below. The rooms above are spacious, while those on the ground floor, with their thick walls and vaulted roofs, remain cool in the heat of a Lebanese summer and warm enough in winter. The locality has evolved a style suited to its wide range of temperature, eminently liveable, and most pleasing in architectural effect. This style in the simpler one-storey cottages with vaulted roof and arched façade or arched portico is probably indigenous and its architectural origins go back a long way. The same type is found in Arab villages southward into Palestine. The origin of the more complicated two-storey house, with the pointed triple window on the first floor balancing the arches below, presents rather a problem. It has about it something Italianate, and the general effect of the façade is reminiscent on a small scale of Venetian architecture. Eighteenth-century prints of Beyrouth apparently reveal no trace of such houses, and the style seems to have been introduced into the country something over a hundred years ago. It has been tentatively suggested that it was brought in by Italian workmen who may perhaps have been employed by the Emir Bechir. Wherever it came from, it was a happy importation.

The traveller who visits these houses on the Mountain finds them as attractive inside as out. They are apt to be tidy and clean, while the white slips over the chairs and sofas, and the treasures in the 'best' room have a pleasant period flavour, which might be described as Lebanese-Victorian. Cheap coloured prints of medieval romances – knights in armour, ladies and enchanted forests – unmistakably English in origin, must at one time have had a great vogue in the country. They share the walls with faded wedding groups and with (for some unaccountable reason) the crowned and bearded heads of an almost forgotten Europe.

The master of the house sees to it that the visitor is in a mood to enjoy his surroundings: the ritual of entertainment, involving home-made *arak*, or wine from the vineyard, and little dishes to stimulate a thirst, begins coincidentally with arrival. In winter the ritual probably takes place in the snug downstairs room where a piping stove soon thaws out numbed hands and feet; in summer in the large room above that runs the full width of these houses, where a mountain breeze comes freely in through the triple windows and the view falls vertiginous down rock and hillside to the Mediterranean haze below. In a country of believers and architects, the Church has built liberally. Not only every village and every isolated hamlet, but in some districts almost every naturally distinguished site, has its church or chapel. As a general rule the poorer and wilder the district, the more satisfactory is its church architecture. One common type of small unassuming church is of considerable interest. Built of fine masonry, as everything else in the Mountain, it is characterized by a flat roof, round-headed windows and a complete simplicity, relieved only by a light cornice or by shallow stone pilasters, and a solid little belfry. One comes to regard these square belfries, of which half a dozen will sometimes be in view at once, as an integral motif of the landscape. Along the roads one also meets with those touching shrines – a virgin or a saint in a small hutch, a paper rose and a bit of tinsel – familiar in the Austrian Alps. The visitor cannot forget that these are Christian hills.

In the Mountain there is no Baalbeck that one must see at any price, no particular excursion that is inevitable. With the proviso that one keeps north of Beyrouth, attraction is fairly evenly distributed. The charm is general. Each village, each river that carves its way with winding and spectacular labour to the sea, almost each mountain shoulder and hamlet, has something to offer. Perhaps if one wished to indicate an unspoilt yet accessible cross-section of the country – though in the Mountain it must be borne in mind that the Best is the Highest and that mule tracks usually offer more than roads – it would be the road from Batroun over Hardine to Hadet and the Cedars. The route is reasonably spectacular and characteristic. It introduces the traveller to the sense of mountain struggle and achievement, to the tough hospitable stone-built villages, the belfried churches, the open-faced peasants labouring at the vines, the impossible places where no one labours, the fir-trees rooted in the rocks, the stream that eats away the road, and, always recurring, the glimpse of distant flat blue sea, so irrelevant in that upper world. The road passes also, on a ledge above a tremendous waterfall, the ideal mountain valley, sensuous in a cradle of rock, where the Nahr-el-Djos glides down from Kfer Halda among poplars and orchards: a place one will always remember, and to which the memory will return from very different scenes.

Another place which makes a similar impression, though these impressions are personal and hardly to be handed on, is the curious plateau of Lacluc, which for five months lies under snow. It is reached from the valley of the Adonis River by a road that leads up through the most barren of gorges to emerge, at the top of everything, on a pleasant, grassy plateau. Only the jagged peaks are higher. Here the Bedouin migrate with their beasts in the early summer and set their brown tents beside the snow-drifts. These men and their cattle are strangely and movingly out of place, and there are camel tracks in the snow. Sitting before the tents you exchange cigarettes for unleavened bread, white cheese, honey and goats' milk. The woven tents are pitched as in the desert, and all around the camels graze in their usual craning, hungry way – but among Alpine flowers. The attraction of the Mountain consists partly in just this type of contrast. Things Arab and Turkish, the characteristic beasts and gear of the Middle East, you had associated, rightly or wrongly, with flat waterless spaces, with heat and sand. Yet to some extent they have been siphoned up into the Mountain, and have been absorbed into the lives of the mountaineers. The resulting blend is unexpected and poetic. To see mountain guides smoking *hookahs* jerks the imagination out of its usual and travelled paths. To see a train of camels – as you may – plodding ankle deep in snow across the passes, lifts you into Central Turkestan, or anywhere you wish. The traveller's eyes are continually opened; moved by the strangeness of such things, he sees the ordinary paraphernalia of the Mountain, the merely Christian and Alpine, as new and startling.

The heart of the Christian Mountain, both historically and geographically, is the Kadischa Valley. As such, and for its natural beauty, it is a spectacle that the traveller should not miss. This great gorge, winding its way inland from the sea and climbing to over six thousand feet, was the cradle of the early Maronite Church and for centuries its protection. There lay (and lies) the monastery of Kanoubin, founded by Theodosius the Great in the fourth century, and later the seat of the patriarch and the administrative centre of the Church. It was only one among many religious retreats. The gorge, which Lamartine described as a vast nave with the sky for a ceiling, was honeycombed with chapels and the grottoes of anchorites. A seventeenth-century traveller reports eight hundred such dwellings in the rock. The very name of the gorge means the Valley of the Saints, and though these saints are now fewer in number the tradition continues, and the patriarch maintains his summer residence at Diman, just across the gorge from Kanoubin. Becharré, established in a strategic position at the head of the valley, was, as we have seen, the centre of civil resistance to Turkish domination, and it remains today in some sense the spiritual, though no longer the political or economic, capital of the Maronite nation.

The landscape of the Kadischa Valley is unforgettable. The approach from the sea is through orchards of gnarled olive groves beneath which grow in spring iris, anemone, cyclamen, narcissus and orchid. Where the gorge begins, revealing a break in the apparently unassailable mountain face, an awesome Turkish road, which Lamartine described as 'cette route horrible, ou plutôt cette muraille presque perpendiculaire', hairpins its way up the southern side. For the adaptation of this road to wheeled traffic the traveller is apparently indebted, as for so many travel facilities in various parts of the world, to the royal progresses of the Kaiser Wilhelm. The gorge perhaps has never been better described than by an English clergyman who visited it from Aleppo, no mean undertaking, two hundred and fifty years ago. 'There is', he says, 'a very deep rupture in the side of Libanus, running at least seven hours' travel directly up into the mountain. It is on both sides exceeding steep and high, clothed with fragrant greens from top to bottom, and everywhere refreshed with fountains, falling down from the rocks in pleasant cascades, the ingenious work of nature.' The 'rupture' deepens as the road rises, and where the latter creeps along its monstrous lip assumes a terrifying magnificence. Characteristically the economy of mountain life, fighting for a square yard of ground, pushes to the very verge. The cliffs are prolonged as the walls of peasant houses, and fruit trees overhang space. The void is curiously vocal and when the spring snows are melting is full of the echoes of waterfalls that rise to the villages above.

Where the gorge reaches, at Becharré, its wedgelike end, driven in vain against the solid rock, the traveller's attention has already wandered. He is looking up at the snow-covered mountains above and the smooth snowy bowl at their feet, where stand an isolated group of huge dark trees – the Cedars of Lebanon. As the traveller climbs another thousand feet and approaches the trees, their majesty and drama come home with immediate force. Almost the last remnant of the great cedar forests that once covered these slopes, they stand in a spectacular setting. Their position and their age (a dozen of them are well over a thousand years old) have always impressed the mountain people, as the splendour of the original forest impressed the classical world and found a place even in Tacitus' laconic pages, who speaks of the Mountain as *inter ardores opacum fidumque nivibus*. A mass is yearly celebrated in the small chapel under their spreading branches, and the cedars long ago assumed something of the importance of a cult. Locally they are half believed to be tree divinities, and it is said that they are endowed with foreknowledge and can anticipate changes of season. As the first winter blizzard strikes the Mountain, they contract their vast branches like limbs and point them earthward so as to support in the ensuing months the minimum weight of snow. In the spring, or so it is said, they shake off the melting snow like dogs, and extend their branches once again. Though for generations excommunication threatened anyone who dared to damage the trees, the 'forest' steadily dwindled. The outlook now appears to be brighter, for goats which had no regard for the Church's anathema are amenable to other sanctions. The young shoots are now protected and, as the giants fall, other cedars will in due course replace them.

In this bowl the snows are extraordinarily deep. Lamartine, with his horse ploughing up to its knees, failed to reach the cedars in mid April, and had to contemplate them from a distance sitting on a boulder. But the snow which once closed the higher Lebanon in winter now does the reverse, for every year more people come up the Mountain to ski. French officials landing in Beyrouth to set up their mandate saw snow nine thousand feet above, and thought of the Haute Savoie. Soon two pairs of skis arrived; others followed, with waxes, skins and the skier's armoury. It was not long before a small band of enthusiasts each year eagerly awaited the December snow. Their assaults on the Mountain with their curious boards were viewed with incredulous amazement by the Maronite peasants. In due course the best climbs were mapped, the peaks were named and the Club Alpin Français built its refuge huts. By 1937 Lebanon ski-ing was launched.

Snow conditions in the Lebanon are excellent and usually comparable to spring snow in the Alps. The sun in this latitude is hot in the day-time, but there is a correspondingly large drop in temperature at night. This alternating process of thaw and freeze very soon produces an ideal surface, for the variations in temperature are usually too intense for 'breakable crust' to last any length of time. Though the early morning snow is frozen hard, by ten o'clock the sun begins to do its work, and before noon conditions are perfect. The skier in the Lebanon also has the comfort of knowing that avalanches, except in the two or three days after a heavy snowfall, are unknown.

The peculiar charm of ski-ing on the Mountain consists largely in its setting. From the Dome du Loup or the Col des Cedres you look down, from the snow world, eastward to the oasis of Baalbeck, distinguishable as a splash of darker green in the Bk'aa Valley, and to the Anti-Lebanon beyond. To the west the gulfs of the Kadischa Gorge fall away from the snowfields on which the Cedars stand to orchards, orange groves and the coast line shimmering in the Mediterranean haze. Where you stand, the wind whistles over the mountain crests at nearly ten thousand feet and has whipped the snow into frozen waves. Your hands grow numb with cold as you pull off your skins; you must stamp your feet to keep the circulation moving. Yet a few hours earlier you were bathing in that flat blue sea below, drinking an *arak* in a café beside a banana plantation, stopping to pick cyclamen in the olive groves, or talking to monks in a prim monastery garden. The almost immediate juxtaposition of sea and snow, of the frozen mountain-tops and the turned red valley-earth, of tense solitudes and villages below – whose friendly bustle seems almost perceptible – is stimulating and disturbing. The range of colour, of atmosphere, of association, that the eye and mind take in is so wide and so unusual. Later, the memory of snow will remain inappropriately blended with oranges, snow waves with sea waves and monks with guides. The whole Alpine practice will be deeply tinged with the colour of the Christian Mountain.

CHAPTER IX

THE CONTEMPORARY SCENE

———— ·◁ ▷· ————

A VARIETY of forces contributed to raise the Syrian monuments which have been the preoccupation of this book. Traders made Palmyra, a martyr created Resafa, and a pasha's taste and luxury built the Azem palaces. What, it may well be asked, has been the contribution of the twentieth century? Outside the indigenous and unassuming tradition of architecture which finds expression in the Lebanese villages, it is difficult to think of modern buildings in Syria calculated to give pleasure either now or in the future.[1] The governmental and administrative buildings show little architectural sense, and the taste for which private enterprise caters can be gauged accurately enough by the style of such buildings as the Hôtel St Georges in Beyrouth. Contemporary misbuilding was confined to the main centres of population, until the Second World War created, and then deserted, hundreds of camps in the depths of the previously unpolluted Syrian landscape.[2] The shoddy huts are falling, and the corrugated iron will disappear. But the concrete floors remain, enigmatical scars that in the dryness of the steppe will last for millenia. It is curious and discomforting to think of later archaeologists excavating these remains and finding nothing but concrete and the imperishable razor blade. The period of the 'Blue Gillette', they will say, left few remains of artistic importance on Syrian soil.

Though modern Syria has added little of value to the stone stratifications of time, the stranger will none the less wish to know something of the contemporary economic, social and political conditions of the country in which he moves. Such information this book does not set out to provide; but the present chapter, briefly and by way of

[1] The new museums at Beyrouth and Damascus are honourable exceptions.
[2] The army did not always build with the worst materials in the most expensive way. At Raqqa and one or two other places, the indigenous building tradition was adapted with the happiest results. Domed, mud-brick constructions not only proved far cooler in summer and warmer in winter than the usual army huts, but were decent to look at.

epilogue, indicates the main outlines of certain complicated problems and provides the traveller with a few indispensable bearings.

In Syria goats and men contend for numerical superiority. Of the latter – excepting the migratory Bedouin – only a small minority have not at some time or other tilled the soil or pruned a tree. They are thus predominantly a peasant people. That they are not a prosperous peasantry, but the reverse, is due partly to the inequitable system of land tenure. They are, and have been for centuries, thoroughly exploited. There are few independent farmers. Most of the arable land is in the hands of large landlords who often are absentee landlords. As a result of prolonged mismanagement many of their unwieldy *latifundia* are heavily mortgaged. On these great estates the peasants scrape a living by renting their acre or two of land on the old system known as *métayage*. Such leases are usually yearly and terminable at the will of the landlord, and the rent consists of a proportion of the annual yield of the ground. This proportion is most commonly fifty per cent, but may even rise to eighty. Such a system has nothing to recommend it, and even presents disadvantages from the landlords' point of view. Insecurity of tenure makes the peasant reluctant to put capital into the land. His object is a quick return even if this involves exhausting the fertility of the soil. Again, he often works only the minimum necessary to secure the necessities of life to himself and his family. He argues, and with reason, that there is no point in working more when the product of his labour goes, not to himself, but to his landlord. Lastly, such a system reduces the position of the tenant to that of a serf, and gives the landlord an undue social and political control.

The position, of course, varies a good deal from place to place. In parts of the Lebanon, although the Maronite Church is a large landowner, conditions are better and there are a number of small and relatively prosperous independent agriculturists. In the hinterland, on the other hand, the independent peasant is rarer. The following figures give an idea of the land tenure situation in the Damascus Oasis. At Duma, where a population of fifteen hundred work some of the richest soil in Syria, a quarter of the land is in the hands of five large landowners. Many tenants get as little as twenty-five or thirty per cent of the annual yield on their land. No services, however, are required from the tenants. At Jarba, a poorer village on the oasis edge with a population of about two hundred and fifty, nearly *all* the cultivable land belongs to a single owner. The tenants receive a third of the produce.[1]

[1] See J. A. Tower, *The Oasis of Damascus*, Beyrouth, 1935.

It is in the Alawi Mountains, however, that the system is to be seen at its worst. There agricultural exploitation is linked with compulsory services of various sorts, and forms the basis of an extreme social and political absolutism. The landlords' word is law, and from them justice and protection must be bought, if it is to be secured at all. The local system has the further unpleasant feature that much of the best land is owned by Orthodox Muslims and that the *métayer* peasant is often not even working for one of his own religion. It is, in fact, a feudalism (a *jus primae noctis* still exists in certain places) without the organization and the advantages which that system once offered. In the Middle Ages payments and services ensured corresponding rights, such as justice and protection, but in the modern feudalism of the Alawi territory (which is by no means unique in Syria) the overlord recognizes no obligations. Whatever payment is made everything still remains to be paid for. The peasant is the victim of a perpetual blackmail.

These *métayer* peasants, and others more fortunately situated, are not all employed in the same types of agriculture. The picture from this point of view is, however, not of great complication. In the Lebanon, the Damascus Oasis and the newly developed areas near Homs, the emphasis falls on arboriculture: olives, apricots, mulberries for silk (especially in the Lebanon) and every kind of fruit tree are cultivated. (Olive oil was before the war the most valuable of the Syrian-Lebanese exports.) In the Alawi district and around Latakia, the emphasis falls on tobacco and on the cotton crop (the latter an economic development due to the French). In the hinterland – the Bk'aa, the Hauran (once the granary of Rome) and the great plain south of Aleppo – the peasants grow almost exclusively cereal crops (wheat, barley and oats), and raise sheep. (Wool was the second most important export before the war.) The Jezira, the vast triangle of land stretching north-east beyond the Euphrates, still remains largely undeveloped, only one-third of the cultivable land being at present utilized. The area is the most fertile and the best watered in Syria, and is capable of producing large quantities of corn, rice and cotton. It has not been more exploited because of its isolation and for lack of labour. Also, lying at the foot-hills of the Caucasus where Turkey and Iraq meet, it has always been exposed to political disturbance, and its future has seemed in this respect so uncertain that the shrewd Syrian business man has been unwilling to put money into it; yet capital outlay is an essential prerequisite to the development of the Jezira.

The towns where the produce of the Syrian countryside finds its home market are, in order of size, Aleppo, Damascus and Beyrouth. The last is growing from day to day, and between them the three towns have a population of well over three-quarters of a million, a figure unduly large for an agricultural country whose total population is only three and a half millions. While a proportion of the population of Damascus and Aleppo remains agricultural (i.e. consists of peasants who happen to go out to their fields from a town rather than a village), the three towns are essentially commercial. Industry remains negligible. There are those who believe that the Syrian skill and aptitude for selling things across a counter, for turning goods over at a profit, is today doing the country as much harm as good. The Syrian business man is unwilling to vary a money-making technique of which he is perhaps the supreme master, and he therefore does not put his profits into capital enterprises and the development of industry which are seriously needed. There are more people engaged in commerce than the economy of the country warrants.

Looked at along these broad lines – peasant agriculture and town commerce – the Syrian picture looks deceptively simple. In fact it is bewilderingly diverse, and there can be few areas of comparable size that present such a variety of traditions, outlooks and beliefs.

Even the racial composition of the population, despite its pre-dominantly Semitic nature, is by no means straightforward. An earlier Aramaic-speaking Syro-Phoenician population, who also originally came from the south, has been subjected to continual pressure and infiltration from the Arabian deserts. Their absorbent powers have proved enormous. As, generation after generation, Bedouin tribes pene-trated into Syria and reached the cultivated belt, they shed their migratory habits, took their place in the standing economy and became thoroughly Syrianized. This process has been going on from the earliest times. There was, for instance, a considerable Arab influx from the south during the Seleucid period, and at the period of the Arab conquest it has been estimated that as many as a hundred thousand came in to swell the existing population (which then amounted probably to somewhere between five and six million). A high percentage of the present popula-tion derive from these later Arab waves, rather than from the earlier arrivals, the Syro-Phoenicians. Southward, in Palestine and Trans-jordan, it is thought that the descendants of the Arab immigrants even outnumber the original stocks. Though they left behind their desert ways, the Arabs at the conquest brought their religion and the language of the Koran, with which the former was inseparably bound up. The resistant quality of the Syro-Phoenician peoples may, however, be judged by the persistence of religious minorities into our own time, and by the extraordinary survival of their Aramaic tongue, in its Syriac form. After the dominance of Arabic for over a thousand years it is still the spoken tongue of one or two villages in the Anti-Lebanon, and is still preserved wherever the Maronite liturgy is read.

This racial amalgam of Syro-Phoenician and Arab has received additions through the immigration or transplantation of racial minorities from the north and east, such as the Kurds and the Armenians. Fleeing southward from the Turkish massacres, the Armenians took refuge in Syria mainly after the First World War, and were settled with the help and co-operation of the Mandatory Power. It has been estimated that over a million died on the roads in their exodus from Turkey; of those who reached Syria some hundred and twenty thousand have remained in the country. Their settlement has further served to complicate a picture already confused, but has benefited Syria. After a period of initial unrest, when the activities of their secret societies – the *Tachnak* agitating for the Free Armenia of 1918, and the *Hentchak* at one time affiliated to the Third International – caused trouble, they have settled down satisfactorily and are becoming valuable citizens.[1] Established mainly in the towns (there are over 50,000 in Aleppo), their mental endowments, and their ability to work hard and with system, enables them to supply not only efficient doctors and lawyers, but the skilled technicians of which a developing Syria is seriously in need.

It is not, however, the racial but the religious question that creates the real complication of the Syrian picture. Religious differences are profound and varied, and the social cleavages that they effect most harmful. Centuries of discrimination, and sometimes of persecution, have given the minorities an extraordinary solidarity. Each faith tends to coalesce into a compact social and political block whose first allegiance is not to the state and whose assimilation presents a problem for the administrator.

The following round figures, which omit some of the smaller but very compact religious minorities such as the Ismailis and Yezidis, give the approximate size of the main religious blocks. Sunnites (Orthodox Muslims) 1,920,000; Shi'ites (heretical Muslims) 175,000; Nosairis (Alawis) 275,000; Druzes 135,000; Christians 705,000; Jews 30,000. The strength of the Sunnites, who make up about half the population, is

---

[1] It is estimated none the less that a large majority would migrate to Soviet Armenia if they were allowed to do so.

mainly in the towns, though they also comprise the Bedouin tribes. The degree in which their faith modifies their way of life and their attitude to their unorthodox or non-Muslim fellow citizens varies considerably. The Bedouin takes his faith easily, while the stronghold of Muslim fanaticism is in provincial towns such as Hama and Homs, and in sectors of Damascus. The Shi'ites, followers of the Prophet's son-in-law Ali, are usually despised by the Orthodox Muslims, but, since their release from centuries of persecution, have shown much initiative. Situated chiefly in the Lebanon they maintain excellent relations with the non-Muslims. The Alawis comprise most of the peasantry in the Latakia district. Their interesting hermetic faith, whose origins are ultimately Shi'ite, is controlled by a hereditary priesthood, and includes, as does the Druze religion, secret rites and an initiation, the latter lasting in this case for a period of nine months. They worship a curious trinity, believe in metempsychosis and preserve a rich symbolism whose significance they have forgotten. They have no churches or mosques, but revere the tombs of saints, and like the Phoenicians before them make a cult of the natural sites in their wild landscape – springs, trees and hill-tops. They are very poor and very backward. Of the Jebel Druze something has been said elsewhere. It is worth remembering, however, that rather more than a third of the Druze population is still to be found in the southern Lebanon, the original stronghold of the faith before a migration to the Jebel in the latter half of the nineteenth century. The Christians, something less than three-quarters of a million in all, divide as to numbers fairly evenly into the Orthodox and Uniate Churches. The latter is mainly restricted to the Lebanon, where (as the Maronite Church) it acts as a single political unit and has long had close cultural affiliations with France. Though only amounting to twenty or twenty-five per cent of the Syro-Lebanese population, the Christians owing to their education and their higher standard of living exercise a social, economic and particularly, intellectual influence disproportionate to their numbers.

The position of the Christians has been further strengthened by the tradition of emigration. Since the second half of the nineteenth century the Lebanese Christians have emigrated in considerable numbers – 300,000 in all are said to have left the country – seeking opportunity in the United States, South America and nearer at hand in Egypt. Their industry abroad has brought them wealth and consideration, and modern Egypt in particular owes a great deal to their enterprise. This emigration fortunately for the Lebanon has been essentially a two-way movement. In the first place the successful emigrant has sent back remittances to his family at home, and thus yearly a large sum of money has entered the Lebanon from abroad (these remittances are estimated to have reached in the twenties as much as four million pounds a year). Secondly he often returned to end his days on the Mountain. Naturally he has brought with him western ideas, a wider outlook and a higher standard of living. Since 1930 the outward flow has declined. Depression abroad and the growth of stability and opportunity at home have made emigration less tempting (in 1931 and 1932 more returned to the Mountain than left it), but the tradition has already modified Lebanese life, and its effects will continue to be operative for at least a generation. Another factor which has primarily benefited the Christian population has been the tourist traffic.[1] The Christian strength is in the Lebanon, and it is to the Lebanon that foreigners come from the surrounding countries to escape the summer heats in the Mountain. They, too, bring money and new ideas and ways.

The bewildering differences of outlook which characterize modern Syria are partly due to the impact of the West upon groups of people variously equipped to receive it. There is a certain homogeneity, certain grounds of contact, between an Alawi and a Sunni peasant. Both of these again know something of the way the mind of the desert Bedouin or the Damascus merchant works. On the other hand, the new business man, the new technician, the westernized intellectual, these live in a different world. Between the unchanged peasant and the scholar educated in America are intermediary types who have lost much of one world and acquired only something of the other. They are puzzled and bewildered. The interpenetration of the old world and the new raises social and cultural problems which far surpass in importance and urgency the contemporary and temporary political conflicts which receive so much attention. After centuries of foreign rule it is not enough that Syria is independent politically. The country is sorely threatened by a cultural and ideological invasion from the West that is likely to suffocate the local genius which survived the cruder dominations of the past. There can be no question of repelling the invasion. It is not to be repelled. But it can perhaps be directed and controlled. Indeed, it must be, if Syria is to exist as a living force, and not simply as an independent area on the map. The West, its thought and its methods, must be fitted into the cultural and traditional framework of Syria, without destroying that framework, and with it the real identity of the country.

[1] The tourist trade before the Second World War almost equalled in value the total of Lebanese exports.

The troubled variety of Syrian life was further complicated from 1919 onwards by two interconnected problems which loomed large in the Syrian consciousness: the national boundaries, and the question of the French Mandate.

Syria existed before Christ or the Prophet, and there never was in the past any serious dispute as to what constituted the geographical and historical boundaries of the country. The writers of the past – Strabo, Pliny, the later Arab geographers – all assume that Syria comprises roughly the area covered by the Lebanon, Syria, Palestine and Transjordan. This is the Syria of history, the Syria of the Greeks, the Romans, the Mamelukes and the Turks; it is moreover geographically a single unit, a country whose frontiers – the Taurus, the Euphrates, the sea and the deserts – Napoleon thought as good as any in existence. It is a very different country from the truncated state which we know as Syria today. This state came to birth in the tortuous conferences after the First World War. It was essentially the creation of Anglo-French rivalry. Had either power taken over the whole area comprised by historic Syria, it would have been better for the country, and incidentally it might have robbed the Jewish problem in Palestine of some of its acuity. Strategic considerations, however, led to the division of the country into French and British mandates. 'The permanent dividing line between the British and French spheres . . . violated almost every known law of physical and human demarcation. It has stood ever since as a crippling obstacle to trade and other forms of intercourse: as an artificial wall on either side of which each of the two Powers has established her own language and currency, and instituted altogether different systems of administration, of education and of economic regulation and planning.' [1] Though the British and the French have gone, and Israel has appeared, the dividing line remains.

The Syrians bitterly resent their artificial boundaries on two main scores: they are arbitrary and humiliating, and they deal a deadly blow at the country's economic prosperity. To understand what they mean in the way of humiliation it is only necessary to think of the educated Damascene, perhaps once the governor of a province, who for a generation had to present his papers to both French and British officials each time he wished to cross the Palestine or Transjordan frontiers in order to visit his property, his friends or his relations, situated on the wrong side of a purely artificial fence. The peasant with his donkey and baskets was subject to the same galling restrictions. It was as though some

[1] George Antonius, *The Arab Awakening*, London, 1938.

foreign power should establish a frontier, with customs and passport control between, say, Devon and Cornwall. Psychologically the effects of the frontiers have been undesirable enough, economically they have been disastrous. Before the First World War Syria was the distributing channel for the whole eastern end of the Turkish Empire. The handling of goods in transit formed an essential part of the Syrian economy. Northward, eastward and southward, from Aleppo and Damascus, there was a free flow of trade; and Syria derived a relative wealth and prosperity as the commercial centre of a trade basin stretching from Anatolia to Egypt, and eastward to the confines of Persia. Damascus served, and was served by, Transjordania, Palestine, Egypt and, via the Medina railway, Nejd and the Hedjaz; similarly Aleppo was linked with Anatolia, Cilicia, Mosul, Baghdad and Persia. With the First World War and the ensuing settlement, this activity came to an abrupt end. Frontiers arose overnight, and the free movement of goods ceased. Southward lay the Palestine and Transjordan frontiers, eastward the Iraq frontier, and to the north the impassable tariff barrier of a hostile and protectionist Turkey. To make matters worse, further amputations effected in the north by the Ankara Agreements, and the arbitrary seizure of Alexandretta, fatally compromised the already reduced possibilities of Aleppo. Situated within fifty kilometres of the frontier – a frontier no longer defensible since the Turks held the Gates of the Taurus – the town, once the most important trade junction in the country, was left without either markets or security. Even the sources of the Kouek, from which the town derived its water-supply, lay in Turkish hands.

The Anglo-French jealousy, which had brought about the insensate restriction of the Syrian frontiers, occasioned between the wars the increasing isolation of Syria from her neighbours. Everywhere else Britain had succeeded to a controlling interest in the dismembered Turkish Empire. Egypt, Iraq, Palestine, Transjordania and Arabia, followed in the British wake, and set about building up their national economies with British encouragement and capital. Their political connection and policy, and not least their finance, drew them in varying degrees into the orbit of the pound. Syria was surrounded with a sterling wall which the weakened franc was powerless to surmount. As a prominent Syrian nationalist wrote in 1937: 'Over a period of fifteen years, and with the perseverance and continuity of aim which characterize British imperialism, a tariff and sterling chain has been forged link by link about this country.'[1] As the economy of the sterling countries developed,

[1] Edmond Rabbath, *Unité Syrienne et Devenir Arabe*, Paris, 1937.

H

their mutual bonds tightened. Haifa diverted the Baghdad trade from
Syrian channels, and Palestine and Iraq formalized their closer relationship by a commercial agreement in 1937. Two years earlier passports and
customs had been abolished between Iraq and Transjordania. Syria,
politically isolated and pegged to the franc, could do nothing to
revive her transit trade. This senseless state of affairs, as damaging
in the long run to Palestine, Transjordania and Iraq as to Syria
itself, was one of the chief causes of trouble between the two World
Wars.

The reduction of Syrian territory, and the economic evils which
resulted therefrom, were a joint Anglo-French responsibility, and may
be logically separated from the administration of the mandate for which
the French were answerable alone. The mandate was acquired, as were
other mandates in the Middle East, against the wish of the majority of
those who had any political consciousness.[1] Given this fact, and given
the possibilities at the disposal of the mandatory power, it is the duty
of the detached observer to try to ascertain with what degree of
efficiency the mandate was carried out.

Except in sectors of the Lebanon, there was always some degree of
opposition to the mandatory power though the French made various
fruitless attempts to secure co-operation. The national governments
they set up they could rarely work with, and the assemblies they created
rarely achieved anything constructive; Syrian nationalism simply did
not accept the framework of the mandate within which these bodies
were called upon to function, and the latter could only propose measures
tantamount to the abolition of that mandate, and which violated
obligations undertaken by the French vis-à-vis the League of Nations
Commission. It was politically a hopeless situation, and it is remarkable
that the French were able to secure any co-operation at all. That they
did secure it in varying degrees, and over varying periods, was due to
the fact that on the whole they adopted a policy of veiled or indirect
control, as opposed to the policy of direct control adopted by the
British in Palestine. They used with considerable skill, in every type of
post, representatives of those minorities and sections of the population
who were, if not always favourable, at any rate not avowedly hostile.

---

[1] Those interested in the Syrian attitude towards the mandate should read the
findings of the King-Crane Report (published in full in George Antonius's *Arab
Awakening*). The country, with the exception of 'considerable groups' in the
Lebanon, was overwhelmingly against a mandate of any sort, though they were
very ready to accept 'assistance' which they stipulated should be American or,
failing that, British, but on no account French.

Outbreaks, none the less, occurred almost yearly until 1925. It is noteworthy, however, that in spite of the open opposition of the Syrian Nationalists there was less political persecution than might have been anticipated. Incidents and individual injustices did occur, but they have been exaggerated. Indeed, formal relations between the French and the Muslims were usually correct, and there was more social contact between the foreign officials and the local population than was the case in Palestine. This constitutes a tribute to both sides.

Apart from the difficulties deriving from the unpopularity of the mandate, France suffered from three initial disadvantages altogether her own: the weakness of the franc, shortage of efficient personnel (both in part the result of the sacrifices made by France on behalf of herself and her allies in the First World War) and, paradoxically enough, her peculiar cultural and historical position in the Levant. The economic drawbacks of the first have already been mentioned. The second led to corruption in certain branches of the administration which, though less widespread than that to which the country had in Turkish times been accustomed, was a bad advertisement both for France and western methods. The third initial disadvantage deserves special consideration. France's connection with Syria went back as far as Charlemagne, who secured from the Caliph Haroun-al-Raschid the protectorate of the Holy Places. In modern times it began with Francis I, who negotiated the first capitulations with the Turks on the model later adopted by the other western powers, and inaugurated the French policy of alliance and friendship with the *Grand Signior*. Later came Colbert's brilliant organization of the French trade posts in the Levant, and renewed capitulations which insisted clearly on France's religious and economic protectorate of the Holy Places. By the middle of the eighteenth century France had come to be regarded as the hereditary protector of Catholic interests in Syria. A century later it was France that landed an expedition to restore order and safeguard Christian rights after the massacres of 1860. It was mainly French missionaries who worked in the country and French education that strengthened the Christian minorities and set them culturally ahead of their compatriots. As a result, long before the question of a mandate arose, the French, as traditionally associated with Christian interests, were profoundly suspect to the Orthodox Muslims. The very cultural and educational achievements, which had earned them the devotion of the Christian minorities, were a major disadvantage in assuming a mandate over Syria as a whole.

Any review of the administration of the mandated territories of Syria and the Lebanon, an administration which lasted roughly a generation, must draw attention to errors and omissions. Many of these the French themselves would readily recognize. First, public works were sometimes inadequate; no major port works were undertaken at Beyrouth before 1933, although such works were essential if the port was to compete with Haifa. (The weakness of the French financial position had something to do with this. Capital was lacking.) Secondly, the towns were encouraged at the expense of the countryside, a grave error in a primarily agricultural country; money went to providing municipal water, electricity and public buildings, which should have gone on agricultural development. In other words, a disproportionately small percentage of the budgets was spent in and on the countryside. On the one hand this resulted in a gravitation towards the towns with consequent unemployment; on the other it led to the neglect of rural drainage problems and of the malaria endemic in certain regions. Thirdly, little effort was made to prepare Syrians for the task of self-government when the mandate should expire, and no cadre of efficient and responsible civil servants was trained. The Syrian official too often remained, as in the old Turkish days, slow, lazy and corrupt. Fourthly, many will regard the introduction of the mechanism of democratic government, with the bureaucracy that it entails, and in the direct form developed in the West, as premature. Not only was the machinery involved expensive out of proportion to the financial resources of the states concerned, but experience, and the example of Egypt, had shown that for countries in the stage of development reached by Syria and the Lebanon such government does not give effective expression to the needs and wishes of the people.[1] It bordered on the ludicrous to confer upon the Lebanon, a country with a population of less than a million, and that population mainly peasantry, the expense and the machinery of a bicameral parliament.

There remain two major charges to be brought against the mandatory power: first, its attitude of complaisance in the face of Turkish encroachments on Syrian territory, and secondly its separatist policy. There is little doubt that the French – though the other member states of the League of Nations must take their share of the blame – did not wish to antagonize Turkey, and therefore did not oppose with sufficient vigour the Turkish pressure in the north which ultimately resulted

[1] Recent events seem to show that Syria has decisively abandoned the form of democracy imposed by the West.

in the seizure of Alexandretta. The French and the League of Nations may be said to have given away, without a struggle, territory which was held in trust, territory, moreover, which comprised the town of Antioch, for many centuries the capital of Syria and the focus of Syrian life. Although the League gave its approval to the changes, the French seem morally to have contravened Article Four of the League Mandate, by which they had guaranteed 'la Syrie et le Liban contre toute perte ou prise à bail de tout ou partie des territoires et contre l'établissement de tout contrôle d'une Puissance étrangère'. This breach of trust was doubly serious since its effects are permanent.

The separatist policy pursued in Syria (as opposed to the Lebanon), involving the creation of the Sanjak, the Alawi territory and the Jebel Druze, was most ill-advised. By the terms of Article I of the League Mandate the French guaranteed to favour 'les autonomies locales dans toute la mesure où les circonstances s'y prêteront'. They went, in fact, further than this. They not only safeguarded minorities but fostered them, and in every region were accused of encouraging separatism. Their primary object in doing this was clearly political, and they hoped to strengthen French influence thereby. The policy only succeeded in increasing economic and administrative dislocation, and in creating further political unrest owing to the extreme dissatisfaction of the Muslims. On the other hand, in fairness to the French, it must be emphasized that the Alawis and the Druzes constitute very real historic minorities with their own religions, costumes and traditions. Experience further seems to show that minorities in Syria, and particularly the Christians, still need adequate and enforceable guarantees. Many of the ill effects of the French separatist policy were fortunately offset by the *de facto* reintegration of the autonomous states in most important matters. Posts and telegraphs, finance, customs, railways and a dozen other vital services, as from 1922, were handled throughout Syria, the Lebanon and the other states, by the central administration. The budget of these Common Interests, as they were called, was as large as that of the separate states. Though the economic ills of separatism were thus largely avoided the political grievance remained.

The problems raised by the creation of an independent Lebanon were, and are, more complex. In 1919 the autonomous Sanjak of the Lebanon was made an independent state. This independence was recognized by the League of Nations, which mentioned Syria and the Lebanon separately in the terms of its mandate. On the other hand, the size of the independent Lebanon was not initially determined. Under Turkish rule its boundaries had fluctuated widely, and there had as a result arisen two different conceptions as to what constituted the Lebanon, conceptions which found expression in the terms *Little Lebanon* and *Greater Lebanon*. The Little Lebanon meant the strongly Maronite and Druze sector of the Mountain between Sidon and Tripoli, and the coast between this sector of the range and the sea (excluding Beyrouth). The Greater Lebanon was envisaged as an area extending southward as far as Tyre, and comprising also Beyrouth and possibly Tripoli. Historically the Greater Lebanon had tended to emerge, as the creation of semi-independent Lebanese emirs, whenever the Porte was weak. Thus the Emir Fakr-ed-Din in the early seventeenth century and the Emir Bechir in the early nineteenth gave the conception of the Greater Lebanon its widest territorial expression. Conversely a strong central government tended to restrict the area of Lebanese semi-autonomy within the limits of the Little Lebanon and its mountain fastnesses. Between 1842 and 1860 the Turks made determined efforts to destroy even this restricted autonomy. Disturbances resulted, culminating in the massacre of Christians in 1860. Thereupon the foreign powers intervened to re-establish the Little Lebanon as a wholly autonomous sanjak within the Turkish Empire. Both the French and the first Christian Turkish governor of the new state, Daoud Pasha, suggested the re-establishment of the Greater rather than the Lesser Lebanon, but the Turks and the British for different reasons were both violently opposed, and the scheme fell through.

The Lebanon had been particularly hostile to Turkish rule, and the restriction of the Lebanon was therefore a natural feature of Turkish policy. On the other hand, when the French received their mandate it was among the Lebanese Christians that they had most friends and most support, and it was therefore equally natural that they should wish to give the Mountain the greatest possible extent and influence. The Greater Lebanon was therefore recreated, but with territorial limits so wide as to be historically unjustifiable. The population of the Little Lebanon had been somewhere about 400,000; that of the new state was rather more than double, the new accretions being mainly Orthodox Muslims and Shi'ites. Apart from questions of French foreign policy,[1] there was one argument *for* a Greater Lebanon: it would form a workable unit economically, whereas a Little Lebanon without a satisfactory port

---

[1] The Greater Lebanon situated the terminus of the pipe-line (at Tripoli) and the best aerodrome in the mandated territories (at Rayak) within the boundaries of a state where it was hoped that some form of French influence might prevail almost indefinitely.

would be a travesty as an *independent* state, picturesque but almost as ineffective as an Andorra or a Lichtenstein. (The cogency of such an argument depended on the idea of Lebanese *independence*. It would, of course, in no sense apply to an autonomous Lebanon in a Syrian Federation.)

The arguments *against* the Greater Lebanon as recreated by the French were many, and its existence posed serious problems. In the first place it included territory, particularly in the Bk'aa and the Anti-Lebanon, which had never been comprised in any Greater Lebanon, and which could only be regarded by the Syrians as an unjustifiable seizure. Secondly, it created a Muslim minority in the Christian Lebanon who wished for union with Syria, while in Syria itself it created an irredentist party. Thirdly, the new Greater Lebanon incorporated without justification a sector of the Syrian railway linking Damascus, Hama and Aleppo, and so acquired a grip upon the very spine of Syrian economy. Fourthly, and perhaps most important, the new state by incorporating the ports of Beyrouth and Tripoli blocked Syria's natural access to the sea. As long as the regime of the Common Interests existed the ill effects of this last drawback were largely offset, but Syria none the less remained insecure. There is still no guarantee that at some time in the future, perhaps with the support of a foreign power, the Greater Lebanon will not erect tariff barriers and close its ports to Syrian trade.

Even in the Mountain itself there was initially considerable misgiving about the new frontiers. It was felt that added territory had been dearly purchased at the price of Syrian hostility. The Orthodox Muslim minority of the Greater Lebanon naturally resented the new state of affairs bitterly. No revision was, however, undertaken. Such a revision, while retaining Beyrouth as the port of the Lebanon, should have handed back Tripoli and the Bk'aa valley to Syria, while allowing the southern Lebanon, where sentiment is divided, to settle its future by plebiscite. With the passage of time, new interests have inevitably created new ties within the Greater Lebanon, and habit and custom have done much to lessen internal opposition, even among the Sunnites. No less than the Maronites, the other communities have become aware of the advantages of belonging to a unit whose standard of living and education is higher than that prevailing in surrounding Arab countries. Further, an interesting and significant process has become apparent, which has tended to reconcile the most irreconcilable: the Muslims, who are for the most part the poorer and less educated part of the population, are increasing more rapidly than the Maronites, and a situation is to be envisaged in the future when the Greater Lebanon will cease to be predominantly Christian.[1] It is ironic that the very measures – increase of area and population – taken by the French to bulwark the power of the Mountain, and to ensure its position, should in the end appear likely to threaten its existence as a Christian state.

The major administrative errors and omissions of the mandatory power have now been considered. They constitute a serious debit balance. It is a balance against which a number of solid and lasting achievements can be set. In the first place the practical modernization of Syria and the Lebanon was taken a long way: those unromantic but invaluable adjuncts to modern life – light, water, public buildings, efficient postal services, good roads and, not least, security – were made generally available. Before the French mandate only Beyrouth had main water, and only Beyrouth and Damascus had electricity. Today both exist as a matter of course in the major towns of Syria and the Lebanon. Apart from the routine supply of such municipal and administrative services, much was done, within the financial limits possible, for the general economy of the country. Even in the troubled days before 1926 irrigation and reafforestation were undertaken on a considerable scale: thus the large Ghab plain north of Sheizar was made cultivable and over four million trees were planted in the Homs-Hama district. Before and even during the Second World War, such schemes were pushed forward at a vastly accelerated pace, and it is no exaggeration to say that the aspect of large areas of the country was totally changed. Much was also done, through research, planning and administrative supervision, to increase the yield of valuable crops and to introduce others. Thus the area under cotton cultivation had risen by 1926 from 800 to 40,000 hectares. Through the development of rural services, agricultural tax reform, and the wise policy of leasing out a million and a half hectares of the State Domains among small farmers (thus, incidentally, providing an exemplary contrast to the *métayage* system), the condition of the peasants was considerably improved. It is no exaggeration to say that Syria in twenty-five years advanced in many respects further than it had done in several hundreds. The advance occurred in spite of the weakness of the franc, the sterling wall that surrounded the country and the disastrous effects of the world slump which intervened just as new schemes were getting under way. Two things speak clearly for the French achievement: the land under cultivation increased by

[1] This will not occur if the 160,000 Lebanese *émigrés*, who have retained their nationality and who are mainly Christian, secure the vote, as they wish to do.

over fifty per cent, and the population rose from two to three and a half millions.[1] From another angle, the budget figures give a striking idea of the extraordinary change and development that the mandated territories underwent. The Syrian budget under Turkish rule amounted to one million Syrian pounds; in the early nineteen-thirties it had reached twenty-five times that figure.

Before passing from the practical and economic achievements of the period under review, it may be well to refute four common, but unfounded, charges brought against the French administration. It is claimed that the French allowed the country to pile up an adverse trade balance. There are two things to be said here. In the first place the League Mandates Commission imposed the policy of the 'open door' as a matter of principle in all mandated territories, and there was thus nothing the French could do to stop certain countries dumping their goods. In the second place, the French found Syria in 1919 exhausted after Turkish rule, famine and military occupation. They started from scratch. To build up the country it was necessary to import goods of every sort, from textbooks to drain-pipes and agricultural machinery. The adverse trade balance was in fact an investment for the future, and the best type of investment that could have been made. (The balance was not as serious as appeared on paper, since it was to some extent offset by the tourist traffic, the remittances of emigrants from America and the carriage of goods in transit.) Secondly, it is sometimes claimed that France used Syria for dumping her own goods. The official figures clearly refute this. In 1938 the tonnage of British imports was more than twice that of French imports. Thirdly, it is widely maintained in Syria that France drained the country of her gold. This belief is based on such irrelevancies as the substitution of a paper currency for the old gold currency of the Turks, the fact that the Syrian gold reserve was kept in France, and that at one time a French bank held the monopoly of gold purchase in the mandated territories. Finally, there is the groundless accusation that the French destroyed the Lebanese silk industry because it competed with Lyons. The facts of the case are very different. Vast numbers of mulberries were cut by the Turks during the First World War, and the orchards were subsequently ploughed for wheat owing to the huge prices fetched by cereals. The French, on assuming their mandate, did everything to revive the industry, and the

---

[1] The figures for railway transport are also significant. Between 1933 and 1938 the takings of the Syrian and Lebanese railways more than doubled. (*Rapport à la Société des Nations sur la Situation de la Syrie et du Liban. Année, 1938.*)

* H

output was more than tripled between 1920 and 1926. In the latter year an intensive propaganda campaign was launched for the Syrian product. That it failed, and that the output subsequently dropped, was due to two main causes over which the French had no control: the development and popularization of artificial silk and the competition of raw silk from Japan.

The practical achievements of the mandate represent only part of the picture. French cultural influence long antedated the mandate, and had been felt in the Lebanon since the seventeenth and eighteenth centuries (the Capuchin Mission was founded in 1625, and the Jesuits followed before the end of the century). In the education of the local populations and in the creation of an intelligent and informed Lebanese upper-middle class, France has done much. No foreign power spreads its culture in pure altruism, but this should not obscure recognition of the benefits which France has conferred on Syria and the Lebanon through numberless schools, scholars and teachers, over a period of generations. In this context it is important to realize that the work of France and of her religious missions is inseparable. Though the latter represent the Church, they also represent France. It is French culture and French ideas that they diffuse in the course of their multifarious educational and humanitarian activities. The French are well aware of this intimate connection, a connection which foreigners sometimes overlook. Even during the French Revolution, when priests were being executed at home, the government continued to give its support to the religious missions abroad.

It has sometimes been claimed that the French missions have concentrated too much on advanced education, and the formation of an educated upper class, at the expense of primary education. No one conversant with the Middle East and with the weaknesses of educational programmes in most Middle Eastern countries, can doubt that it is just this, a fully educated upper class, responsible and informed, that is everywhere needed. A more pertinent criticism is that French in the mission schools was often developed at the expense of Arabic. Thus it is not unusual to find upper-class Lebanese with a perfect command of French, and sometimes also English, who are unable to write Arabic. Such a state of affairs is obviously undesirable.

Though the French may have neglected the teaching of Arabic in their schools in the realms of scholarship and archaeology, they have given tremendous impetus to Islamic studies, and have shown particular understanding and initiative in their efforts to preserve and interpret the Syrian past. The *Institut des Lettres Orientales* with its fine library at the Université St Joseph at Beyrouth and the *Institut Français* at Damascus have long been among the most active centres for the study of Islamic letters and archaeology in the Middle East.[1] The achievement of the *Service des Antiquités* under French direction was also notable. When the French took over Syria there was not a museum in the country, and buildings of importance were yearly disappearing through neglect or wilful destruction. They created museums of outstanding importance, admirably arranged and managed, at Beyrouth, Damascus and Aleppo, and a collection by no means inconsiderable at Soueida. Effective steps were taken to preserve existing monuments; and restorations, usually in excellent taste, were carried out on a wide scale. The restoration of Krak of the Knights was in itself a major achievement. Further it must be emphasized that the intelligent and sympathetic preservation of the Syrian past was not confined to sites and antiquities, but extended to traditional aspects of Syrian life. A conscious effort was made to preserve local costume and custom, and to encourage local crafts. The printed stuffs of Hama, the Mayadin carpets, the Djezzine knives, and not least the woven materials of Aleppo, owe something of their renown and persistence to the interest and historical sense of the French.

The mandate is a thing of the past. As it recedes, the Syrian is better able to disentangle the idea of a foreign rule which he opposed, and the division of Syrian territory which he bitterly resented, from the practical record of the mandatory power. In time he may conclude that, if there were omissions, there were also important achievements, and that he and his countrymen owe much to the period of the mandate.

The Second World War hastened the full independence of Syria and the Lebanon. Independence came however at a particularly difficult time, accompanied by inflation and a grave political threat. Of the tragic events of 1948, and the shadow which Israel casts over this corner of the Arab world, it is still too soon to speak without anger. Though no solution to the political threat, or to social and economic problems equally serious, is yet in sight, the good genius which has preserved the identity of Syria and the Mountain through successive invasions and catastrophes will surely not desert it now. Nearly two thousand years ago prosperity and strength peopled the hills of the desert, and built great monuments. An independent Syria believes they will return.

[1] The only other comparable centres are the French Institute in Cairo, Fuad University at Giza and the Hebrew University in Jerusalem.

BOOKS

BOOKS

THE following titles may prove useful to those interested in Syria and the Lebanon.

Chapter I

INTRODUCTION

The most readable general history, in spite of a certain bias, is HENRI LAMMENS's *La Syrie* (2 vols., Beyrouth, 1921), though it has in some respects been superseded by P. K. HITTI's *History of Syria* (London, 1951), an accurate and scholarly work. Other books of a general nature include:

La Syrie antique et mediaevale, Paris, 1931, by various authors.
Syria (an official quarterly publication devoted to the life and antiquities of the country).
GERTRUDE BELL, *The Desert and the Sown*, London, 1907.
C. P. GRANT, *The Syrian Desert*, London, 1937.
Syrie, Palestine, Guide Bleu, 1932. (Indispensable to anyone visiting the country, but not altogether reliable in certain respects, e.g. desert tracks. Many new roads have been built since 1932.)
JACQUES EDDÉ, *Géographie Liban-Syrie*, Beyrouth, 1941. (Useful for facts and figures.)

Good books on the flora are: G. E. POST, *Flora of Syria, Palestine, and Sinai* (Beyrouth, 1896); and F. BOULOUMOY, *Flore du Liban et de la Syrie*, 2 vols., 1930.

Chapter II

THREE TOWNS

H. LAMMENS, *La vie universitaire à Beyrouth sous les Romains et le Bas Empire* in *Revue du Monde Egyptien*, X, 1921.
WULZINGER and WATZINGER, *Damaskus*, Leipsig, 1924.
J. SAUVAGET, *Les monuments historiques de Damas*, Beyrouth, 1932.
J. A. TOWER, *The Oasis of Damascus*, Beyrouth, 1935.

There is a brilliant, readable and inaccurate review of the characteristics of the Syrians and their towns in Chapters 58 and 59 of Lawrence's *Seven Pillars of Wisdom*.

Chapter III

PHOENICIAN COAST

G. CONTENAU, *Civilization phénicienne*, Paris, 1926.
E. RENAN, *Mission en Phénicie*, Paris, 1864.
CLAUDE SCHAEFFER, *Ugaritica*, Paris, 1939 (for the Ras Shamra excavations).
JAMES FRAZER, *The Golden Bough*, vol. IV (Adonis, Attis, Osiris).
PAUL JACQUOT, *L'état des Alouites*, Beyrouth, 1931.

Chapter IV

THE ROMAN PEACE

P. JOUGET, *L'imperialisme macédonien et l'hellenisation de l'orient*, Paris, 1926.
ROBERT COHEN, *La Grèce et l'hellenisation du Monde Antique*, Paris, 1934.
E. S. BOUCHIER, *Syria as a Roman Province*, Oxford, 1916.
Baalbeck (ed. THEODOR WIEGAND), Berlin, 1923.
MICHEL ALOUF, *History of Baalbeck*, Beyrouth, 1938.
Palestine Exploration Fund, vol. XXI, 1890. Contains a reprint of the earliest account of a modern trip to Palmyra, made in 1691.
Palmyra (ed. THEODOR WIEGAND), Berlin, 1932.
J. G. FEVRIER, *Essai sur l'histoire politique et economique du Palmyre*, Paris, 1931.
M. ROSTOVTZEFF, *Caravan Cities*, Oxford, 1932.
GERTRUDE BELL, *The Desert and the Sown*, London, 1907.
J. MASCLE, *Le Djebel Druze*, Beyrouth (no date).

Chapter V

A RIVER AND BYZANTIUM

V. CHAPOT, *La frontière de l'Euphrate*, Paris, 1907.
A. POIDEBARD, *La trace de Rome dans le desert de Syrie*, 2 vols., 1937.
GERTRUDE BELL, *Amurath to Amurath*, London, 1911.
SARRE and HERTZFELD, *Archäologishe Reise im Euphrat – und Tigris Gebiet*, 4 vols., Berlin, 1911–20. (For Halebiyah, see vol. II.)
LOIS MUSIL, *Palmyrena*, New York, 1928 (for Resafa).
SPANNER and GUYER, *Rusafa*, Berlin, 1926.
H. C. BUTLER, *Early Christian Churches in Syria*, Princeton, 1929.
J. MATTERN, *Les villes mortes de Haute Syrie*, Beyrouth, 1933.
Ammianus Marcellinus, available in the Loeb Classics, gives a graphic account of the Emperor Julian's march down the Euphrates.

Chapter VI

BEDOUIN AND DESERT PALACES

R. A. NICHOLSON, *A Literary History of the Arabs*, London, 1930.
PHILIP K. HITTI, *History of the Arabs*, London, 1937.
For Kasr el-Heir see:
ALOIS MUSIL, *Palmyrena*, New York, 1928;
ALBERT GABRIEL, *Kasr el-Heir* in *Syria*, vol. III, 1927;
and especially K. A. C. CRESWELL, *Early Muslim Architecture*, vol. I,
   Oxford, 1932.

Chapter VII

CRUSADER CASTLES

HILAIRE BELLOC, *The Crusade*, London, 1937. (Excellent on the relation
   of the castles to the manpower problem and the strategic difficulties of
   the Crusaders.)
K. A. C. CRESWELL, *Early Muslim Architecture*, 2 vols., Oxford, 1932 and
   1940 (see index under Kasr el-Heir, Ukhaidir, portcullis, machicoulis,
   bent entrance, etc.).
PAUL DESCHAMPS, *Le Crac des Chevaliers*, 2 vols., Paris, 1934.
PAUL DESCHAMPS, *Les entrées des Châteaux des Croisés et leurs défenses*
   in *Syria*, vol. XIII.
C. ENLART, *Les monuments des Croisés dans le Royaume de Jerusalem*,
   2 vols., Paris, 1934 (for Tortosa see vol. 2).
ROBIN FEDDEN, *Crusader Castles*, London, 1950.
T. E. LAWRENCE, *Crusader Castles*, 2 vols., Golden Cockerel Press, 1936.
   (Stimulating but inaccurate.)
CHARLES OMAN, *A History of the Art of War in the Middle Ages*, 2 vols.,
   London, 1924. (The present author's account of siege tactics (pp. 205–
   208) is largely based on information contained in this work.)
E. REY, *L'Architecture militaire des Croisés*, Paris, 1871 (out of date, but
   a classic; excellent plates).

The *Memoirs of Usamah Ibn-Munqidh*, New York, 1929 (translated
by Philip K. Hitti), and JOINVILLE's *Vie du Saint Roi Louis*, are among
the more accessible and entertaining contemporary records.

Chapter VIII

TURKS, TRAVELLERS AND THE MOUNTAIN

For the life of the Europeans in Syria in the seventeenth and eighteenth
centuries, see A. C. WOOD, *A History of the Levant Company*, Oxford, 1935:
F. CHARLES-ROUX, *Les échelles de Syrie et de Palestine au xviii siècle*, Paris,

1928; and contemporary travellers' accounts (Maundrell, Pococke, Volney and others).

JOAN HASLIP, *Lady Hester Stanhope*, London, 1934.

LAMARTINE's *Voyage en Orient*, and CHURCHILL's *Mount Lebanon* (3 vols., London, 1853) both give a good impression of the Mountain in the nineteenth century.

Chapter IX

THE CONTEMPORARY SCENE

La Syrie et le liban sous l'occupation et le mandat français, 1919–1927, Nancy. The official annual Reports of the Mandatory Power to the League of Nations.

SA'ID B. HIMADEH, *Economic Organization of Syria*, Beyrouth, 1936.

EDMUND RABBATH, *Unité syrienne et devenir arabe*, Paris, 1937.

GEORGE ANTONIUS, *The Arab Awakening*, London, 1938.

ALFRED BONNÉ, *The Economic Development of the Middle East*, London, 1943.

A. H. HOURANI, *Syria and Lebanon*, London, 1946.

A. H. HOURANI, *Minorities in the Arab World*, Oxford, 1947.

The Middle East. A Political and Economic Survey. Royal Institute of International Affairs, 1950.

APPENDIX
ON TRAVEL IN SYRIA

APPENDIX

ON TRAVEL IN SYRIA

------------- ◄ Ɔ► -------------

IT may be worth while giving a few practical hints and warnings, in the manner of Baedeker, to enable the traveller to attain his objectives with a minimum of discomfort.

The Mandatory Power provided two of the primary necessities of travel, roads and security. Both were inadequate in Turkish times, and it was impossible to visit many of the best sites in Syria without an escort and the paraphernalia of *laissez-passés*. It is now possible to get where you want, quickly and safely. A word of warning is, however, necessary. Many sites in the steppe and the hinterland are isolated, and are only to be approached by desert tracks. These tracks, where the going is often good enough in dry weather, may become impassable after rain. Again, the isolation of these sites means that a mechanical breakdown becomes a serious matter. In principle, one should not venture into the deserts without two cars, or at least a competent mechanic who knows the country and can, if necesary, get help through the Bedouin.

The West has done less well for Syria where accommodation is concerned. There are modern hotels, many of them pretentious, but almost none are well run, and the service is usually deplorable. In these respects there is nothing to choose between the 'best' hotels in Damascus, Aleppo and Latakia. The trouble is that there is no one who *knows* how to run a hotel; the knowledge is lacking, and plumbing in itself is not enough (especially when it is a good bet that the hot water, if it does run, will probably do so from the cold tap).[1] This, it should be recalled, is in a country where hospitality was once a ritual. What has happened is that the old Turkish tradition of hospitality has been largely supplanted, while the tradition of the good European inn has not yet taken its place. The traveller suffers from an interregnum. The same thing applies to cooking. Good Turkish cuisine has disappeared from the Europeanized restaurants, but the French tradition has not taken its place. Probably the most serious fault which the traveller will personally have to find with the period of mandatory

[1] Exception must be made of at any rate one hotel in Beyrouth where the service is good, and of two or three of the hotels in the Lebanon which cater for the summer tourist traffic. At the time of writing (1945) all hotels in Syria were extremely expensive. It was possible to pay two and three pounds sterling a day and get nothing for it. They were, however, very cheap before the war and may well be so again.

233

rule is that the French, so assiduous and so successful in spreading other aspects of their civilization, did not impose their cookery to any real effect. In Beyrouth, where French influence has been supreme for over a generation, there is hardly a single good public restaurant – and by that is meant a place where the *patron* is interested in fine cooking, and his dishes are worthy of the critical sense of his clientele. Neither does this wealthy flourishing town provide agreeable gaiety at night, the mildly rakish pleasures with which a stranded traveller may while away an evening. Even the *boîte* with the marine flavour, that he has a right to expect in every Mediterranean port, though it exists, is not easy to find.

Faced in most places with a poor version of western cooking and accommodation, the traveller will do well to reach back wherever he can to the indigenous tradition. It is no exaggeration to say that off the beaten track, where no hotels exist, it is possible to go from one end of Syria to the other and find everywhere the most courteous and ready hospitality. The stranger has only to turn up at some isolated village at noon or nightfall for the sheik or headman at once to throw open his doors. The fare will not be luxurious, but it will be honest and adequate: eggs, freshly made *leban*[1] and honey, in a courtyard under a spreading vine; or white cheese, olives and meat balls, taken on a low divan in a clean whitewashed room, with afterwards the long pipe, and Arab coffee flavoured with cardamom. Money, of course, must never be offered in payment, but it is often possible, when you leave, to find some suitable present to give in return for your entertainment.

More ambitious Syrian food is to be had in the larger towns, and especially Damascus, where the *Restaurant des Princes* in the Suk Hamidieh is excellent. Many of the dishes eaten locally will repay experiment. There are, in particular, numbers of excellent rice dishes, of which *waraq ainab* (rice, flavoured often with pine kernels and raisins, wrapped in young vine leaves) is among the best. Other common dishes which can be recommended are *lahm mishwi* (pieces of mutton grilled on a skewer), *kufta* (meat balls flavoured with various herbs – a very favourite dish), and *kubeba* (a basis of finely crushed wheat with meat or fish). For sweetmeats Syria and Damascus have always been famous, and there is an infinite variety (of which *baklava* seems particularly suited to western taste). The Syrian desert also produces a species of brown truffle, both plentiful and cheap at the right season, which is excellent when properly prepared. It is not dug up by camels. As regards drinks, the European will probably find sherbet, in spite of its poetic associations, a little insipid. *Arak*, the local aperitif, is good; made from a grape basis and flavoured with aniseed, it is vaguely reminiscent of *pernod*, and has, further, the advantage of being something of a specific against the intestinal troubles which so commonly beset the traveller in the Middle East. Quite good wine is also made in certain parts of the Lebanon, particularly in the Bk'aa Valley in the neighbourhood of Chtaura. It is relatively cheap. On the other hand most of the wine in the out-of-the-way villages is hardly recognizable as such, and is best avoided.

[1] = *yoghourt:* usually excellent, and altogether one of the most useful words in the traveller's Syrian vocabulary.

The European travellers who visited Syria in the past automatically carried their own hotel with them; they took, in fact, full camping equipment. This still remains the best method of procedure for anyone who intends to penetrate beyond the pleasant villages of the Lebanon into the hinterland. There is no doubt that in places like Palmyra one's own camp-bed at the edge of the oasis is far preferable to anything the village can offer, while at such sites as Resafa and Kasr el-Heir, miles from any habitation, there is no alternative. Even in more civilized regions many will rightly prefer the stars to a dubious hotel. Outside the Lebanon, the country is so sparsely populated that it is always easy to get away from people and set out one's bed in solitude. A mosquito net should always be used, except right out in the desert or at an altitude of over four or five thousand feet, since malaria is common in many places. Finally, even in late spring and early summer, the traveller should take warm clothes. After a scorching day the desert, where there is no vegetation to retain the heat, can grow bitterly cold before dawn, and it is well to remember that in the Lebanon and Anti-Lebanon there may be patches of snow as low as five thousand feet until the beginning of June.

INDEX